Why they don't buy

Why they don't buy

The science of selling online

Max J. McKeown

FINANCIAL TIMES
Prentice Hall

An imprint of PEARSON EDUCATION

Harlow, England • London • New York • Reading, Massachusetts • San Francisco
Toronto • Don Mills, Ontario • Sydney • Tokyo • Singapore • Hong Kong • Seoul
Taipei • Cape Town • Madrid • Mexico City • Amsterdam • Munich • Paris • Milan

PEARSON EDUCATION LIMITED

Head Office:	*London Office:*
Edinburgh Gate	128 Long Acre
Harlow CM20 2JE	London WC2E 9AN
Tel: +44 (0)1279 623623	Tel: +44 (0)20 7447 2000
Fax: +44 (0)1279 431059	Fax: +44 (0)20 7240 5771
	Website: www.business-minds.com

First published in Great Britain in 2002

© Max McKeown 2002

The right of Max McKeown to be identified as author of this work has been asserted by him in accordance with the Copyright, Designs and Patents Act 1988.

ISBN 0 273 65674 0

British Library Cataloguing in Publication Data
A CIP catalogue record for this book can be obtained from the British Library.

10 9 8 7 6 5 4 3 2 1

Typeset by Pantek Arts Ltd, Maidstone, Kent
Printed and bound in Great Britain by Biddles Ltd, Guildford & King's Lynn

The Publishers' policy is to use paper manufactured from sustainable forests.

Also by

MAX J. MCKEOWN

E-Customer: Inspire the wired generations

For Deborah, my game-free zone.

Contents

Acknowledgements xi

Preface xiii

How to use this book xix

1 The e-customer experience – what's it all about? xxii

2 Get this thing on the road 20

3 Understanding *your* e-customer 38

4 Creating the e-customer offer 82

5 Creating the ultimate e-customer experience 108

6 Experience creation teams – the individuals, culture, skills, and the stress 196

7 Trends and technologies for creating experiences 232

8 Keeping it fresh, staying in business 278

9 Do it, do it now, and do it again – next steps 298

Complete checklist for all activities: get them checked off 318

The e-customer manifesto: an open letter 320

Music that produced this book 324

Notes 327

Index 335

"Excellence costs, but in the long run **mediocrity costs** far more. **"**

A NATION AT RISK, THE REPORT OF THE NATIONAL COMMISSION ON EXCELLENCE IN EDUCATION

Acknowledgements

SUCH A WORK DOES NOT, AND CANNOT, COME ABOUT in isolation. It achieves heights because it stands on the shoulders of giants. Academics and practitioners who have inspired me to go much, much further than simple customer service or marketing or CRM or e-commerce texts.

Included here should be E. F Schumacher, Eric Berne, Brad Templeton, Queens of the Stone Age, Peter Checkland, Tom Peters (for *Thriving on Chaos* – still a fantastic book), Tom Stonier, Gordon B. Hinckley, Clifford Cocks, James Ellis, Martin Hellman, Whitfield Diffie, Alan Turing, Charles Babbage.

Many thanks to my tireless research leader, Carla Bule, who manages to locate vital references and examples from around the world in four different languages without complaint. To my resident creatives (if you type that term in Microsoft Word you are asked if you want to "Ignore All" – it makes you think), my cool e-kids (Reuben, Zak Bronte, and all those in the future), Haydn, Spen, Ellie, Judge, and Greg.

The help of the e-customer experience community was immense. I didn't want to send out a book that had not been forged in the fires of their experience as well as mine and, as a result of their dedication, this aim has been achieved. Thanks are due to Bruno Girin, Tracy "Trev" Ashdown, Morgan Lynch, Ian Maltman, all the people at ebates.com, the Centrica team, and Maverick and Strong for its permission to publish its framework and diagrams in book form.

Let me not forget the dedicated Pearson team, led in the UK by Richard "never at his desk" Stagg, a man who understands what his online customers want and is building far more for them than a publisher has ever attempted before. Rachael Stock for caring that the books she works on make a real difference. Thanks to Tim Moore for ensuring that this book could get real and get local in the market of markets.

Preface

Excellence is not dead. It got speeded up and turned around, but it is more important than it has ever been. Not excellence in the eyes of the business – that won't save you; it needs to be excellence in the eye of the customer. Above all it is excellence that will need to reach out to the unconvinced 85 percent of internet users who surf but do not buy, and to the unconnected 85 percent of the general population who do not feel the need to use the internet at all. The 15 percent of net users willing to buy are driving forward the growth of electronic commerce, but their purchases are still only a small proportion of customer expenditure each year.[1]

> **Excellence** is not dead. It got **speeded up** and turned around, but it is more **important** than it has ever been.

If you want to do business with an online customer and make a profit at the same time, then admit to yourself that these are tough but rewarding objectives. To achieve them you will have to learn a lot. You can learn through hard personal experience or the experiences of hundreds of others whose expertise has been collected and structured in this book.

You may have already worked out that an e-customer doesn't want to be sold to, but, to make business work, you need to sell. He has to buy, but hates shopping. He likes life and he likes the net. He cares about interconnection, but doesn't understand how it is all achieved. "He" can be a she, old or young, from any race, location or level of techno-literacy. And you have to do business with him. You have to play the games that he is playing. You have to become his third place – where he goes to get away from home and work, somewhere to relax and be fulfilled, but there's a lot of competition.

Anyone who has to make money from online customers (now that the gravy train has pulled out of dot com city) will want to know how to build a profitable, differentiated, sought after, world-beating customer experience. That's why I have written this book on how to design companies, products, user interfaces, marketing, and packaging to attract, amuse, interest, satisfy, and retain the e-customer. This is the decade of systems integrity. It is the age of the big picture, the smallest detail pursued with relentless brilliance, so that it all combines to heighten the holistic impact of your proposition.

I have been on a worldwide, seat of my pants quest to find the businesses in North America, Europe, Africa, and Asia that have understood the needs of the linchpin e-customer. They're profiled and analyzed in case studies ranging from the one-person business to the mega-corporation and across every sector. I was told again and again that it is not (never was) enough to make the page pretty or functional or funky. It is not enough to be on the web or WAP or digital TV. It has to be profitable and harmonious. It has to be a world-beater in some key aspect or it will not move beyond a defensive use of funds or a hobby.

66 It is not (never was) enough to make the page pretty or functional or funky. 99

My own interest in the relationship between customers and businesses started young. You might say that I was a customer prodigy. My father was a successful sales manager in the (then young) computer industry and I would accompany him on sales trips, sitting in the car listening and discussing his approach to his customers. Much of his wisdom has remained with me, including, "never discuss the deal until you are out of sight of the customer," "don't give in to the short term," "respect the secretaries," and "never make price your key selling point."

This interest also showed itself in my fascination with the automobile industry. This went far beyond an interest in the vehicles themselves and was centered on the reasons for a customer buying one model or make rather than another model or make. It was soon apparent – as I collected brochures, hung out in showrooms and discussed it with drivers – that what was bought and sold went far beyond the technical characteristics of the automobiles. A Ford was not bought simply because it was faster, more economical, or safer than the equivalent General Motors offering.

Instead, it was a complex combination of image, history, service, and the experience of buying and owning a Ford. In those days, the "Ghia" badge meant something and it – along with velour trim, luxurious marketing documentation, and the ever-present garage that worked alongside every dealership – meant that the car-buying public was exchanging its money for something worth every penny.

> ❝ **The conclusion** I have come to again and again is that **only respect**, value, **humanity, and** integrity win the day. ❞

The conclusion I have come to again and again as I observe the customer – business relationship is that only respect, value, humanity, and integrity win the day. The impact is not always immediately apparent. Some businesses manage for a while, sometimes decades, to show condescension and a lack of appreciation while remaining profitable. Lack of competition can protect them, lack of sophistication on the part of customers can protect them, or some lingering advantage in the eyes of customers can tip the balance and keep them buying, but, eventually, the competition increases, customers become better informed, and the advantages dwindle. Then, the customers happily wreak their revenge. Businesses that listen to their customers will learn, before this damage reaches the critical point, the sources of dissatisfaction and the dreams that customers have that the business can play a part in fulfilling.

Examples? Ericsson mobile phones were fashionable for a short while in the mid 1990s, they were loved by those who admired engineering while phones remained a technological purchase. Since then, they have dwindled as a must-have purchase because they no longer speak to customers' needs and hungers. Where Ericsson failed, Nokia succeeded because it understood that customers wanted to have fun, show off their purchases. If Ericsson had asked its customers, it would have found out that including cool games, ring tones, graphics, and exchangeable covers had become higher priorities than sound quality (which was expected) or tri-band coverage (which was featured in a phone that looked just like the cheaper versions – where is the fun in that?) They didn't ask, though, the screens stayed small, and, when they finally started to wake up, the bond between phone and customers was firmly established with Nokia, which, in the words of Mr Kallasvuo,[2] had "the design, the branding, and the technology."

My work allows me to say what I really want to say and do on behalf of every customer in the world – every full-of-expectations customer, every evolved, enhanced, eclectic, full-of-life customer. For every single one of those, I want to grab the company by the lapels and beat the living daylights out of them. Not because I am against the person who is serving me – that person I recognize as an individual – but the company – the company has organized itself to irritate me. Why didn't it organize itself to help me? It is such a waste of resources when I am told that, "It's not me that you want to speak to; it's the great big brand in the sky."

> **Who wants to** just lead a boring working **life delivering** mediocre, indifferent, lukewarm, average services to customers?

My research has revealed a strong link between revenue, customer satisfaction, and employee satisfaction. The explanation is that when people (employees) are allowed to have pride in doing a good job, they serve customers better. *They* are happier, *customers* are happier. Who wants to just lead a boring working life delivering mediocre, indifferent, lukewarm, average services to customers? What is the point in living your whole corporate life and going out with a whimper? The customers sure don't appreciate it. Should the whole world be mired in mediocrity? Why should customers be unhappy? Why should customer service staff be unhappy? What makes the difference between happy and unhappy people? Desire for excellence. There are too many miserable people and far too many miserable, miserable companies. This simply will not work in a surplus society that wants to encourage customers to spend precious time and money online. You will need much better than that to attract them in and keep them happy and profitable.

Paco Underhill, author of *Why We Buy: The science of shopping* (Simon & Schuster and Orion, 1999) examines the behavior of customers in the real world and describes over 900 different scenarios and what they mean for effective real-world store design. He makes it clear in one chapter of his entertaining and insightful book that he feels the electronic world doesn't measure up to the real-world experience. It is too cold, he says, and, if it is to compete, it must be fun.

Unfortunately for the reader who wants to make the electronic experience competitive, he doesn't go on to say what should be changed. He does not look in detail at "why they buy" online. He does not answer those questions. This is what this book seeks to do. We intend to justify your purchase of this book by filling it full of value, but we cannot do 20 years of research into online shopping because there have not yet been 20 years of online shopping! The statistical reports do not equal the "science of online shopping," but this book makes a bold start in that direction by applying the rigor of other disciplines to the question of why customers buy online.

I hope you have read my previous book, *E-Customer* (FT.com, 2000) and now want to know how to put that rich understanding of the e-customer into practice. It was an impassioned plea for creativity and innovation to be applied to improving the life of the e-customer. Services and stuff with a soul were demanded. It introduced the mind of the evolved, electronic customer so that businesses could start to understand why and how the demands of successful business have increased.

Readers inspired by the e-customer manifesto will want to put that inspiration to good use by practically applying it. This book sets out a structure for designing so that the online customer is enthralled. There is no other book published in the world that takes a holistic view of what it takes to build the e-customer experience from organizational structure to website design with everything in between.

Alternatives to reading this book are:

- lose your business;
- lose your mind;
- read a web design book (don't worry about the bottom line);
- read a "how to get into e-commerce" book (don't worry about the customers);
- miss out on the killer advances.

Following the steps in the book will ensure that e-customer hearts, heads, and credit cards are won over by focused and effective creativity. You will start to increase margins, roam across borders and maximize returns per online customer – all this through aligned design of organization, training, project management, user interfaces, packaging, business models, and more. Indeed, everything *has* to be aligned if it is to magnify the resources utilized in the service of the online customer. It is all good, practical, thought-provoking, inspiring, sensational, logical, common-sense stuff. It will include hot (and not) examples of this fledgling art and science. It will also feature insights from those who have proved their expertise by creating enthralling customer experiences. And lots of checklists. Game on!

Note

To save endless repetition of "he or she" we have mainly used the male gender indiscriminately to denote both genders.

How to use this book

Objectives

Why They Don't Buy is a field book, a travel into the practicalities companies need to put in place in order to create an experience that is capable of delivering what customers want, concluding with the steps companies need to take in order that the necessary projects and initiatives are launched, maintained, and succeed.

This book brings together my expertise as the original online customer and my knowledge of the corporate world. Its aim is to enrol you and your company in the great cause of the e-customer experience program.

Structure

The book starts with a passionate plea for excellence in the preface, builds up throughout the nine chapters based around different parts of the experience framework and culminates with the e-customer manifesto.

It can be read from beginning to end, which allows you to have a complete view of the online customer universe, or it can be read in bits, which allows you to go directly to the specialist elements that compose the program.

Each chapter is structured the same way:

> experience framework
> experience studies
> stuff to think about
> activities.

Experience framework

Each framework involves identifying the key aspects to consider when building each stage of the e-customer experience and identifying the dangerous pitfalls to avoid when ensuring that the online customer is the company's focus.

Each experience framework has been designed to include all the issues, components, and subjects that you need to deal with in order to deliver electronic experiences that can sell to your customers. There are reasons for most experiences not reaching the majority, and a rigorous application of the framework will identify and provoke solutions so that the experience can be adapted to fit the needs of the customer.

Experience studies

The electronic experience – everything that your customers feel when they are in your space – is a consumer product, service, an entertainment venue, and a work of art. It will be judged on all those levels and not only on one occasion, but throughout the experience over time and at each stage of the relationship. That is why experience studies are presented with features that are reminiscent of consumer product, film, and music reviews. We are rigorously subjective, just as your customers will be – the difference is that the customer rarely tells your business how well or badly the interaction has gone and, even when he does tell you, he lacks the framework to explain why it went wrong and how it can be improved.

We also look at the aims, objectives, history, technology, and people related to the experience to see the impact that they have had on the experience reviewed. The experience is the product of the people and the actions of those people. To understand its strengths and weaknesses, it is vital to see the experience in those terms.

Stuff to think about

The e-customer is ever-changing, his universe is multifaceted and you and your company needs to grasp and understand that same universe using all the means you can. To help you, we have gathered together a list of books, articles, TV shows, and websites, stuff we have pondered, that illustrate some aspects of what we are preaching about and expand your vision for the complexity of the online customer experience creation and delivery process.

Activities

At each stage of the implementing process of the online customer experience, we have created a set of activities that you can find at the end of each chapter. By using the activities, you and your team will be able to assess how far you are from the e-customer's heart and how good the experience you are providing is.

The aim of these activities is to implement the "thinking about and acting according the e-customer advantage" culture, where you start to feel like he feels and, as a consequence, be in a position to create the unique experience he's looking for.

Using the activities, you'll also be able to compare the experience you're providing with the competition and learn from it. The activities, more than their intrinsic value, are valuable because they allow discussion groups to be formed around each chapter.

Around the book you will also find hyperlinks that link paragraphs and chapters throughout the book and link this book to my previous work, *E-Customer*, in order to provide you with an inspiring and enriching experience just by reading it.

Enjoy the trip!

" New websites are currently being added to the internet at a rate in excess of four million sites a day. By the end of 2002, the number of websites will exceed the world population. More than 80 percent of the pages on these sites will be no more than a year old. Your customers have plenty of places to spend their time and money rather than with you so your experience needs to attract, reward, and bond, creating real relationships. **"**

MAX MCKEOWN, *E-CUSTOMER*

The e-customer experience – what's it all about?

Can't make it easy but we can make it simpler to get yourself organized to get closer to those evolved, demanding customers

The five practical steps of an e-customer program

What brings together every business on this fair planet? What they all share – whatever the industry sector, geographic location, or size – is their absolute reliance on customers as their only source of income.

> ❝ **What brings** together every **business on this** fair planet? Reliance on **customers.** ❞

That makes sense doesn't it? It means that every effort in a business should be aimed at ensuring that customers keep on providing that income in ever-increasing amounts. Each person involved in the business needs to know how the work he does relates to customers. There should be a link between all work done and how the customer perceives the business.

Focusing on online customers' needs involves all areas of the business. Marketing people cannot do it alone because the offer they make must be delivered. Customer sales and service people cannot do it alone because their team must be supported by operational structure and flow and by technology applications and infrastructure. Each project and the performance of each individual or group should be judged on the difference it makes to a profitable, sustainable online customer relationship.

In the world of e-customers, expectations are running higher than anywhere else. Fueled by science fiction and dot com advertising, these expectations mean that the e-customer is not grateful nor passive. He knows that everything is possible in this post-DNA world and he expects that anyone who wants his money (because that is what you want isn't it?) will do everything for him.

Of course, business has always been based on meeting customers' needs, but don't make the mistake of minimizing the radical changes in the customer relationship that have occurred. He is faster and smarter than ever before and the previously impossible, unaffordable, or unprofitable can now be delivered to him with margins intact and time to spare. That's the power of e and it's the power that the online customer is depending on to make life better.

The e-customer program recognizes that the business is not relevant simply because it spends a lot of money and time trying to convince customers to buy. It is relevant to the extent that it makes a difference to customers' lives. The real reasons that your particular business is successful may not be known. The truth is to be found "in the online customer's opinion" and in his life.

There are five vital, vital implementation steps that should be followed when launching an online customer initiative, change program, project, or product. These are set out below. There really is no end to an e-customer program, only a series of new beginnings and both incremental and radical improvements. Nevertheless, to get started you will have to go through the sequence once.

66 There **are five vital**, vital **implementation** steps that should be followed **when launching** an online **customer initiative**, change program, **project**, or product. **99**

Each time you go through the steps, you will benefit from a virtuous circle of implementation and refinement. Pretty soon, you will find that killer advances become more frequent, but more about that later in the book (check out the index for more references). Back to the steps you need to take.

Step 1: understand *your* online customer

The stereotypical descriptions are not only inaccurate and out of date but also dangerous to your business objectives. The e-customer is as likely to be a she as a he, old as young, tech-novice as tech-expert. Online customers are as diverse as humanity and becoming much more so. Statistics may give you a starting point, but understanding summary statements about someone else's e-customers will not be enough. You need to dive into the mind of *your* e-customer – those you have and those you want. Not liking this "techie stuff" or not thinking that you are in the dot com business will not save you. If you have customers, then you already have online customers. If you want more profitable customers then you need *more* online customers. To build a relationship requires more than software stamped with the legendary acronym "CRM" (customer relationship management), it requires a self-sustaining exchange between two individuals who know and like each other. He doesn't yet know that you are worth spending time with, so the first move is up to you.

Step 2: figure out what difficult stuff he wants that you can give him

As a lover of people, culture, and cool stuff, you will be better placed to figure out something really valuable: where is the difficult stuff? There are so many problems in the world for which the e-customer wants solutions. Once you are in his head, you can walk around and see where the friction and the dreams are. Zowee!

Using the Malkovich method (you recall the film *Being John Malkovich* where various characters *were* John Malkovich for a time?) you are surrounded by potential, unrealized value. You just have to quickly step through what the solution would look like. Then ask, how much would the online customer pay for it? Can we solve his problem with the capabilities that we already have? Which of the many difficult problems available can we solve that will be more difficult for our competitors to solve? Which of these life enhancers creates the greatest difference between delivery cost to your business and purchase value to the online customer?

Now you are ready for the next stage, which is to get more people involved.

Step 3: get a team together to deliver what he wants – a council of ideas

Technology is another word for tools. Tools are the result of specific human expertise applied to solving problems. As the technological component of each new product or service increases, the intelligence in them increases. There are top-of-the-line sports sweatshirts jam-packed full of intelligence – reflecting light, transferring sweat, and reducing my drag coefficient. The same is true of every computer, automobile, television, or piece of designer furniture.

So, ask yourself: where does the intelligence come from? The answer is people. All services and products have people involvement. Better services and products have more people involvement. The best services and products (hereafter referred to as stuff!) have not only the best people involved but also the best of those people. They have not only engineering answers to mechanical problems, they are also filled with humanity! You will need a team that can comment on and create all aspects of the stuff that speaks the language of the e-customer.

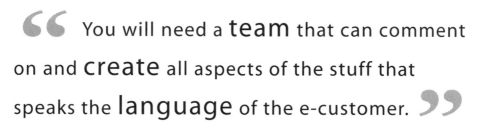

66 You will need a **team** that can comment on and **create** all aspects of the stuff that speaks the **language** of the e-customer. 99

Next, set the team free on Step 4.

Step 4: deliver an end-to-end experience that delivers what the customer wants

You have the team and the idea. Now is the time to wrap it up in an experience. This isn't just dressing; it's not just the nice-to-have. The way in which a service or product is delivered is as vital and as relevant to the perception of reality as the service or product itself – it is the reality. Don't think that products do not deliver an experience because they do. The moment of purchase is an experience. So is the day-to-day life with a product. And so is the moment when there is a problem with the product.

The experience is everything that the e-customer senses when he is involved with your product or service. It's everything that he hears, sees, tastes, smells, thinks, and feels. It all matters and it is what he buys. Brands are only worth what they deliver. First you make the promise, then you deliver – or fail to deliver. This step is all about what makes an experience increase the benefit the e-customer gains from spending his money on your stuff and, as a result, the profitability of your business.

It is foolhardy to expect any loyalty based only brand recognition. Many electronic experiences are so unsatisfying that the customer is only very loosely bonded to the brand. As soon as something better (or even different!) presents itself, the customer is pulled towards the alternative. Need evidence? Well, 68 percent of customers have not remained loyal to one internet service provider, 83 percent have abandoned a shopping cart when they are online because they want to compare prices on other sites before buying anything, and 60 percent stopped dealing with a company online when they had a particularly bad customer service experience.[1] Are you surprised? I hope not.

Don't blame the internet! A large proportion – 62 percent – of customers think that it is "essential to everyday life," 70 percent think it is integral to their work, and a further 20 percent think it will be in the future. You have to blame the experience. You will have to improve that all-important experience. Then, maybe 62 percent of customers will feel that your offer is "essential to everyday life." Isn't that worth aiming for?

Step 5: keep it fresh and stay in business

This is important. Loyalty cannot be bought. The relationship is owned only by the online customer. The only way that you are going to keep on keeping on is to keep the imagination and interaction humming and generating new and improved everything while building real relationships that will mean more than a line in a database. This means processes and platforms that work, day and night, night and day, always and forever. It means knowing what to do when they fail (which they will even though you have built them not to). It requires cultural vigor and playfulness, the science of foolishness.

The importance of the five steps

These are not just steps but steps filled with principles. You would be investing your time wisely if you read the e-customer manifesto at the end of this book (and get your hands on a copy of my book, *E-Customer*, from which it is adapted). They are important steps and the practicalities of implementing them are set out throughout the rest of this book in lists, anecdotes, and diagnostics. I have the privilege of having created the principles and steps; you will have the privilege (and profits) of implementing them for your online customers.

Check back here through the steps to see whether or not you are making progress on the big picture. The steps will inform your efforts to reap the rewards of this approach. The great truth is that no efforts in any one of the steps will be wasted as long as you seek to understand your e-customer so that you can help him out.

Is this soft-hearted nonsense?

> Every action that's been attacked in this case was Microsoft working on behalf of consumers.
> BILL GATES

At this point, some will ask (not you surely?) if these steps describe a fairy-tale world somewhere beyond Judy's rainbow. Too many do not believe that their work can be based on genuinely helping the online (or any other kind of) customer.

Is this true? Nope. A business is successful because, by chance or planning, it meets some kind of customer need. A business will continue to be successful only when it continues to meet the needs of the e-customer. You might be lucky – let's hope so – but the weight of history over the centuries, and particularly the past few decades, is against you. If you're not feeling lucky, it's no time to be a punk.

Stress relief for e-customer pioneers

An online customer project has to be difficult to be worthwhile, but it does not have to lead to burnout, divorce or psychotherapy. This book compiles the experiences and expertise of those who have made understanding the online customer their life's work.

The five-implementation steps provide a remarkably helpful roadmap for the whole e-customer team. They are a straightforward structure for viewing the entire lifetime of every initiative, project, product, campaign, department, and the business itself.

❝ An online customer project has to be **difficult to be** worthwhile, but it does not **have to lead** to burnout, divorce or psychotherapy. ❞

These steps will be returned to again and again in the book. As you implement the steps, you will find that you keep on referring to the same steps and the questions that accompany them. You will keep asking yourself:

- "Do I understand *my* e-customer?"
- "Have I found something difficult to do for him that he will really thank me for?"
- "Do I have a team and a culture capable of delivering what he wants?"
- "Are we designing and delivering an experience that heightens the value and enjoyment that the online customer gains from our product or service?"
- "How do we keep it fresh and stay in business?"

Each chapter of this book that sets out how a step works is packed with practical advice in a variety of different formats. This not only avoids you dying of boredom but also makes sure that you can find exactly the right answer to any particular e-customer issue that you face.

This book is filled with tools and wisdom for all members of the e-customer team. Each practitioner of the e-customer principles and implementer of the e-customer steps will come to the project with specific areas of expertise, a role in the project, and experience in certain parts of the online customer experience. The book is designed to give answers to each team member relating to their specialist role while at the same time ensuring that those who read (and study it) will have a view of the overall picture and plug significant gaps in their own point of view or experience.

We humans tend to have less empathy for specialties that are not our own. This may have been good enough to land each of us in our current role but it is not good enough when designing and delivering the ultimate e-customer experience. To do that everyone needs to understand exactly how vital all elements of the mix are.

When you redesign a business for any reason, it demands an understanding of multiple disciplines. The more radical the change, the more essential it is to have comprehensive and deep cohesion between each element of the organization. As you know, it is not unusual for good online customer ideas to be delayed for months while business and IT try to understand each other. Each to some extent hides behind their expertise (of their own area) and their ignorance (of the other area).

Make sure when you put together your e-customer team that its members represent each business function who are roughly at the same level of influence within the organization. To avoid the specter of people using authority instead of reason to change the decisions of the team, choose team members.

There are some innovations that can only be created if all elements of the business mix are inside the same head of at least one person in the meeting. This is because people do not tend to innovate in areas that they do not understand. They are just about coping with the basic change in the system needed, let alone moving ahead of the current level of thinking.

The online customer team must be capable of ensuring that the original pure and enjoyable objectives of the project are not hijacked by well-meaning, boring, visionless committees that will translate the thrilling mission of the e-project into gray, soulless, pedantic slop.

❝ The online customer team must be capable of ensuring **that the original** pure **and enjoyable** objectives of the project are not **hijacked. ❞**

Each needs to be so dedicated to the e-customer that, even when busy with the project, the partnerships and the process they do not forget to focus on the e-customer.

This book has been written to help anyone who has to do business with online customers, particularly the teams organized to refocus on their many and varied needs.

I want you to be able to invest your time, effort, and money in making a real difference in your e-customers' lives. This book has been written to save you time figuring out how to tackle the task, what to do next, who should do what, how to manage projects, and how to spot danger and avoid it. It contains checklists, tips, forms, techniques, brainstorming ideas, and tools that have been developed with the aid of painful experience.

Without it, the only way to gain this knowledge is for you to go through the same painful problems, but, in the end, you would only learn lessons that have already been learnt. End result? You will be behind the best of the competition. I view waste as evil. It improves nothing. Reading and applying the lessons here will avoid waste in your project, leading to a better, more profitable, more valuable project delivery for all who invest in it.

The book presents examples and case studies from each continent, from varied sectors, and from the most popular electronic experiences in the world, including Yahoo!, AOL, eBay, Amazon, J. C. Penney, Ananova, MSN, First Direct, Spiegel, Boo, and Real. The combination of screen shot analysis, principles, flow, and structure will improve any electronic experience if the principles are applied.

Warning: you are expected to improve on what this book contains! You will have to make it yours by writing in the margins, writing its checklists up on whiteboards, and adding its principles to your project plans and objectives. Each time you and a million other readers of the book work with its techniques, they will be adapted and improved. That is a key part of the messages: the relationship with the online customer is neverending if it keeps on improving.

> ❝ **The relationship** with the online customer is neverending **if it keeps on improving.** ❞

Let me know about your experiences with this book. Send me your suggestions, your anecdotes, your challenges, and your successes. This is the first of what we hope will be many editions and the lessons learned will become part of each new edition. Use the companion website at **www.maxmckeown.com** to share your ideas and discuss them with the e-customer community. You will be able to benefit from downloadable checklists, spreadsheets, and presentations, and there will be new articles, online customer news, web logs, and the e-mail column that I write (nearly!) every week.

Bookmark the site and you will be kept up to date with the mind and will of the ever-changing online customer. Join us, destroy apathy and create value for and from the e-customer.

Experience study

Who wants to be a Millionaire?
– don't just sit there

The experience is stomach churning. The mood is set by the tense theme music. The pressure increased by the tone of the presenter. We are in the electronic experience inspired by the hit game show and it feels mighty convincing. The room, the chairs, the flat panels, and the screen displays, all in their places.

So how did we get here? A free CD-ROM giveaway with a breakfast cereal provided the specific route into the electronic experience. Here I am, with my son, playing. He wonders if I can win the million jackpot and, fortunately, I manage it by correctly identifying what a "parsec" is.

The CD also encouraged us to look at the online version of the game at abc.com, which, when my son returned from school, is what we dutifully did. It's by far the most appealing item on the abc.com website and also suitably prominent. In a click, we find ourselves in 'WWTBAM' country, complete with photos of Reg Philbin from the US TV edition of the show.

The theme music is used effectively. If you go to the site, try it with and without the music. Huge difference, isn't there? The combination of sound and the layout, which are instantly familiar, send you back to the show. The version of the game for the Sony Playstation benefits from the same instant recognition of theme, but has no representation of the game show host. Strangely, the board game comes without a CD-ROM soundtrack.

The main feature that it is worth you focusing on for this experience study is the offer that is made on the website:

> "Don't just sit there ... interact with ABCs Enhanced TV."

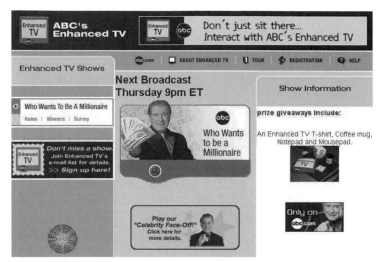

FIGURE 1.1

Don't just sit there ... interact.

What is this "Enhanced TV"? It's not interactive television in the usual sense. Instead, ABCs version of enhanced TV involves both live television and the internet to bring the customer into the television broadcast of the *Who Wants to Be a Millionaire?* (WWTBAM) show.

It's a combined electronic experience that uses two channels and multiple senses to great effect. It has worked even on the skeptical, world-weary world of journalists. Listen to this praise:

Hyperlink

See Chapter 5.

Read all about the seven senses and five or more channels that can be used to enhance the experience.

> The most interactive television application in the United States so far ...[2]
>
> Brings a new level of excitement to a television viewing experience ...[3]
>
> A whole lot of fun to play. This is internet technology at its best.[4]

Responsible for the customer focus and creativity that has produced such an effective experience is the Interactive Team from Disney (that makes sense doesn't it?) The team has also been busy building experiences around other live programing, including US football, that have impressed many who had tired of waiting for the day that convergence would deliver.

Every TV show that is "enhanced" in this way shows a yellow "I" icon on the screen to alert internet-enabled customers (half of the 100 million television households have internet access and 30 million multitask anyway) that they can log on and play along with the show. Each customer can answer the questions as they appear on TV for the contestant to answer. At the same time, customers answering via the internet are competing against, on average, 125,000 other customers who are also playing on a live scoreboard every night.

FIGURE 1.2

Who wants
to be?

This pulls the customer into the experience very powerfully at all levels. He is willing on the player and stepping into the arena with him, while at the same time being connected, however competitively, with many other customers, including friends and family. He hears the music, the voice of Philbin, sees the questions, and becomes immersed for, on average, 41 minutes – more than the internet browsing average for the rest of the web world.

Customers who play along receive points equal to the dollar value of the question each time they get one correct, with bonus points awarded for answering rapidly. Breaks for advertising on the TV means further sponsored bonus questions about what has already happened on the show that night for additional game points.

Customers are not allowed to simply sit back passively and talk during or ignore the advertisements. Instead, the experience and commercial sponsorship combine to continue to be the interactive center of attention, with 94 percent staying to interact even through commercials. This is further strengthened by the full-time sponsorship from McDonald's that uses multimedia advertising (Flash) and questions on special containers of French fries.

There is even now a mobile phone version of WWTBAM. In the UK, text M to 8889 and play for prizes. It is just one more step towards the merging of all channels into an end-to-end cultural experience. No wonder the term "want to phone a friend" has crept into everyday conversation whenever someone takes too long to make a decision.

Sadly, there is no community built directly into the *WWTBAM?* experience. It is still possible to find the bulletin board for the show, but this wastes customer effort and risks them never finding it. For a media

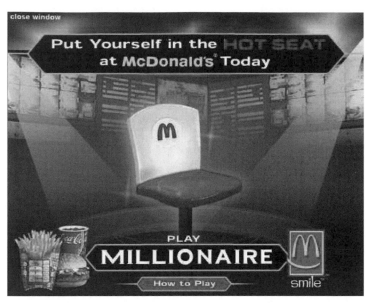

FIGURE 1.3

The hot seat at McDonald's millionaire game.

player founded on advertising, losing customers for no reason seems naive or at least careless. Such lack of care has, no doubt, contributed towards the demise of the portal go.com that hosts the Millionaire game.

There is a newsletter to give customers all the latest news and prompts about the show as it continues. The bulletin boards are a little dull and slow. There is no chat to allow a community to develop during and after the show. Missed opportunity? Yep, but, with e-mail feedback being encouraged and used to enhance future offerings, 80 percent say that they want more and 97 percent will use it again. The result is a success for ABC and a set of significant lessons have been learned for other experience providers to build into their offerings.

Stuff to think about

books, articles, tv shows, and websites

Adams, Scott, *The Dilbert Future: Thriving on stupidity in the 21st century* (HarperCollins, 1997)

A cartoonist, as an observer of life and the people living it, is as valid a guide to the needs of the online customer as any. Scott's book is worth reading for the sections on "Spider Web Marketing Strategy," "Busy

Life," and "Clothing of the Future" alone. His predictions include the very, very likely "Your clothes will become smarter than you."

Cairncross, Frances, *The Death of Distance* (Harvard Business School Press, 1997)

Of course, distance did not really die in 1997, but it did reduce its automatic impact on customer relationships. You can start to act as though your e-customer is in the next room right up until you need to send him something physical. This book is a classic (and now historic) account of how far telecommunications have progressed.

Crainer, Stuart, and Dearlove, Des, *Generation Entrepreneur: Shape today's business reality, create tomorrow's wealth, do your own thing* (FT.com, 2000)

The number one future career plan among MBA students is to own their own business. If you want the top thinkers and doers on your team, it makes sense to recognize what they seek in entrepreneurship. Then simply (!) build it into your online customer culture. Free them to be rewarded based on profitably pleasing the e-customer. You will find that this "new" breed of customer and manager are both much happier than they have ever been.

Dixon, Patrick, *Future Wise: Six faces of global change* (HarperCollins*Publishers*, 1998)

The future that Dixon predicts may be faster, more urban, more universal, more radical, more tribal, and more ethical. He argues that market research is not enough because it only shows what customers (think they) want today. By the time you get to market, their needs will have changed. Better, then, to try to look ahead and depend on futurologists?

Peters, Tom, *Thriving On Chaos* (Alfred A. Knopf, 1987)

Love this book. Subtitled as a "Handbook for a management revolution," it covers a complete program for organizational renewal. Peters heralded a complete change in business publishing tone, but few have lived up to this standard. In recent years, Peters has chosen to write more on the importance of work for individuals rather than explaining the state-of-the-art in customer focus. It was to fill this gap that *E-Customer* and this book have been written. Write another customer book Tom!

Ridderstrale, Jonas, and Nordstrom, Kjell, *Funky Business* (Bookhouse Publishing AB, 1999)

It's like being given a breathless synopsis of management thinking of the twentieth century in a funky, Swedish accent. A bestseller, and rightly so, because it fluently demonstrates how time-honored business thinking can be metamorphosed to meet the needs of an altered situation. Funky business for funky e-customers.

Raymond, Eric S, *Cathedral and the Bazaar* (O'Reilly & Associates, 1999)

Raymond looks like a stereotypical picture of a "techie." He has the hair, the mannerisms, and the obsessions. His book is a good taster of what big-thinking techies are discussing. Proud to be called hackers (the good guys who build things) and not crackers (the bad guys who break things), this group fights for better code and a better world with almost violent zeal. You need this power in your business.

Siegel, David, *Futurize Your Enterprise: Business strategy in the age of the e-customer* (John Wiley & Sons, 1999)

It's been criticized by some for failing to explain who the e-customer is or what he wants but Siegel, who became well known for his book on web design – *Creating Killer Web Sites* (Hayden, 1997) – is one more voice arguing that the needs of the e-customer should shape the organization.

Senge, Peter, *The Fifth Discipline Fieldbook* (Currency Doubleday, 1990)

To look after the online customer, your company will have to be a learning organization. Peter Senge examines this learning dimension, or fifth discipline, in an encyclopedic volume full of references, case studies, and lots and lots of thinking. It's not an easy book, but it will pay dividends to those who perservere.

Geus, Arie de, *et al.*, *The Living Company* (Harvard Business School Press, 1997)

The average lifespan of a Fortune 500 company is less than half a century, yet there also are corporations around the world that have been in business for 200, 500, even 700 years. Arie de Geus maintains that the most enduring treat their companies as "living work communities" rather than pure economic machines.

Activity 1.1

Starting to think about the e-customer advantage

Ask each team member to complete this, in written form, before your next meeting. Send it as an e-mail or put it on the company intranet exactly as it is set out. In this way, the whole team will need to start using the e-customer's basic tools. Send them a copy of *E-Customer* so that they can gain new information rather than just depending on what they already know.

The written answers are then given in anonymously, collated in a presentation entitled "Thinking about the e-customer advantage," and distributed. The results will provide a first-level refinement of the discussion of the first meeting and a platform of consensus for the rest of the project.

Think of everything: consensus building

When will we finish this by? _____

1 • In our company, who knows most about how e-customers are evolving?
  • Which groups? Which individuals?
  • Do we involve them in planning or designing for the e-customer?

2 • Where do you love to shop?
  • Which is your favorite online business?
  • Why?

3 • What are the top three reasons for online customers buying your services/products?
  • How do you know that?
  • How often do you interact with your own e-customers?

4 • What/who could stop this working? How could we prevent that?
  • Rate its importance on a 1–5 scale.

5 • Create your first draft e-customer web.
    – Write the word "e-customer" in the middle of a piece of paper.
    – Add the channels (real and virtual) he uses/uses with you.
    – Add the senses that he uses/uses with you.
    – Add the locations that he uses/uses with you.
    – Add the relationships that he has at home and at work.
    – Add the problems/objectives that he has.

6 • What problems does your business face now/over the next five years.

• How could understanding what your online customer wants help to solve those problems?

7 • What would you want your online customer to say about your business?

8 • What do you hate about your own business from the point of view of an e-customer. Think hard now!

9 • Name something that you do for the online customer that no one else does?

10 • Share a quote from *E-Customer* that had the greatest impact on you.

Activity 1.2

E-customer vision: stuff to get the team arguing, thinking, and agreeing

When will we finish this by? _____

Who will attend? _____

Share thinking about the online customer advantage

If you have completed Activity 1.1, share the group's viewpoints by using the presentation to promote debate.

Remember, all the comments should be anonymous. This should be the general rule for the group. Everything it publishes should be from the group, not named individuals. Everyone should sign up to everything but be free to disagree within the group up to the point that the majority has decided to take a particular stance.

At the meeting, organize your team around a table. Break up any natural or historical seating arrangements. Get the marketing representative to sit with operations and arrange for the technology person to work with someone from human resources. The answers should be documented. Preferably, this will be done directly into a presentation so that the group can see the results of the discussions.

Create an existing e-customer model

Draw the diagram up on a whiteboard and ask them how each of the areas contribute to building a profitable online customer experience. Expect the discussion to take about an hour. List in the relevant box short descriptions of the characteristics of the existing contribution. Once the draft is complete, stick it up on the wall.

Create an aspirational e-customer model

Draw the same diagram up on a whiteboard and ask each team member to tell you how he would like the model to look in the future (one to three years). Focus on what the e-customer really wants, what unique service propositions you would like to be able to offer him, and how process, platform, and people can strengthen the killer proposition.

The result of this task is a top-level description of the customer experience that you will offer to your e-customers. Your online customers will experience the results of your organization's components working together (for better or worse) through planned and ad hoc processes. Where these are electronic, it is even more vital that they should be thought through completely from the viewpoint of the e-customer.

After the session, each of the models and explanatory text should be written up and distributed for comment and agreement. Once agreed, the aspirational model provides a consensus that should inform the rest of the initiative, whether this is at project, departmental, or company-wide levels.

Customer experience thinkers

There's another important factor that is radically changing the way organizations have to do business – and that's the customer. Customers have come to expect that we do things their way, rather than that they do things our way. So it's no longer "we'll make whatever we like and the customers will take it because it's the only option they've got." The customer now has many options. Many choices. There are many people competing for the same order and for the same customer dollar.

MICHAEL HAMMER, AUTHOR OF *BEYOND REENGINEERING: HOW THE PROCESS-CENTERED ORGANIZATION IS CHANGING OUR WORK AND OUR LIVES*
(HARPERCOLLINSBUSINESS, 1996)

So again, it's not about product cost, it's about product value. It's about giving customers what they need, which is to help them reach their goals. A lot of people seem to forget that the only way to make money is not through the products but through the benefits those products bring to the customer.

ELI GOLDRATT, AUTHOR OF *PROJECT MANAGEMENT THE TOC WAY*

Being nice to people is just 20 percent of providing good customer service. The important part is designing systems that allow you to do the job right the first time. All the smiles in the world aren't going to help you if your product or service is not what the customer wants.

CARL SEWELL AND PAUL B. BROWN AUTHORS OF *CUSTOMERS FOR LIFE*
(POCKET BOOKS, 1998)

Success is never **final** and
failure is never **fatal.**

WINSTON CHURCHILL

Get this thing on the road

Quick start, quick wins

DESPITE THE VERY GOOD REASONS FOR RESTRUCTURING efforts to build superior online customer experiences, there are many reasons that your good intentions may provide hell-bound paving rather than heaven-bound stairways.

Whoever you are in the organization, you will have to do some convincing, get some money, jump some project queues, educate the willing but ignorant, overcome mucho skepticism, and just plain figure out how to fit "one more project" into the business calendar. That could take some time and, meanwhile, the online customer is getting away and you have no proof that these e-customer principles work in practice in *your* organization.

> **66** **Whoever you are** in the **organization,** you will have to do some convincing, that could **take some time** and, meanwhile, **the online** customer is **getting** away. **99**

What could slow you down?

- A lot of people will think that they have heard it all before. They will minimize the differences between the e-customer approach and customer service in general. It is a sad fact that many view customer services as the lowest of the low and will only begrudgingly give it the focus and the respect that it deserves.

- Achieving consensus (or anything useful that is close to it) takes time and effort. Without it there will be no clear idea about what you are trying to achieve. Result? Many of those who the approach depends on will build their version of whatever it is and the components will not fit. So, consensus of a kind is worth working towards because without it there is no e-customer approach, no total CRM (customer relationship management) just a bunch of individual, departmental efforts, which is what you have now.

- Those who grasp the size of the difference between your existing business approach and the online customer approach will want to avoid what they see as a lot of work (for them) and a lot of risk (for the business). Alternatively, they will decide that the approach would help them better if they were responsible for it or feel that the approach will damage their standing and power. You know how that goes.

Wait, wait then go, go, go!

The flipside of this problem is that when you do get the green light, it will come with an impossibly rapid delivery date. First you are stalled for a year, then you have to deliver in three months. It happens again and again and again. The bane of internal and external project teams everywhere. It leads to lost sleep, legal fisticuffs, costly organizational friction, partially finished "all or nothing" information systems and missed opportunities. You don't want that.

The solution – apart from stoically gritting your teeth and getting on with it – is to stop viewing the creation of the ultimate online customer experience as a particular project with a start date, budget, or end date. Instead (listen carefully here – this might save your career, marriage, and health) you start now. Document each initiative and spread your efforts as far as you can without seeking time-costly approval. Record the successes and add them to the justification for each new budget increase or policy change beyond your immediate control.

This stealth approach has numerous advantages.

- The e-customer gets some benefit now and, as soon as he knows that you are listening and adapting, he will start to return the favor. This is a permanent shift of thinking. The online customer is being invited in, to become part of what you do rather than simply some mug you sell things to. Getting on to his radar will take time and might as well start soon.

- Your experience in e-customer initiatives grows with every small effort. This experience and its resulting expertise will mean that you can better shape each successive initiative. Your confidence in your own abilities and the technique will also grow so that you can speak convincingly and inspirationally as a champion of the online customer.

- Large future projects are given solid foundations and the best chance of success. In the world of businesses shaped around the e-customer, all parts of the business have an impact on the experience and the relationship. The database bone is connected to the CRM bone, which is connected to the customer service bone, which is connected to the marketing bone. Many projects fail because they are not sufficiently well founded, but, by the time those involved find out, no one wants to admit the truth. The time to prepare is now.

- Others will join the ranks of the true believers (!) as they understand the realities of such an approach, the advantages that it brings, and the relentless justification for its adoption. As resistance reduces, the momentum of the project can move forward naturally based on the driving force of successes to date.

As you trial individual techniques, you will gage the level of returns possible from a total online customer approach. As you do this, you and your team should be building up a cost–benefits model for your business that allows investment to be obtained.

What advantages could you expect in the short term from getting into the mind of your e-customer and building the ultimate e-customer experience around him?

- Oversupply and undersupply both reduce profits and they both result from a lack of understanding about what and how the online customer wants to buy.

- Once you reach out into the e-family (the extended network of people for whom the e-customer is a trustworthy influencer), your costs per sale will drop and your sales totals will increase.

- Building each new process around the way that your e-customer thinks, acts, and lives will reduce the friction between the buying signal and the buying action.

- Organizing around the online customer is simply more efficient. You want an example? He doesn't like having two departments to handle complaints, so only have one. He hates being transferred to specialist departments for anything, so get the power to the frontline – it's less costly and creates hypervaluable goodwill that you can turn into supernormal profits.

- Once the e-customer is working for you, with you, he will be prepared to try buying more from you. It's the easiest decision in the world to go to someone you trust for help. As online customer veterans know, integrity is not a luxury it's a necessity. You could call it cross-selling and up-selling if you like, but it's actually just the online customer feeling comfortable with spending more money and time with you.

Put in place some basic measures and you can show how altering the nature of the e-customer relationship and creating humanity-filled experiences is ultra profitable. Linking your efforts to help the e-customer with achieving your own performance objectives will add weight to your opinions and prepare minds to hear your future plans.

View your business, its shareholders, and your management as other e-customers. They have particular needs. They view the world in a certain way. They want results and, once you have proven the link between online customer focus and profitability, they will let you get on with it. Just make sure you speak their language when you explain how it works and why they should get involved.

This stuff isn't just soft-hearted, qualitative or touchy-feely. It works and nothing else will, but you should get measures in place to ensure that there is no other explanation for the improvements than that you and the e-customer are making friends with each other. Rather like these examples:

> **❝ This stuff isn't** just soft-hearted, qualitative or **touchy-feely.** It works and **nothing** else will. ❞

- Recruiting specialist programers (Java architects) is a tough business when demand is so high and supply so limited. Over at Sun Microsystems, one of its team found that the most effective and cost-efficient method for hiring new experts was to spend most of her day online in the technical and job chat rooms where they hang out. It's cheaper and she gets to offer jobs before other recruiters even know that the programer is looking. It's a closed loop relationship.

- Knowing exactly what enhancements real online customers want means that there is no wasted effort building features that will not have an impact on the purchase (or repurchase decision). When dataviz.com sends out e-mails regarding upgrades, it asks for feedback that "will shape the future shape of dataviz software" and provides a simple online form to allow e-customers to become software designers.

It is not only possible to start small and still get big results; it is actually better to do it that way! Let the projects evolve, as you understand the benefits of doing business on the online customer's terms and turf. Then you will see how far empathy and incrementalism takes you and understand what you really want to spend big bucks on.

> **❝ It is not only** possible to start small and still get big results; it is **actually better** to do it **that way! ❞**

Remember that the customer predates e-commerce and exists independent of the internet. He will not wait for your next great project and is, instead, spending his money now on what is available now – a point that is eloquently (if sarcastically) put as follows by one commentator:

> I had always thought of them as people who had never shopped before the introduction of the internet. Then, I imagined, they emerged naked and emaciated, their sole possessions being the credit cards they had been hoarding for years while awaiting the coming of the web.[1]

In the next set of stuff to do, I have put together activities, tasks, and suggestions that are meant for the short term. Some can be started now (by you and your team) and some have no direct monetary cost. They should all be assessed (again, by you and your team) to put them in order of benefit to the e-customer. You are not expected to make a loss at any point here but generally you will find that the needs of the two groups coincide if you just think about it long and creatively enough.

Experience study

Eyestorm.com – "art meets the net"

It's beautiful, and so it should be. Plenty of white space, provocative images, and delicate framing make it quite clear that the customer is now inside an art gallery. Lest you forget that this is a commercial offer, the word, "buy" is appropriately pinned next to the word, "browse." "Have fun," the experience invites, "enjoy, admire, and, then (please) buy a part of this to enhance your own real world environment."

FIGURE 2.1 Eyestorm – home for art.

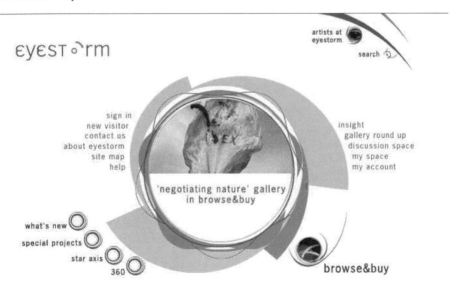

Every option is listed in a highly usable menu that includes everything the customer needs on the first page in fewer than 40 words. Choosing to hide any of the options would be unlikely to simplify the customer's experience as he would then either not know that they were available or have to hunt around each time he needed them. Each option includes additional help information and is positioned with other options in the same group.

As you orient yourself to the structure, your eyes are provided with a range of changing artworks interspersed with information and competitions. The zones of interest are designed to be deep and central to the customer's line of focus rather than distract him.

It even appeals to a sense of fair play. It is all about "empowering the artist and circumventing the layered bureaucracy of art galleries worldwide that oftentimes overcharge buyers while pocketing hefty commissions" – what could be fairer than that?

It explains why a money-making artist such as Damian Hirst – contemporary British artist responsible for the sheep in formaldehyde – is selling limited edition works via the Eyestorm experience. A man who says that: "becoming a brand name is an important part of life"[2] understands that the buying experience needs to be deep and all-inclusive.

Using the expertise of a cross-Atlantic team, Eyestorm has focused on creating all the content that a hip, art-loving, online customer could want amid flow and structure that encourages interaction and that all-important purchase. Focusing first on interaction, the experience offers the art-curious browser the ability to look through an online gallery, trying before you buy. Definitely not just a set of images, the gallery allows the customer to "delve" into art via a gorgeous interactive display built in Flash that uses art concepts and history as navigational aids.

Clicking on a category brings up a selection of artwork for the customer's viewing pleasure. Another click on the artwork that is of interest gives a larger image and – wait for it – the buying details. This is not an experience that is scared about selling, I found myself wanting to buy and possess what I was looking at on the screen.

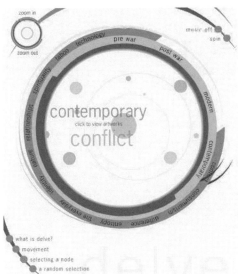

contemporary
conflict

Arnold Crane
Deck Crew aboard USS J F
Aircraft Carrier [$200]

FIGURE 2.2

Eyestorm's innovative navigation process.

Eyestorm feeds the collector in me by allowing me to create my own online gallery in what is known as "My space." Once I have done so, I have my own space in Eyestorm's world and have started to bond with the Eyestorm experience. All that it asks is that I sign up with my details and suddenly I am one of the group, the crowd, and the supporters.

While the customer is feeling pseudo-intellectual, he can also read the discussion board entries. Cleverly, Eyestorm has cajoled or paid thinking friends into writing suitably wide-ranging debates on brands, art, and value. This ensures that the discussion is setting the right tone to match the desire of the customer to structure his time in a "fulfilling" way. Take the following discussion entry from Eyestorm's online editor as a highly appropriate example:

> Nicholas Negroponte claimed that add-on-value was the way to seduce customers in the future. The service industry would no longer make money simply by offering one service but would exceed customer expectations and woo new clients by offering add-on extras. Extra services get you more customers. Negroponte's example was how Fed-ex might offer a dry cleaning service – hence if one was shipping clothes from one end of the country to another (as businessmen often ship shirts from one city to another so they don't have to carry them) the clothes would be dry cleaned free of charge en route, and waiting for you on your doorstep when you arrived home from your travels. Add-on value for customer satisfaction. And the more you offer (as add-on) the better the profit.

I have reproduced this comment here because it kept me thinking and left me with the feeling that the experience was run by intelligent, well-informed people with whom I was happy to have a commercial relationship. In a similar vein, the discussion board is moderated, with comments being vetted (censored!) before they arrive on the site 24 hours later. One critic was allowed to speak openly in the early days of the discussion board. He wanted to know why there was a list of people the experience wanted contributions from:

> It's like you're only asking for those people to contribute, and nobody else. Not very friendly.

There ensues a little "debate" between the online editor and the critic that ends fairly rapidly. The trouble with moderation is that when customers feel they cannot speak freely, they do not speak at all. This reduces the free-flowing debate but does it suit the calm and measured nature of the Eyestorm experience better than some "vulgar" criticism?

What happens when you need some help? It's cool! There is a floating telephone icon that follows the customer around as he uses the scroll bar or moves to another page. Click on it when it works and you can arrange for a call back at your convenience. Click on it when it doesn't work and it gives you a telephone number that you can call at your convenience! Not quite as impressive, but at least the experience's designers built safety into the flow and structure.

While I am waiting for my phone call, I am encouraged to listen to the music, reassured by the no questions ten-day returns policy and the free delivery, and generally beguiled by the experience. This is how the electronic world should be on the whole. It would be great if there were more browsers, it could do with some live help, and they should consider putting part of the gallery within a 3-D world, but, these things aside, it's pretty good.

Stuff to think about

books, articles, TV shows, and websites

Goldratt, Eliyahu M., *It's Not Luck* (Gower, 1995)

It's a good read as a novel and an inspiring read as a business book. Alex, the hero of the book, saves his company (again) by applying lateral thinking to the problems faced by his business and his customers. Set in a manufacturing environment, it could be described as an online customer program prototype in action. Luck should have nothing to do with it.

Sewell, Carl, and Brown, Paul B., *Customers For Life* (Pocket Books, 1998)

Fantastic, down-to-earth account of what customers have always wanted but focused on the real-world experience. The web was not an issue in Sewell's world in the late 1980s, but doing business with Cadillac buyers was (and is). If you can just transfer the essential lessons to the virtual world, you will gain valuable insights. I certainly did (and have).

Activity 2.1

Get thinking (quickly)

This activity is pretty simple but very powerful. If your mind is open to the possibilities, you will be able to make significant improvements in your e-customer experience that will lead to enhanced loyalty and more productive sales/marketing efforts.

Some of this you will already have. Great. Some of this you will already know about. Fine. Are you doing everything on this list, though? Isn't it about time that you did?

	Valuable e-customer experience stuff	Do we?	Could we?	When?
1	A search facility on the first page of the site is the simplest way to allow online customers to find what they want and be in control.			
2	A newsletter service, offering information, special offers, games, and humor relevant to your e-customers.			
3	A bulletin board that allows online customers (fans or critics) to publicly comment on your business and how it relates to them.			
4	Getting team members, of the same age and general interests as your e-customers, to write content, including help files and FAQs, using their natural tone and vocabulary.			
5	All key menu options available on the first (and every page) of your site.			
6	A human adviser, available 24 hours, 7 days a week to answer questions by text, video, or voice chat.			
7	Video footage of your team at work fulfilling the requests of real online customers.			
8	Tools that allow the e-customer to manage his account with you.			
9	Interviews with members of staff or those you sponsor.			

10 Recommend-a-friend reward schemes that reduce the cost of your products and services to the e-customer, pay real money, or add points to the various online currency schemes.

11 Contact/call centre support that allows the team member to see what the online customer can see on screen so that they help them through it.

12 The ability to save and come back to partially completed orders or application forms.

Activity 2.2

Something for everyone: a taster

When will I finish this by? _____

Dealing with the e-customer effectively will require you to keep those plates a spinning. There is no way you can hide from multiple, concurrent responsibilities, and still be successful.

This activity invites you and your team to do a little of something from each key step to delivering the ultimate online customer experience. It gives you a flavor of the complete steps and helps prepare you to take them.

Activity	Details
Understanding *your* e-customer	**When will I finish this by?** _____
Start sending mobile phone text messages to your team.	Find a team member who can teach you (he or she will probably be young!)
Establishing an e-customer team culture	**When will I finish this by?** _____
Organize your very own "idiot police" intranet page to find and get rid of stuff that hurts (or does not add to) the online customer experience.	The key here is to ensure that everyone is free to add anonymously, that everyone is able to vote for other people's suggestions (with no duplication) and that action is taken.

Creating the ultimate experience	When will I finish this by? _____
Use your own service relentlessly (particularly online) and become your severest critic.	Ideally use yours and your best of breed competitor's service continually to allow real comparisons to be made. List improvements and add them to the transition plan.
Keeping it fresh	**When will I finish this by?** _____
Give every team member a small budget to buy something ultra-cool or fun from an electronic source.	Make sure that they write two paragraphs explaining why they chose their purchase, what the whole experience was like, and what stuff they found out that you can adapt to improve your own online customer experience.
Staying in business	**When will I finish this by?** _____
How could your business offer an affiliate service?	Figure out how your service – such as your information or application form – could be added to an affiliates site securely by "just adding a few easy lines of code."

Activity 2.3

Thought shocking: what changes do we want to make?

The only way of coping with the needs of so many different personalities among your online customers is to let the personalities of your own team out of the box. You cannot do this if you just pretend to go through the motions.

You have to make sure that you can communicate your firm desire to understand the nature of the online customer and allow that understanding to improve the way that the business supports the e-customer. You will have to believe (and be prepared to argue) that this is the route that will lead to increased, and sustainable, profitability. If you have problems with this, go back to *E-Customer* and read it again!

Before undertaking Activity 2.3, you will need to have completed copies of the basic e-customer organizational model (a result of Activity 1.1) and the e-customer relationship web (a result of Activities 1.1 and 1.2). You will just shoot yourself in the foot (or some other more vital part of your anatomy) if you try this in the wrong order.

What are you trying to achieve?

The objective of this activity is to figure out and agree the order in which you will tackle all the changes needed to move the business from where it is now (the existing model) to where it wants to be (the aspirational model or online customer vision) over the next one to five years.

Re-call your online customer council of ideas. Remember that you will need people from different specialties but without any obvious differences in authority that will restrict completely open interaction.

Step 1 (15 minutes)

Distribute the model and the e-customer relationship web to the team. Give them each a pen and ask them to list all the changes necessary to implement the e-customer vision on a prepared flipchart with a diagram similar to the one shown in Activity 2.3(b). This is the master list.

Step 2 (30 minutes)

Then, score by vote and discussion the proposed changes in terms of the value they deliver to the online customer. Compare the online customers' priorities with the capabilities of the business and, for each, write down any reasons for the group thinking that it might not work or happen at all. The e-customer will not be helped by you closing your eyes to difficulties ahead; he will be helped by you recognizing and solving them.

As a result of the "thought shocking" session, team members will have challenged each other's ideas and the status quo within their departments and the organization as a whole. They will have listed the changes, tasks, projects, investments that will be necessary to deliver the desired e-customer vision and experience. They will have prioritized those activities and then put them in order on a timeline so that they can see the implications of the priorities that they have agreed and the real-world limitations (as they stand) that they have recognized.

Activity 2.3(a)

Prioritizing the improvements to the online experience

Suggested improvement	Desirable? 1–5	Feasible? 1–5	Profitable? 1–5	Capable? 1–5
A				
B				
C				
D				
E				
F				
G				
H				
I				
J				

Note:

- **Desirable** means the extent to which the online customer is likely to notice, appreciate, and be willing to pay more for the privilege.
- **Feasible** means the likelihood that the change can be delivered.
- **Profitable** means the level of extra revenue/profit that the change would bring.
- **Capable** means the ability or capacity of the organization to deliver the change today.

All are scored on a scale of one to five.

Ideally, document the suggested changes and distribute the list to the team. Then, score them by vote and discussion according to the value they deliver to the e-customer. Again, compare the online customers' priorities with the capabilities of the business and, for each, write down the reasons for the group thinking that each change might not work or happen at all. Ask the group to vote quickly for each change in each category.

Activity 2.3(b)

The transition plan: vision meets reality

Once you have completed Activity 2.3(a), it is time to introduce the prioritized changes to the world of time and scheduling. Sometimes organizations hide away the planning process at this point so that secret deliberations can produce mysterious project diagrams. However, transparency is a quality of working effectively in the world of the e-customer because your internal processes and rules are made visible.

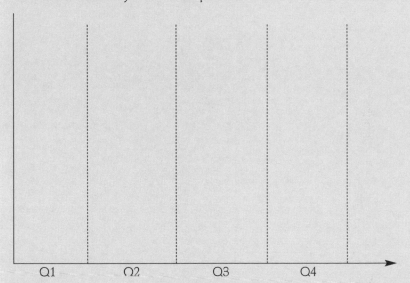

The aim is to keep the process as fluid as possible. With a team that has all the necessary expertise, there is no reason that it cannot be fairly rapid. It will not be the last time that you come back to this chart! However, it does represent the team's view of desirable and feasible change over time.

Where there are dependencies on anything not on the original list (legal, personnel, technological, marketing), these should be noted. Solutions should be quickly sought and the person responsible for the dependency should be identified. The aim is to get the big picture in a spirit of can-do and set it as the shared objective before anyone starts to feel scared.

Activity 2.4

Would you buy from you?

It's very nearly the ultimate test. Would you (do you?!) spend your own precious time and money on the stuff that your business provides? Are you a Nike man who wears Adidas ... ?

So, it's time to briefly (half a day) compare the online customer experience delivered by your business with that of your competitors. Here we go.

1 Choose two competitors:
- the market leader _____
- the best of breed _____

2 How did you choose the best of breed (give three reasons)?

1 _____
2 _____
3 _____

3 **E-customer experience testing zone**

Use and then rank each of the experiences. If the channel is not used, leave it blank. Visit as a guest, request some information, play around, buy something. This is not a comprehensive exercise, but one that allows you to compare the general look and feel of e-customer experiences. Put your hand up if you have never done this before.

Channel	Market leader	Your business	Best of breed
Website			
Mobile phone			
Interactive television			
Kiosk			
Call center			
In store or face to face			
	Market leader	Your business	Best breed

4　Based on your online customer experience alone, which would you buy from?

5　Name the three improvements that should be made to your business' e-customer experience?

　　1 _____

　　2 _____

　　3. _____

Get the whole team to do the same exercise before coming back to the next iteration.

I am amazed at the number of businesses who do no competitor analysis of online customer experiences, nor mystery shopping of their own e-customer experience. How can you judge how to compete for the heart and wallet of Mr, Mrs, Miss, and Ms if you have not shared their online customer perceptions?

Customer experience thinkers

No skill is more important than the corporate capacity to change per se. The company's most urgent task, then, is to learn to welcome – beg for, demand – innovation for everyone. This is the prerequisite for basic capability-building of any sort, and for subsequent continuous improvement.

TOM PETERS, AUTHOR OF *THRIVING ON CHAOS* (HARPERCOLLINS, 1989)

Improvement is an innocuous term. Even innovation is fairly innocuous. Change is not. Change means disruption, by definition. Whether it's holding a welding torch at a slightly different angle, moving a file cabinet ten feet, or installing just-in-time inventory management across ten plants, change is disruptive. Constant change by everyone requires a dramatic increase in the capacity to accept disruption.

TOM PETERS, AUTHOR OF *THRIVING ON CHAOS*

The greatest personal skill needed for this decade will be to manage radical change. There is unlikely to be any business or institution which will escape radical change in the nineties and the choices before us are to manage ourselves or to have change forced upon us.

SIR JOHN HARVEY-JONES, AUTHOR OF *MANAGING TO SURVIVE*
(HEINEMANN, 1993)

"Each person's map of the world is as unique as the person's thumbprint. There are no two people alike. No two people who understand the same sentence the same way ... So, in dealing with people, you try not to fit them to your concept of what they should be."

MILTON ERICKSON

Understand *your* e-customer

Dive into the minds of your e-customers and come back inspired by their hang-outs and their hang-ups

AS SOON AS A PERSON MOVES FROM THE REAL WORLD into the electronic world, he undergoes some behavioral changes. It is at this point that he becomes an online customer. He is the same person, but has entered the electronic world for a set of reasons and so his behavior is likely to be modified by the differences between the electronic and real worlds.

This chapter examines why it is important to understand online customers in general, what you can do to understand your e-customers in particular, and the impact of interacting with electronic interfaces on online customer needs, wants, and behavior.

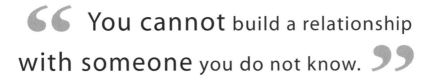 **You cannot** build a relationship **with someone** you do not know.

You cannot build a relationship with someone you do not know. Simply collecting a lot of data about him does not equate to a relationship (if it did, dating agencies would have a higher success rate), so you need to go beyond data. The relationship is not in the E-CRM software or in the marketing statistics or the database segmentation, important though these may be (see later in the book).

The relationship starts as you learn about the other person: the e-customer. To effectively serve him you will have to get into his mind. To find out what he wants, you will have to walk in his shoes. You have seen the *What Women Want* film and the Mel Gibson lipstick and stockings scene haven't you? Or maybe *Freaky Friday*, the film where a teenage Jodie Foster swaps bodies with her mother and they both learn more about each other's lives.

Why bother? Because you can avoid the misunderstanding that most businesses have of why their customers visit websites and what they want. Businesses still think that name recognition and convenience[1] are the main selling points for the electronic experience. This is why they have spent so much on advertising at the expense of making experiences that customers would pay for, complete with extensive merchandise selection, ease of use, and availability of goods when they are wanted.

So it's a mind and body swap. What to do about the knowledge that you have gained is discussed later in the book.

Ask yourself the following questions.

• Who is your typical online customer?	This may be a trick question.
• How many of your online customers do you meet/ interact with weekly?	If the number is a fraction, you'd better change a few things.
• How many e-customer requests by any electronic/ remote channel do you answer personally each week? then give yourself a (little) pat	If the answer is zero then send me an e-mail confessing all. If the answer is more than ten and you are in senior management, on the back.
• Which of the following do you use as a customer?	Internet and mobile phone. Personal digital assistant. Home PC. Interactive TV. Online chat.
• How often over the past year have you bought music for yourself that was currently in the pop charts?	Once? Twice? More?

Why all the questions? To point out the kinds of activities that anyone who wants to understand the nature of his e-customer will have to get into – pop culture, gadgets, chatting online, answering real questions from real customers. This is how you start to explore using the Malkovich method, trying to get into their heads, see with their eyes.

Example

Getting into the head of the customer is what brought Dyson his insights. He knew that the world wanted a bagless vacuum cleaner because he had asked his wife. For his next major innovation, he went again to the source, mothers, and asked what they wanted from a washing machine. They said they wanted one that could wash faster and take greater care of their delicate clothes. He watched how they washed these delicate materials by hand and invented a washing machine that finished each load in only 30 minutes by mimicking the hand-washing movement.

All the people who work (even those who pretend to work) are going to have to know this stuff if the online customer experience is to be as good as it can be. This could be considered a huge task, changing the empathy and knowledge of a whole business, but there is good news! People like to know stuff and they like to play with stuff. They only avoid it and resist it when they think it's some kind of win or lose test or that the punchline to them bothering to learn is that the business didn't really value their effort anyway.

The point here is that the sociodemographics have to be brought to life because it is simply ineffective and demoralizing (in fact, impossible) to try to create, innovate, and work the ultimate experience for a faceless, characterless database record. You can do a lot with shallow data, but you need rich understanding if you are to build relationships. Below are examples of each kind of source.

Shallow, cold data	Rich, warm understanding
Name.	What music they listen to.
Social security number.	What makes them angry.
Phone number.	What they think of authority.
E-mail address.	What tone of voice/ type of text they prefer.

Home address.	If they do or don't find your service a chore.
Credit card and bank account details.	How they *really* use your stuff.
Recent purchases.	What the hottest net toy of the moment is.
Letters or e-mails sent or received.	What the top ten searches are.
Credit rating.	Which sitcom is making them laugh.

Collecting details like his name, social security number, phone number, list of recent purchases, and his address can be considered the bare minimum. They are just hygiene factors, stuff that any business just has to know to keep making a living over the next little while. They are not motivational factors. They will not allow your business to let sufficient humanity out to captivate the online customer.

> **❝ Collecting details** like his name, social security number, **phone number**, list of **recent purchases**, and his address can be considered the **bare minimum.** They will not **allow your business** to let sufficient humanity out to **captivate** the online customer. **❞**

Telecommunication businesses know your name, address, telephone number, socioeconomic status, tastes and buying habits, but, despite all of this, they are terrible at integrating the different communication channels their customers actually use. Only a small proportion of them give online access to their bills, online payment options, automatic phone payment, live web chat or co-browsing. When you call up your telephone company they will ask you for a customer reference number every time, but even your local pizza delivery place has already mastered the technology that allows them to answer your call already knowing your name and address and what flavor pizza you ordered last time.[2]

You need to find out what your potential e-customer's looking for. The complete answer cannot be found by looking at the most popular search results, but it can give you hints. "Sex" is the top word searched for, but is still only about 1 percent. The other 99 percent of searches are for other items and it requires much more digging around if you are to see patterns of interest emerging and, more valuably, the nuances that your experience can use to learn to adapt more effectively to the customers' interests.

Research and play

> If you listen to the customer, they can't tell you anything. You have to watch the customer to really learn something. That's how you get at what they think and feel.
>
> DAVID KELLEY, DESIGNER, *WIRED*, JANUARY 2001

Think about it: no one should want to rely on his competitors for all new innovations. Where do yours come from? How do you know where the next big thing is coming from? How do you figure out the mind of the online customer so that the stuff you want to sell clicks with him?

❝ Think about it: no one should want to rely on his **competitors for** all new **innovations.** Where do yours come from? **How? ❞**

In early 2001, there was a frenzy of speculation about a new mysterious device that had been patented in the USA.[3] Harvard paid $250K for the rights to the book about the device, code-named "GINGER." Guesses about what it could be have been intriguingly wild, including anti-gravity, a new form of energy, and a one-man jet pack.

Is this an indication of e-customers' eagerness and belief in the next big thing? It certainly shows how high expectations are. Despite e-customer skepticism, they still believe that everything is possible. What can amaze such an innovation-glutted generation? Each time we open our eyes, there is progress at a pace that suggests that the ideas of sci-fi will be one day within reach. Didn't the gene-altered monkey with glow in the dark fur make you think?

To understand what the market will buy requires an understanding of hide-aways, hang-outs, and hang-ups of individual e-customers, and those of the many groups that each belongs to. We will not naturally share the views of others, but others are who our online customers are. It is wise not to rely on your own preferences and bias in determining what others (including the nebulous "most people" and the ethereal "niches") need, want, or appreciate.

Does the digital generation care? Each

generation has a different perspective on technology. For example, as a child of the moon landing, I expect everything to happen eventually, but am not bored with it and not therefore alienated from the society that creates it. Contrast this with the (growing) subsection that plays with the results of technology but doesn't understand it, expects it but doesn't appreciate it, and is bored, bored, bored.

This particular subgroup can be identified in part by its music, as represented by chart-topping Limp Bizkit, who sing of their "digi generation" that, "doesn't give a **** until you give a **** about them." It is tempting for those of a different generation to dismiss what they do not find personally attractive rather than consider what it means for the development of society in general and the development of electronic experiences in particular. What kind of offer do you make to the electronically apathetic?

As a creator of value for and from the e-customer, you can see that we cannot allow our interests and pastimes to be limited to what we like to do and like to read. That road leads to myopia of the type that allows Microsoft to be blinded to the possibilities of the web. It was big, ruthless, and rapid enough to remedy its error. Are you certain of your own ability to make such blunders and recover? Do you want to waste effort on doing so?

Don't limit your search to the local or national, push outward to discover the cultural, technological, physical, and spiritual characteristics of each region and nation. Innovations will be discovered and can be modified for international application with cultural sensitivity. Make the cross-cultural comparison in some depth and you will find simple explanations that can be turned into valuable insights and new online customer-winning strategies. Why, for example, has the experience with the mobile internet been so different in Japan, Europe, and the USA? Has it been as different as we think?

Is it a technology issue? Japan had full HTML and Java (key building blocks of the net) on its mobiles at a time when Europe was only enjoying a cut-down version called WAP. Meanwhile, the US had full internet access but only in limited regions and only via radio technology. Is it a pricing issue? Japan signs up websites that are allowed on to the mobile network and then pays them for their content via charges that are added to their 12 million mobile users' phone bills. Europe charges its e-customers for getting on to the mobile internet, keeps the funds to itself, and lets anyone on to the network.

This is where understanding needs to be sought not just for clean answers to questions like "Which one will work best?," but for a grasp of online customers' behavior that makes subsequent decisions more likely to capture revenue and respect. You need to look at why one is more attractive than another so that you can highlight those benefits in marketing and emphasize them in the design and delivery of content, flow, and structure.

Is the difference explained by societal structures – smaller Japanese families with more children living at home – or by great population density – more Japanese per square mile than in the West – or by education levels – more Japanese able to grasp the demands and benefits of fully wireless internet while many Europeans can only grasp the benefits of wireless Post-it Notes? Understand, explain, and improve.

Control and freedom To understand the e-customer,

businesses need to understand the differences between control and freedom. This necessitates a grasp of the conflicts between efficiency and innovation. Control is good, but it should be used as a specialist tool, not applied to problems it is not designed for. The controlled approach to market research tends to be statistical and deliver a narrow focus, highly rigorous, study that answers very limited, preconceived questions. It is good for deciding which of two shops a product should be sold in, but not of any use in deciding whether or not there is a much better location for selling the product than a shop.

Only free minds will peer beyond the obvious. Only innovative minds will see opportunities in the midst of threats. Consider the experience of manufacturers who find that their products are being modified by hackers eager to experiment. The Furby Hack competition led to a winner (Jeffrey Gibbons) who created a fully programable Furby that can read e-mail and answer the phone instead of merely turning spoken words into gibberish. The reaction of its makers was to make the Furby more difficult to modify because they assumed that they had to protect their design. Lego, on the other hand, viewed similar hacking as a great opportunity and decided to release the code behind its product into the public domain and let the hackers loose. Result? Functionality increased, sales increased and a mature product was given a new lease of life.

" Only free minds will peer beyond the obvious. Only innovative minds will see opportunities in the midst of threats. "

In pursuing the online customer, we must find his third places – those areas where he gets away from work and home. These include recreation and vacations within both real and virtual worlds. Chat, 3-D environments, gaming consoles – these constitute placeware, capable of creating the structure within which the e-customer can and does live.

Getting into their space: where are they?

So where are online customers hanging out? The answer is less and less certain because the electronic society is fragmenting as it matures to reflect the rest of our diverse world. Once the top ten web locations would account for 50 percent of the time spent on the internet; in 2001, they accounted for less than 20 percent. Here's an introduction to the most popular/cool top ten at the time of writing just to give you a taster and get you thinking about why they matter.

Location 1: "double power" chat rooms

Chatters spend more than twice as much time on the web, click on twice as many banners, and spend twice as much money as anyone else.

You might want to ask yourself why? Why is the web more interesting for those who chat? It's because they are socializing and building real (and weird) relationships. What can you learn from that?

Some businesses are already capturing the comments and discussions in chat rooms to identify trends before they happen. Analyzing the content allows the online chatters who influence those around them to be spotted and then assume that their influence will shape future trends. This can be done in person – just get in there and observe customers speaking freely – but already some research companies are applying computing power to the task.

One of these is Opion, which claims to be able to pick up on which phrases, ideas, and words are being passed from chatter to chatter. The company calls these "semantic pheromones," relating these to the chemicals that we use to attract other people, and claims that it can spot these tag phrases and the source of them from data gathered from around 400,000 people online. In the words of Opion's founder:

> It's like watching gorillas: you can tell how much influence the alpha males have, without speaking their language.[4]

Location 2: "watch but don't play" gaming

The electronic gaming industry is bigger in financial terms than Hollywood and has come a long way since the first asteroid arcade machines and tennis-playing home consoles. The future is, beyond doubt, in multiplayer, virtual, networked games across continents, language barriers, and time zones. It's a tough industry to play in (selling more than 10 million consoles couldn't make it profitable for SEGA, which has given up manufacturing to focus on software), but you should learn from the experiences of many.

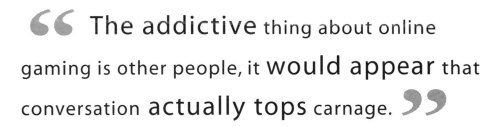

❝ The addictive thing about online gaming is other people, it **would appear** that conversation **actually tops** carnage. ❞

The addictive thing about online gaming is other people, and the hottest games of the moment are those that allow general chat and strategic discussion rather than simply playing against a more violent computer opponent. It would appear that conversation actually tops carnage among web game-loving online customers. That should start you thinking about how to attract and keep money-spending e-customers with you longer.

Location 3: music swaporiums

Have you used Napster yet or another of the free-for-now music services? The attraction of them to online customers is undoubted. Napster had 38 million after only 12 months based only on word-of-mouth marketing. Misguided efforts by the music industry to close Napster down may yet work, but it will have missed the point. You, though, will be able to understand it and use it to your e-customers' benefit.

Mess with this desire to copy music at your peril. Sony, with its feet in the camps of both copyright owner and gadget manufacturer, has attempted to saddle its digital music players with obstructive anti-piracy software. The result has been a reduction in sales and popularity among even those who wanted to make legal copies of their own compact disks.

Location 4: Flash cartoon or video streaming

It's growing, growing, growing, and then, suddenly, boom, it will rock the online customers' world. As the pipes grow bigger, the stuff you can shove down them becomes increasingly multimedia. Already the impact is being felt in terms of what can be done with this fusion of traditional movie values and ultimate interactivity. What's next?

Interactive television events that invite the customer to watch and participate via television and the internet have increased dramatically the number of people who have had streaming software installed. Realplayer.com and Microsoft.com both have strong positions, with more than 150 million in their installed base. Customers have enjoyed watching contestants on *Big Brother* and having some input and are now ready for more content.

Meanwhile, Flash.com and the macromedia Flash products are transforming websites, allowing comic books to come to life on Marvel.com and films and games to become a rich addition to the web kingdom. From providing simple animation, Flash has grown to the point where it has now been installed on 180 million computers and allows 3-D worlds to be created that challenge the traditional differences between television, games, and the internet.

Location 5: part of a web ring

Web rings are part of the quaint magic of Terra Electronica. They are the groups that get together to promote each other's, often amateur hobby-based, websites and homepages, joined together in a common love of whatever obsession it happens to be. Once a member of a web ring, an online customer must place the web ring's graphic on his site. On clicking it, a visitor will be taken to the website of another member of the web ring and so on and so forth until he finds himself back on the original site (if he lives that long).

Why do these sites matter? Because they demonstrate to you and your business many important characteristics of people that electronic channels tend to amplify. One of those strong characteristics is the desire to have a place of our own, the homesteading instinct, the push towards My Space and My Web where I can say what I want to say without being interrupted.

Think that this is insignificant? Just consider the work put in by customers on the top largest providers of free web space homesteads. On Geocities, there are 5.5 million pages, on Tripod 2 million pages, and on AOL 1.7 million pages. Count them up and you will find that that is 9.2 million pages created by customers for no commercial gain. They just like to build and exercise their individuality. What are you providing that allows your customers that privilege?

Location 6: trying to find out how to get somewhere

We live in a world of lost people, judging by the very large number of people who search every hour and minute for maps to get here, there, and everywhere. They turn to electronic channels because of their oracle-like status in the eyes of the converted (but cynical) online customer. Some of the most popular services on the internet have been grown around showing people the way to get where they want to go or speak to someone or find something. What is the lesson here?

Portals will continue, direction-based services via mobile phones will eventually be designed helpfully enough to be usable, satellite navigation will become a standard feature on cars, just as CD players have and DVD players are starting to be. Customers do not like being lost, so there will be a continued attraction toward anything that gives the power of the web without all that stuff customers have needed to know. They don't all want to read idiots guides to the net; they want to never feel like idiots in the first place.

Location 7: seeking their fortunes

Gambling is becoming more popular electronically than any other way. Entrepreneurs and day traders are busy getting burned on their way to ephemeral millions, but the most searched for fortune on the net is the horoscope. There are people who just want to know what the future holds, play a little with the occult, or poke fun at the tarot card afflicted.

Betting has made it to the interactive television (for example, U Bet in the UK) and the web (for example, paddypower.co.uk with its outrageous advertising). It will grow and grow in popularity because customers worry about money, think about being rich, and prefer to risk money than boredom.

Location 8: the world of UR4ME

It caught a whole telecommunications industry by surprise – Gen Y likes to write! With the vocabulary of amateur graffiti, perhaps, but sending little notes by mobile phone is a vital part of life for many of them all over the world. They write text messages in the bathroom, during school, while at their evening job making hamburgers, on the bus, and watching TV. They even send them – which involves beaming via base stations up to satellites and back again – when their friends are in the same room. They use combinations of letters as shorthand that are reminiscent of third-grade love notes and buy best-selling books showing them the latest codes and abbreviations.

❝ It caught a whole telecommunications industry by surprise – Gen Y likes to write! ❞

Expect to see the rapid movement toward community and group applications that are commonplace on the web. In Japan, one of the first such applications was put together by Neeraj Jhanji for fun, in about two weeks. It is called ImaHima,[5] which means, "Are you free now?," and allows customers to send messages to a group of people simultaneously. The big boys at AOL, MSN, and Yahoo! already have early generation mobile phone messenger applications. If two-way chat already inspires such frenzied obsession, just watch the fun that will be had with groupwide mobile communication.

Location 9: shopping (if we must)

A lot of money is being spent by e-customers, but that doesn't mean shopping is their favorite or natural use of electronic channels. Get that into the heads of your team! They cannot rely on shopaholics to go wild with those credit cards. As it stands, more browse than attempt to buy. For the moment, more start to buy than complete their purchases. Once you get them into the habit, though, it's a different matter. Online shopping must deliver something extra, something more, which overcomes the twin enemies of net shopkeepers everywhere. Consider how you will overcome them.

> **❝ A lot of money** is being spent by e-customers, but that **doesn't mean** shopping is **their favorite or** natural use of **electronic** channels. ❞

- **Enemy number 1** Most shopping online is still not natural as the real world.
- **Enemy number 2** Just a click away there is more fun to be had!

Location 10: counting all their money

It's almost too dull to write about, but here goes anyway. People are interested in money, wealth, and lifestyle (among other things) and they have spent a lot of time on financial websites trying to find pearls of wisdom that will make them yet richer. They watch the results, read the tipsters' advice. Some have jumped in and become day traders. Others just watch. The interest level in "what could be" (see Location 7) is greater than the desire to see what is.

Online banking has, often, been a missed opportunity. It is not interactive, fun, helpful, and does not offer any of that relationship stuff. Not any. Nada. Nothing.

Location 11: looking good and watching others

Voyeurism and (the closely related) news fetishism are stalwarts of the wired and wireless worlds. Thousands of sites exist just to show you what someone else is doing right now (or in the recent past).

Such sites often use web cams (little video cameras) to show moving pictures of what is happening. Quality of pictures is variable. Subjects covered include bedrooms, landscapes, bird's nests, and company coffee machines.

Elsewhere, e-customers binge on up-to-the-minute news coverage, delight in being first in on the world's gossip, and enjoy the feeling of connection with the global villagers.

Location 12: out in the real world missing the best of the electronic world

Shock! Web user seen in the real world. Shock? Well, not really.

Evidence shows that, on average, they only spend around an hour a day actively online, so, by clever deduction, this means that they spend 23 hours off-line. They spend most of their time building up their real-world habits and skills. The more advanced online customers will, though, note the deficiencies and disconnects in the real world and wish that they could have the best of both worlds.

Real-world retail, busy having its own tough time[6] at the moment, could benefit from electronic enhancement. Too many fail to do anything special with the characteristics of either real or electronic channels. Kiosks in real-world shops could be used to ensure that "if it's not on the shelves" and "we don't know when it will be back in stock" are less well-used excuses.

What these locations tell us

These locations give a good idea of where e-customers like to hang their virtual hats and, in the activities section at the end of this chapter, you will be invited to visit with them personally. This is how you will begin to learn their tone, pace, language, interests, and concerns. If you can walk and talk like an online customer (even temporarily) then you can make shoes and write speeches that will make him feel at home.

Of course, location is just one way of looking at the online customer. There are many others that we can consider together through the rest of this chapter as we move step by step toward understanding your own existing and future e-customers.

At the end of this chapter are activities and resources that will support your efforts to put this into practice and reap the rewards of doing so. First, though, ask yourself these questions.

- In how many ways are you different to other people?
- What do different e-customers need?
- How many different kinds of online customers do you have?
- What do you mean by "e-customer" anyway?
- What dimensions of the online customer is it useful to consider?

- How can we make the differences come to life in our business?
- Does your understanding of the online customer change the way you do business?
- Are there simple ways to increase understanding of the e-customer among all the people working in your business?

Other important questions to answer are what do you mean by *your* online customer? Is this a generic term to cover all web customers in the whole world who may at some time buy something from your business? Is it someone your business has already received money from? Should it include all those who use your services or products? What happens to those who have requested information from you? The list can go on and on.

66 What do you mean by *your* online customer? 99

Each definition will affect the scope of the e-customer experience that you create and the discussions you need to have in order to know what to build. You need to consider who you are serving and how many of them there are. Choosing to use a very narrow definition can appear to make life easier, but this may be deceptive. A wide definition would be something like this:

- your customers are those you must keep pleasing to avoid losing revenue;
- your online customers are those you serve via (or with the help of) electronic channels and hardware.

The further away your e-customer is from direct contact with you, the more effort you will have to make to get in touch with and understand his concerns.

Having determined what you mean when you talk of your e-customers, you will need to use as many perspectives as possible to understand them in as multidimensional a way as possible. These dimensions will include age, gender, income, aspirations, objectives, location, interests, hobbies, occupation, family circumstances, income, and beliefs.

Later in this chapter, I will come back to how to use these individual dimensions to create full, rich views of your online customer. Look at Chapters 4 and 5 in particular to see how to use this understanding to create propositions that give to online customers what they really value and deliver experiences that enhance that value.

Have you built a customer lab where you can observe real customers using your electronic experience? IBM has with its involvement in the world's first wireless community – Helsinki's Virtual Village, which opens for business in the summer of 2001. It will include a wireless network linking back to broadband fiberoptic cable that will allow residents to connect to internet services from anywhere. The same connections will allow the online activity of every resident to be tracked and added to their profile. This will be used to produce recommended product lists based on previous purchases. As the location of every resident will be known by using cell phone signals, the customer can be told where his nearest petrol station is or receive adverts from a local fast-food restaurant in the immediate area. The benefit, hopes Kurt Lonnqvist from IBM, is that this living laboratory can be used to, "test how the different technologies work with the real people in real situations."[7]

Such facilities will be beyond many businesses, but something of the kind is possible for all. Find a way of observing your customers, or potential customers, using your electronic experience. It will pay back every cent, franc, penny, or whatever else you spend on it.

The games online customers play

Commercial relationships are no simpler than other relationships. They may not have the same level of meaning, but they do have a complexity of form that is often ignored. This complexity could be reduced if purchases were carried out in a laboratory, free of influences and circumstances, while, at the same time, the differences between the products and services on offer were set out clearly and factually. It could be made simpler if there was no difference between how the stuff works and looks in practice.

You could strip down the choice until it was a matter of choosing "Product A: the best" or "Product B: the worst" and you would still see that not everyone would choose Product A. Of course, in the real world, the choices are surrounded by the needs and differences between individuals. This is good news because an understanding of these differences can help you:

- ensure that the overall offer delivers what the customer is willing to buy.

By all means hire someone to do the CRM software project but do not automatically think that they are experts in the relationships or in the games that e-customers play. They will be informed, it is hoped, they will have experience, but make sure that you and your team understand what you need the tool to achieve. To do that, you need to be your own expert in what customers want and how they behave as they try to get it.

Going back to basics (we do that a lot in this book) makes it clear that, first, customers are people who feel that it is worth making the exchange that the business asks (everyone else is a potential customer) and that, second, until the customer feels that the experience is sufficiently rewarding, they will have to play games that guarantee some pay-off on their own terms.

People strive for their whole lives to regain the complete comfort that they had, or wished that they had, as infants. By compromising, most people replace their infant stimulus – hunger – little by little – with recognition hunger. They seek to feed themselves with recognition and, over time, each person becomes more individual in that need. From sports stars to film stars to anthropologists and others.

Your online customers are, first and foremost, people from whom your business would like to receive money in exchange for something. This exchange of value is sometimes described as a "transaction" and is usually thought of as being purely mechanical in nature. Only what is formally involved in the transaction is considered in the accounts. The intangibles are recognized in a vague way, but are seldom analyzed to see what it is that the online customer bought.

> ❝ **Only what is** formally involved in the transaction is considered **in the accounts. The intangibles** are recognized in a vague way, but are seldom **analyzed to see** what it is that the **online customer** bought. ❞

Remember, the e-customer is seeking recognition, because he has learned to compromise, structure, because he needs to avoid boredom, and stimulus, because that is what he really hankers after. Where the transaction with your business also fulfils some of his need for "ego strokes" or, even better, for "stimulus," then he will be more willing to buy and then buy again, often at a premium over and above the competitive cost of providing the "stuff itself."

Why are sex sites so popular? There is the potential for meaningful stimulus, even though, ultimately, this cannot be fulfilled. Why are chat sites so popular? There is recognition *and* structure. You can learn from both in delivering more of what e-customers are seeking. As you prepare to move to the next step – creating the online customer proposition and experience – you need to know what kinds of sensations and recognition to build into your offer.

Any such social intercourse is better in his inner view than none at all. Shopping is just one more way that people can gain both recognition and stimulus. If e-commerce is low on these stimuli, then it will always have to work harder to catch up, and sometimes you need a lot of tangibles to outweigh even a little of the intangible stuff.

Example One charming example of how electronic experiences can feed the customers' hunger for recognition and stimulus was the result of work by experience designers over at GlobalBeach. They created an astonishingly inventive virtual fish for Hewlett-Packard (HP) that swims around the customer's desktop in its own aquarium. To survive, the fish needs regular feeding and attention. Each day MOPy fish owners are awarded 40 points and each time they use the multiple print option they gain 20 points. The points can then be exchanged (via the HP website) for aquarium accessories, which enhance the environment of the fish.

How many customers felt an emotional connection with the MOPy fish? 16 million! It became the world's most downloaded cyberpet and is listed under that category by the *Guinness Book of Records*. It increased awareness of a particular feature of HP printers (the Multiple Original Print function) but more importantly created a personal relationship between HP, the fish, and their customers worldwide. It was known for customers and MOPy fish owners to contact GlobalBeach in a panic to know how to look after their virtual pet while they were away on holiday. Couldn't your business benefit from the MOPy fish effect?

The customer is crying out for things to do, which is the reason for the popularity of shopping, obscure hobbies, graffiti, and vandalism.

It also explains why a small team of enthusiasts wrote a modification of a commercially produced game called Half-life. The modification known as Counter-strike was created, distributed, and tested under the leadership of a programer known as Gooseman,[8] and made freely available to anyone over the internet. The team itself and the hundreds of thousands of people who tested it over its two-year development period found the project as engaging as the product itself. The game's popularity was such that it has been officially recognized and released as a separate product.

66 What could you find for your customers to improve for your business? 99

What could you find for your customers to improve for your business? The online customer experience's creator should be working to feed these stimuli and learn from the vocabulary and tradition of sensation creators through history. This includes the animator and the chef. You will find many more of the lessons that can be drawn in the rest of this book.

The process that is wrapped around the essential commercial exchange is part of the exchange itself, for good or ill. It provides the structure of that exchange and will itself be found surrounded by the social programing of those involved. The longer the customer and the business interact, the more likely it is that they will both develop customized views of what is expected, what is liked, and when the other is not playing fair. If the interaction meets some of these needs, then, in the long term, the original formal reasons for the transactions may be overtaken in importance by these deeper but inexplicit needs.

Example

Take, for example, the following situation. An e-customer uses an online chat tool on the web to ask the technical support team a particular question. While asking his questions, he seeks to feed some of his recognition stimulus. As time passes, he needs fewer formal reasons to use chat – the chatting itself comes to justify the use of the service. It stops him feeling lonely in the middle of a busy office.

The objective for the provider of the support service is to find out how to use the need that the customer has to communicate to the advantage of the business by somehow connecting sales and service.

When a person goes shopping, they are looking for more than they admit. When they return having accomplished the explicit objective, they may be deflated and unsatisfied because the emptiness has not been satisfactorily filled. Loyalty is only built when the exchange seems to the customer to give him much more than exchange of the product in the bag. That's a valuable insight.

> **66** **Loyalty is only** built when the exchange seems to the **customer to** give him **much more** than exchange of the **product in** the bag. **99**

The next step is to provide you with tools for conceptualizing and analyzing the transactions that make up this value exchange. This will require enhanced understanding of the psychology of the online customer because behavior comes from feeling rather than the other way around. This leads you to the idea of "ego states," where the e-customer exhibits behavior consistent with the ego state that he experiences at any point in time.

Parent	The same state of mind as a parent or similar figure used to have.	• Act as a parent • Automatic • Saves time and energy • Routine
Adult	An autonomous, objective state of mind that reaches non-prejudicial decisions and actions.	• Survival • Data • Computation • Regulates • Achievement
Child	The same state of mind that he used to have as a child (natural) or the way that his parents wanted him to act (adapted).	• Intuition • Creativity • Spontaneity • Enjoyment

During any commercial transaction, somewhere a customer has encountered a business and has interacted to the extent possible with it or its representative. Where there is a real person available, one of them will usually opt for some level of interaction by making the first move, or "transactional stimuli." The other will then do or say something that is termed the "transactional response." Where there is only a computer or a machine of some kind, your e-customer will still be in one of the ego states but may have a hard time determining how to transact and try a range of possibilities in pursuit of the needed stimuli.

As long as each party receives a complementary response (adult to adult or child to parent), then the transaction can proceed unencumbered, indefinitely. If they stop being complementary, they become known as "crossed transactions" and this, dear reader, is going to cause problems between you and your online customer. You will have to find a way to realign the transaction, returning it to a complementary form, before the original transaction can continue.

This demands an experience design that deliberately seeks to identify the ego state of the customers at each stage and allows the customer to choose what kind of response he would like to keep the transaction aligned or realign it when there is a problem. In general, there is no real-time human intervention from the business, so the key here is to first allow that choice all the time. In this way, there are options that cater for all ego states and many of their needs so that the customer can ensure that there is alignment for himself.

Try designing different parts of the screen to speak to child, adult, and parent. In one area of the screen use images, concepts, and language that appeals to intuition, creativity, spontaneity, and the search for enjoyment. Offer the "child" in your customer games, puzzles, competitions, and the ability to instantly gratify his desire to buy. He will not always want to go through a serious buying decision process; his adult ego may not be in play when he visits your experience. If he is not in the mood for what you are offering, he will either leave or be reluctant to follow the paths that you offer to completion.

The e-customer experience includes transactions, so you must consider how to deal with them, keep them complementary, when to use simple transactions, how to utilize ulterior transactions, which is when you act in multiple states at once in order to gain an advantage deliberately, and how to remedy crossed transactions effectively.

When you have created a structure and content that can appeal to each of the ego states, the next stage is to track the choices that the customer is making and judge from those choices what ego state he is currently in. Then, modify the flow of information and the type of experience that you are delivering in keeping with that ego state.

Keep delivering additional funny lines and playful comments if you are certain that he is in a child state. Start looking to more logical arguments if you start to feel that he is in an adult state. Provide references to sensible ways in which the task would be completed in the real world if you think that the customer is acting as his parents have taught him to, for example.

Good, experienced salespeople have used ulterior transactions since trying to get a deal began. The people who are putting together your electronic face(s) to the world typically will not include much commercial experience in understanding the psychological ego states of the e-customer. They will talk about the importance of "user-centered design" but not about the intricacies of "ends-centered design," where the objectives are reflected in the complete experience.

So, ask yourself these questions.

- When an online customer first interacts with you via electronic channels, how do you know which ego state he is currently in?
- Who should make the first move? Online customer or the business?
- How can you utilize ulterior transactions to ensure that your business objectives communicate across multiple, complementary levels?
- How can you adjust when transactions start to get crossed?

To effectively deal with him, you need to understand that, as an e-customer comes into your electronic space, he will call on a range of activities to structure his time while there. These are procedures, rituals, pastimes, operations, and games.

Procedures and rituals are both stereotyped ways of approaching the same situation. Once learned, they are usually followed, unless there is significant interference from another ego state or another person involved does not follow the same approach and therefore challenges the stereotype.

- **Procedures** are the most efficient ways in which an individual in the adult ego state can use the information, skills, and data available to him. This may not be effective because the procedure may be flawed, but it is carried out as understood, with no hesitation or deviation.
- **Rituals** are activities that use time productively without guilt while the individual adopts either an adapted child state, doing what parents or substitute parents expect or acts as a child, without bounds on his activities, nor expecting parental-style acceptance. An example of this is the "greeting transaction."
- **Pastimes** are ways of interacting before the main, formal, interaction starts that are semi-ritualized but allow each participant to get the maximum advantages out of the activity to

the extent that he can adapt to its form. Pastimes are typically more varied than rituals and are usually played by the child who is deciding who he wants to play with. As an online customer experience creator, you should be learning how to play at pastimes in order to achieve your adult goals, whether this means playing to win or breaking the rules deliberately.

- **Operations** are straightforward, clear transactions that request the help or the pay-off with no ulterior motive. The purpose of such transactions is exactly "what it says on the tin" and, if someone is conducting an operation, the other party can respond with confidence to the request. The challenge is to know when you are faced with an operation or its less obvious cousin, the Game.

- **Games** may contain the words and actions of the other activities, but they are different because they are a deliberate and "hidden" attempt to achieve a pay-off. Sometimes, the e-customer will be playing games and you should learn how to recognize their play and when to do the same.

Games your online customers will play with you

We will return to the practical application of hunger, ego states, and games in Chapter 4 on propositions and Chapter 5 on creating experiences. Here, though, it is still valuable to talk through some examples by applying the methods and concepts described to understanding the e-customer in particular situations.

Example

"Now I have got you" (NIHGY) is the game played by an online customer who will play by the rules until you break them, whereupon he will seize on this infringement with delight and seek to beat you down, put you in your place, and generally act like a stern and critical parent would act when a teenager is late in from a date. In the virtual world, this is characterized by sucks.com, sites set up by disgruntled former e-customers, and by "flaming," the aggressive e-mails and text messages sent by the same.

"Why does this always happen to me?" WAHM is the game played by an e-customer who is looking for a bad story to tell about life in general and the e-commerce experience in particular as people are relatively happy to hear about more bad news in the dot com world. When things do not go immediately to plan, the e-customer finds satisfaction in having another bad news story to relate instead of trying to solve the problem. The harder it is to remedy the problem, the more likely it is that he will choose to win through the easy compromise of blaming you and the web gods of misfortune for the failure.

Where online customers are deprived of the advantages of the game, they will move toward more open and constructive types of exchange. It is to the advantage of the professional experience creator to move the e-customer toward transactions and the relationships that surround them in which they can both win productively.

Meet the e-generations

Now let us look at the differences between age groups and how to start to understand those differences for yourself and your e-customers. The significance is not simply the number of years each individual has spent on earth, but the ways they relate to and interact with electronic channels. This is the significance of the term "e-generations."

Time for a personal question or three or four …

- How old are you?
- When you were young, where did your family buy most of the groceries?
- How many television sets did you grow up with in the house?
- What was your favorite electronic game when you were under 18?
- Do you remember playing Asteroids the first time?
- How many hours do you spend using electronic channels each week?
- Does giving out your credit card details on the web make you nervous?
- Name a top ten album in the pop charts?
- How many years have you been using the internet?
- Have you changed physically, mentally, emotionally, financially in the past 5, 10, and 15 years?

Your age has a significant impact on the relationship that you have most likely built up with all things electronic. Those who were around before the birth of a concept are less likely to be comfortable with that concept simply because they did not grow up as children together. You may buck the trend by having a particularly strong affinity for the concept or by being unusually allergic to it, whenever you were born. In the usual course of events, however, the way we relate to technology is affected by the number of years that we spent with it as an assumed part of normal life. Take a look at the diagram to your left as an illustration.

> 66 **The way we** relate to technology is affected by the **number of years** that we **spent with it** is an assumed part of **normal** life. 99

An affinity with technology and concepts, then, is, generally speaking, affected by when an e-customer was born. Many other characteristics are influenced simply by how many years a person has lived. You should expect your online customers to change physically, mentally, professionally, emotionally, and financially, as they grow older. This is not necessarily for better or worse, but change is the natural result of the friction involved with living.

If e-customers' behavior and needs change over time and differ according to age, then it follows that the experience offered to them should be capable of flexibly changing with them. It should grow with them to avoid them growing apart. Considering just some of the many changes over time is instructive and can be valuable if used with intelligence during the creation and delivery steps of the experience.

- How do physical characteristics differ with age?
- How do emotional characteristics differ with age?
- How do financial characteristics differ with age?
- How do pastimes and interests differ with age?

Here are some of the differences that exist between different generations.

Gen Z These little varmints just got born (2001 to 2021) and look what they will be growing up with! They will take wireless multimedia for granted and be educated using networked personal electronic tutors of the likes of Barney. They will enjoy next generations of AIBO and WILDFIRE.

Gen Y   Born between 1981 and 2001, this group has also been described as Gen E and Net Gen. Members of this generation will take hybrid culture forward with services such as personalized jean production. They spend time online finding out "wasssup" with their friends, organizing online pressure groups, playing on 3-D snowboarding slopes and shopping. They have been characterized as "disrespectful, materialistic, and selfish." So far, they listen to rap, hardcore hybrid music, boy bands, and teen divas.

Gen X   Born between 1961 and 1981, these guys grew up with what was often little hope for the future, no one at home, and, as a result, developed dysfunctional relationships, individualism, and resourcefulness. They have been the key web entrepreneurs to date, numbering among them the founders of Amazon, Microsoft, Oracle, Netscape, and Napster.

It is important to realize that generations are distinct from age and will be modified by it, but history explains behavior and lets us catch a glimpse of the future. The ways in which these generations were raised, the culture, design, technology, political and social environment, will all impact the evolution of the online customer and, therefore, the evolution of any company that wishes to do business with him.

FIGURE 3.1 Generations, innovations, and design fashion.

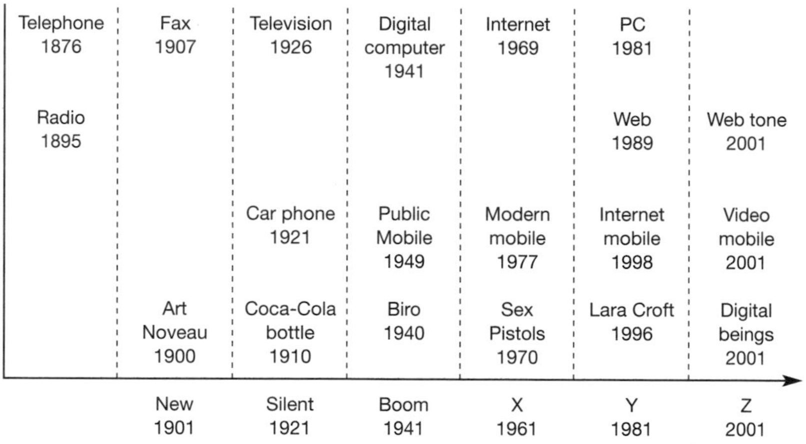

Telephone 1876	Fax 1907	Television 1926	Digital computer 1941	Internet 1969	PC 1981	
Radio 1895					Web 1989	Web tone 2001
		Car phone 1921	Public Mobile 1949	Modern mobile 1977	Internet mobile 1998	Video mobile 2001
	Art Noveau 1900	Coca-Cola bottle 1910	Biro 1940	Sex Pistols 1970	Lara Croft 1996	Digital beings 2001
	New 1901	Silent 1921	Boom 1941	X 1961	Y 1981	Z 2001

At home with the e-family
Your customer should always be considered in the context of his e-family – the network of friends and family, those who surround him. They are the people he

watches, listens to, plays with, and fights against. They are the people he seeks to emulate and those from whom he gains his opinions.

At the centre of the e-family network is, naturally, the online customer. Closest in influence are those he lives with (whether related formally or not) and his most immediate family members. In the case of the e-customer, his immediate e-family is likely to be time-pressured (40–60 percent) and operate as a partnership or team, much like a modern "networked" organization. He will find himself influenced for and against products, services, businesses, and brands by what his closest e-family members buy and do not buy. This is the nature of the modern, democratic family in which the online customer lives.

Consider the ways in which the family interacts and how electronic services can support individual customers in their roles within their family. What are their priorities? Where are their pressures? How does the family work and play together? At what points do family members come into contact with electronic experiences? Who is the most experienced e-customer? Where could your experience enhance and support the objectives of the family?

You can help with shopping lists, DIY, homework, buying gifts. Think about how to become an integral part of family life, in the way that Audrey from 3Com (Palm creators) has tried to do with its latest gift to the world. For just over $500 you can have a device that "can handle your complex life" by synchronizing what the family is doing (plus, e-mail and access to your favorite websites). Just pop it on the side in the kitchen and watch family life take shape. Do you believe it?

Next are to be found his *extended* family – his grandparents, cousins, any grown-up children, aunts and uncles, and so on who do not live in the same house with him. You might want, like family.com, to go directly to facilitating long-distance relationships for families divided by continents and time zones. You could support the creation of photo albums or video footage.

After that, there is his inner network of *friends* – those who socialize and, perhaps, work together. This is the group of people he has chosen (or who have chosen him). This group willingly relies on its members for opinions and news. When do they spend time together? How can you speed up the transmission of opinions that favor and review your experience? Is there a way of being noticed that encourages the influencers in each network of friends to exert that influence in your favor? They spend hours sending terrible jokes, why not something featuring your brand instead? You could even include terrible jokes with your company e-mails!

Beyond family and friends, in his zones of influence are trusted third parties that have either been used satisfactorily or recommended by his personal network. It is to this group that he turns first. They are the first to come to mind when he wants to buy. He may even find excuses or opportunities to deal with them because they satisfy a range of his needs and hungers.

Which third parties do your customers trust? Get yourself associated with them. What makes the difference between being trusted and not trusted? Read the comments on consumer review sites, like epinions.com, and the complaints on sites like ecomplaints.com to find out what creates trust and distrust. This kind of material has never before been self-documenting to this extent. Use the available material on bulletin boards and in chat rooms to increase your understanding of turn ons and turn offs.

Your business does not really want to be any further away than this because it will require even more time, money, luck, and effort to convince the online customer to spend his money on your service. You may move to the possible providers zone because your advertisements have hit a chord or you are on a "best buys" list in a magazine, TV show, or website, but it is not a good place from which to try and make a profit.

The costs of being in the family itself are less than being out there – there is less advertising, more targeted marketing, higher response rates – because you are one of the gang, the group, our kind of people, talking and helping each other. Work your way to the inside track – it's the only one that matters.

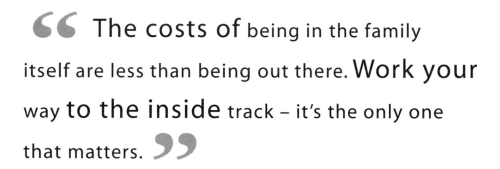

" The costs of being in the family itself are less than being out there. **Work your way to the inside** track – it's the only one that matters. **"**

- Who are the influencers among your online customer networks?
- Do you know what percentage of those networks eventually do business with you? Is that high enough?
- Does your business model assume that it is doing business with isolated individuals or that it does business with networks of connected individuals?

Postmodernist and beyond to a post-ironic peak

The idea of an "online customer" is one with a genealogy based in continuing reaction to the wonders of modernism that developed from the Age of Discovery in the fifteenth century of the second millennium all the way through to the cultural movements of the 1950s and 1960s. Nearly 500 years dedicated to improving on the past, to change, reason, progress, science, secularism, universalism, and skepticism.

This many "isms" were always likely to cause another one and thus it was that a schism developed between those who were still working in pursuit of progress and those who viewed this pursuit as tame and looked for a new radicalism. In the latter case, the emphasis is on combining existing traditions in an eclectic, hybrid style that combines elements of elite and popular culture and science.

Postmodernist society is constructed more than ever by its individuals and their desire to consume and produce. Its leading player, the customer, lives in a world with weakened hierarchies, endless splinter cliques, fantasy worlds, tongue in cheek mixing of original influences, and an antipathy toward orthodoxy, universal truths, and objective knowledge.

The e-customer comes along as a vital, and increasingly recognized, part of the world's economic and political mechanism. It is in his consumption that he has undeniable value for the many businesses that wish to part him from his money. His decisions, his confidence, his votes, and his purchases determine the direction and fate of businesses and governments.

- Do you believe that what you read in advertising and marketing is true?
- Is any of your leisure time spent in or watching fantasy worlds?
- What are the answers to these questions for your colleagues, your family, and your e-customers?
- How does this change the way that you think about your e-customers?
- Can you identify splinter cliques that your online customers fall into? How many are there?
- How are your business propositions, processes, platforms, and people organized to learn more about your e-customer?

From product to fun

The path that customers (people who are in consumption mode) have always taken is to move from being content with products when choice is scarce to hankering after fun when choice is plentiful. For your online customer, time is no longer filled with trying to keep his body from starving; he wants to avoid dying of boredom.

This is not to say that wealthy(ish) e-customers do not have to deal with difficult issues, even tragedy. It does mean, however, that as we expect the basics to be there, no ifs or buts about it, we seek more "bang for our buck" to structure the time that we have in mortality (the bit before we die).

 In the real world, the winning word is "experience," as delivered by a company such as Selfridges in London, complete with its new Vittorio Radice-inspired attitude. In his words:

> The concept of shopping has changed … today when you buy a jumper, you're not buying it because you need a jumper. It's because you want to feel that you're riding a horse in the middle of the Arizona desert, and when you buy a Ralph Lauren jumper, you're halfway there … Shopping is less about commodity and more about emotion.

True to his word, he is delivering shopping as entertainment, shopping as stimulus. In the Selfridges vision there are no self-service trays because it wants to deliver high-quality restaurants that are places to go in their own right rather than simply being convenient places to stave off hunger.

The online customer doesn't merely want fun. Ideally he wants products, service, experience, and fun thrown into the same purchase. Think about it. What happens if his time in the electronic presence only delivers a product? He will keep looking elsewhere for the other desired elements. He will spend less time with you and more time elsewhere that provides these things. He will be happy to accept products from the provider of fun as soon as he is offered them.

The customer's mind (perception) is where the great fight for the e-customer is fought. Get into his psyche and brand brings bonanza. Even Jack, anti-hero of the cult film *Fight Club* (2000), knew that when he explained:

I had become a slave to the Ikea nesting instinct. If I saw something like the clever Njurunda coffee tables in the shape of a lime green Yin and an orange Yang, I had to have it. I would flip [open the catalog] and wonder, "What kind of dining room set *defines* me as a person?"

"WE HAVE LIFT-OFF," *THE ECONOMIST*, FEBRUARY 3, 2001

❝ The online customer doesn't merely want fun. Ideally he **wants products,** service, **experience,** and fun thrown into **the same** purchase. ❞

As he puts it, "The things you own, they end up owning you." Put another way, our inner desires are expressed in what we say, do, and buy, but that doesn't mean that we can find ultimate expression in commerce. For complete self-expression, we (as Jack realized) need, "to talk to a live person."

Why is that? Because humans like to be understood and they feel instinctively that other people will be better able to understand them than computers. Conclusion? Electronic channels work best when they are human, genuine, funny, and honest because, without these characteristics, we are only dealing with machines. We do not want to deal with cold metal, etched silicon, and slender optic fibers, we want to deal with the shadows of humanity. Even better, we want to deal with real people, using technology to make that easier.

We do not demand that our friends be able to determine the 102nd prime number in a sequence. We do prefer that our friends be interesting in some way. It is what explains the popularity of shows such as *Big Brother*.

The intelligent response of technology, answering the telephone or our e-mail requests, is dependent on the level of humanity that is invested in the set-up of the system. The words that are used and the options provided cannot be robotic and still develop relationships with the online customer. The intelligence has to be human. Human intelligence applied to understanding the e-customer in as many ways, across as many dimensions as we can possibly manage.

We've only just begun

To understand the online customer is a never-ending process because he is as complex and ever-changing as the 6 billion faces of humanity itself and its whole history. Naturally, the insights provided in this chapter can provide only a partial understanding and are intended as a starting point for you as a professional e-customer experience creator and student of e-customer behavior.

Use the activities at the end of this chapter to further deepen your understanding. Use them once, then again, and again. Each time you complete a cycle, you will build the level of instinctive empathy that will allow you to create experiences that deliver what the online customer will value (and therefore pay for) the most.

Experience study

Palm.com – mobilize, expand, connect

So, I receive the e-mail that, as a devotee of Palm PDAs (personal digital assistants) I have been waiting for – the announcement of the release of a new model of the sleek, metal Palm Vx, featuring a hot color screen. My attention is 100 percent attracted away from the demands of the day and I want, want, want to get my hands on this baby. The e-mail announced:

> A new era in sleek, expandable hand-held computing – the Palm™ m500 series handhelds. ... Both hand-helds feature a new Arctic Mist metallic silver color as well as a new, gentle curve for easier gripping at the products' waistline.

Hyperlink

Move to page 149 for a discussion of community and how it fits within the experience framework.

Enticing? Well, it was for me. Without waiting, I clicked on the link that was part of the e-mail. In a second, I was on the Palm website, waiting for the new color Palm to appear. When it did, it pulled me, willingly, into the experience, featuring as it did cute little animations of the technology working and a tone that met my happy expectations, including words like "beautiful," "delicious," and "brilliant."

FIGURE 3.2

E-mail
announcing
new, "delicious"
Palm hand-held.

The fan community is fairly well catered for, but, where is the spirit? Where is the freedom? There is no live chat among community members, but there are, at last, live customer-to-customer discussion boards provided by talkcity.com that have over 1700 discussions, each with multiple threads. Of course this is only a fraction of the many millions of Palm users in the world, but it shows the level of interest in the community.

It's a shame, though, that the legal statement, prominently displayed on the discussion boards, is so restrictive in its tone and clauses. Discussions of Palm the business, its policies and procedures, and commentary on the company and its unannounced products are deemed as "not appropriate." This stance and language is not likely to encourage a frank and free sharing of opinions among true zealots and supporters. What are they scared of? This approach is only likely to hide discontent that will surface later. There was evidence that comments critical of Palm are simply deleted (only five posts containing the word "unhappy" among so many thousands?), as with the following comment:

> Looks like I hit a sore spot with the post that I posted because it was deleted from this discussion board …

Meanwhile an unhappy customer at brighthand.com wrote that, "Palm's site is useless as ever," and that he is, "contemplating suing Palm for one hour." His strong comments provoked a passionate war of words between Palm and Ipaq users that is an indication of the way that customers feel about their digital brain enhancements.

The thing that really hurt my feelings as a loyal Palm convert was that it had invited me in but prepared no easy route to information about how to buy my Palm from any other region than North America. I was not alone – the discussion board posting on Palm.com included many such comments and the non-Palm discussion boards and chat rooms were full of discussion on this point. The following comment from a customer in Oman was typical:

> Please let me know how to order the Palm m505. I'm located in outside of USA and my country is Oman (one of the Gulf countries). I have tried to order through Palmdirect.com but it's failed and no one replying. Please help me to get this unit and I'm willing to pay all costs. I appreciate your kind co-operation.

Eventually I tracked down the information in a press release, but, if it was available, why not work out that customers outside the US would be interested? This is a globally connected world after all! And why not personalize the e-mail to let me know as Palm already "knew" that I was not an American customer. Palm should be deeply unhappy that it has snubbed so many of us.

Bottom line?

Palm has spent money on its site, but it can afford to spend more and let more of the vibrancy out that its culture must contain. It should follow up to solve problems, test more of its stuff, consider the global needs of customers, the experience should match the product, and it should learn from criticism. It's got features galore, but could benefit from more fun, more drivers, and more real-time help. Could do better.

Stuff to think about

books, articles, TV shows, and websites

Berne, Eric, MD, *Games People Play: The Pyschology of Human Relationships* (Penguin, 1964)

A superb and sensible analysis of what "games" people like our online customers are playing in order to live with themselves and each other. It spent two years on the US bestseller lists. Unfortunately Dr Berne died in 1970 and it will have to be left to fans of his work, like myself, to popularize his methods and apply them to a post-internet world that he never knew.

Brownlie, Douglas, et al., *Rethinking Marketing: Towards critical marketing accountings* (Sage, 1999)

Put together by marketing academics as a fairly intense examination of the role of marketing and how it has developed over at least 40 years. Lots of valuable material about the failures and the future of communicating with e-customers delivered in an excruciatingly dry manner. It is argued that there will always "be more of relevance outside of [marketing as a field] than inside it," because it has an inherently social nature. Best bit? The insights. Worst bit? The overkill on citations.

Groening, Matt, *The Simpsons* (Fox Broadcasting Company, 1987 to present)

The legend, confirmed by the creator, is that the idea was created in around 15 minutes while he waited in the foyer to James L. Brooks' office.

Why include *The Simpsons*? Because cultural icons (especially those that deal with society and family) are essential to understanding other people and, hence, the online customer, but then you knew that already.

Try **http://www.snpp.com/contacts.html** for more information about everything to do with the show.

Groening, Matt, *Futurama* (Fox Broadcasting Company, 2000 to present)

Futurama begins on December 31, 1999, when the lead character, Fry, delivers a pizza to a cryogenics lab as the result of a prank call, is accidentally frozen, and wakes up a thousand years into the future. Views on technology, advances, changes, and the future of one electronic customer are welcome and funny.

Fans want to keep the show running (see **http://www.crosswinds.net/~algebra/savefuturama/main.html**) for the next thousand years.

Hanna, William, and Joseph Barbera, *Jetsons* (MGM, 1962)

A traditional sitcom family in the distant future. Worth watching and reading about because it represents what the future *should* be like for many of the e-generations. The adventures of George, Jane, Astro, and Cosmo are as instructive now as they ever were.

Scott, Ridley, *Blade Runner* (1982)

It's on the list because of its stunning visual design and because of its story of machines seeking humanity from men behaving like machines.

Conceptual artist Syd Mead worked with designer Lawrence G. Paul and cinematographer Jorden Cronenworth to create a vision of a future Los Angeles that, according to one reviewer, "is a dark, rainy, windswept tomb where garish advertising on giant video screens flash on forbidding corporate towers. Human beings with a place on the economic ladder live sealed off in high-security apartments in the lifeless towers, while most people shuttle about the streets or live in decaying buildings. Nowhere is there a sense of organic growth – all life is secondary to commerce and family life or a sense of community do not even seem to exist." Food for thought indeed.

The Shop Around the Corner (1940)

The classic depiction, starring James Stewart, of how the customer experience should really be. Similar images represent the expectations and fondest desires of a generation of shoppers for their idealized customer experience.

Epinions.com

The best collection (to date) of real e-customer opinions, or epinions, about what they buy, why they buy, and what they thought having used their purchases for a while. Every product imaginable is being used and reviewed. They pull no punches and write revealingly about value propositions and delivery from their point of view.

Cyberatlas.com

A superb resource for those seeking to collect the results of surveys on the comings and goings of the online customer. King of kings is the "stats toolbox" that collects together all the freely available statistics and press releases from the world's net research companies.

Napster.com

Included because you need to know what attracted 38 million e-customers to use Napster in just 12 months. There was no advertising.

It blurs the lines between product and service. It generated a diehard fan base and revealed hidden passions for music among online customers of all ages. It may die a legal death at any point, but its spirit will live on.

Activity 3.1

E-customers: listening, watching, and glad-handing

I will complete this by _____

The objective of this activity is to introduce you to the worlds of various different online customers so that you can walk the walk. Too many great visions are ultimately fruitless because the leader and the team supporting him simply didn't have enough first-hand experience. Just complete the steps and put a tick in the box.

	Date	Done
1 Find out what the top four search items were this week.	☐	☐
2 Visit the top two most popular websites.	☐	☐
3 Buy an internet-enabled mobile phone and use it to buy something!	☐	☐
4 Install one of the graffiti browsers to see if anyone has left messages on your site.	☐	☐
5 Use Napster to download some (legal) music in MP3 format.	☐	☐
6 Bid for an item on an auction site for under a small set budget.	☐	☐
7 Send a video postcard of yourself via e-mail to a friend.	☐	☐
8 Have a meeting with a colleague using instant messaging software.	☐	☐
9 Ask a person ten years older than you what they think of the internet or interactive television. What are the good and bad points?	☐	☐
10 Find and add a new musical ring or graphic to your mobile phone.	☐	☐

11 For a week, buy everything via electronic channels.

12 Open an online bank account and set up your bill
    payments.

13 Play an online game, such as Doom or Yahoo Poker.

14 Find and listen to a sports game (or concert) over the net.

15 Take part in live online chat following a TV program.

Set the team a challenge to complete the above tasks in an agreed period of
time and, each week, during that timespan, share the experience of doing so
with the group, along with the lessons learned about the e-customer from
carrying out the tasks.

Activity 3.2

E-customers: a letter from a stranger

I will complete this by _____

Now you are going to use all the understanding you have gained from the
previous activity to create scenarios for your online customers to show their
lives, their priorities, their trigger points, wants, and wishes.

Step 1

When you have finished, you will have filled this page with a description in
the first person as though the e-customer had written a letter to your
business. Keep it brief and, at the time, include answers to the following
questions and add any depth you can to your as yet voiceless online
customer.

- Age?
- Tech experience?
- Spare-time activities?
- Sex?
- Tech emotions?
- Use of the web?
- Location?
- Key worries?
- Music likes?

- Heroes?
- Hang-ups?
- What do I watch?

- Wants?
- Hang-outs
- What do I read?

- Wishes?
- Link to *your* business?
- What do I care about?

Dear Sir

You don't know me, I'm your online customer.

_____

_____

_____

_____

_____

_____

_____

_____

_____

_____

Yours faithfully

Your e-customer

Step 2

Come up with a title that describes your online customer (the fewer words
the better) and write it below. This is not meant to stereotype your creation/
discovery, but to make him or her more real to you and the rest of the team.
An example would be "Anti-e-mum." Use your imagination, then share your
customer with your colleagues.

_____

Activity 3.3

E-customers: home front

This activity focuses on practical ways of understanding your own online customers better.

The first part takes the form of a quiz to assess how well you understand him at this moment. Once you have completed it, consider how you could keep yourself up to date on this kind of information on a daily or weekly basis. Then do it!

Question	**Answer**
1 How long does *your* average online customer spend on your website?	
2 How many e-mails does *your* average e-customer send to your business?	
3 Which site do *your* online customers visit the most?	
4 How do they rate your online customer experience?	
5 What is their age range (oldest and youngest)?	
6 Which part of your electronic experience do your e-customers appreciate the most? And use the most?	
7 Which part of your electronic experience do your e-customers hate the most? And use the least?	
8 How many online customers start to order but cancel at the last minute? Why?	
9 How many think that your real-world locations offer a better experience than your electronic one? Why?	

10 What music do your online customers like to listen to the most?	
11 What do your e-customers search for on your site? What do they find when they do search?	
12 What do your online customers want more than anything else from your electronic presence?	
13 How long does it take your company to reply to an online customer's e-mail? Try it yourself and test the response time.	

Activity 3.4

Team stuff: talking, arguing, fighting, agreeing

Understanding the e-customer can be reduced to determining what is hot and what is not, rather like the innovative website amihotornot.com has. Eventually it comes down to aiming to be one thing rather than another.

The trick is to keep it up to date and be upfront about what those qualities, characteristics, and behaviors are so that the organization can attempt to become what the online customer wants.

In this exercise, first ask the team members to fill in the columns below, following the examples that have been filled in.

Hot	Not
Saying "yes we will figure it out."	Saying "no, it's not possible."

_____

Once each team member has filled in additional items, it is time to debate for 10–15 minutes which are the three hottest trends or needs and which are the three least wanted on the "Not" list. First, each member should fill in his or her own list (see below).

At the end of the debate, he can score ten points for each item on his list that eventually reached the top three. It's a competitive game that should be played to identify those trends that should be priorities for your own e-customer experience until the game is played again. Play it often.

Top three hot	Top three not
1	1
2	2
3	3

Customer experience thinkers

We have to look at the organization as a portfolio of competencies, of underlying strengths, and not just as a portfolio of business units. Business units are focused on products and markets, whereas core competencies are focused on customer benefits, such as Apple's "user-friendliness" or Sony's "pocketability." We must identify the core competencies which allow us to create new products as well as be successful in existing businesses; and we must act ourselves what we can leverage as we move into the future, and what we can do that other companies might find difficult.

C. K. PRAHALAD, CO-AUTHOR OF *COMPETING FOR THE FUTURE* (HARVARD BUSINESS SCHOOL PRESS, 1994)

If you take a good look at your relationships with customers, you might say, "we're committed to the customer, we're committed to the customer, we're committed to the customer" – but how do you actually view the customer? One senior executive at a major corporation said that he always felt he was committed to the customer, but he eventually realized that he actually saw the customer as his boss. It wasn't until an environment of real trust started to develop within his organization that he could honestly start to feel truly committed to the customer. It was the first time in his professional life that he felt like it wasn't just about pleasing the boss.

PETER SENGE, AUTHOR OF *THE FIFTH DISCIPLINE* (RANDOM HOUSE, 1993)

We don't … have any rules that say all customers must be greeted in 30 seconds, or that the phone has to be answered by the second ring. Rules like that are created by people who assume they know what customers want. We don't assume anything. Instead, we try to find out. If you give customers a chance to talk, and if you're willing to listen, they'll tell you exactly what's important to them.

CARL SEWELL AND PAUL B. BROWN, AUTHORS OF *CUSTOMERS FOR LIFE*
(POCKET BOOKS, 1998)

When I was in Rome, trying to help my sister after she had been in a car accident, I thought the doctors I met who spoke English were much brighter than the doctors who didn't. How illogical. But that was my gut reaction. I could understand them so I liked them better.

CARL SEWELL AND PAUL B. BROWN, AUTHORS OF *CUSTOMERS FOR LIFE*

"The most incredible collection of knowledge in **world history,** **Search it all** in half a second. **"**

4

Creating the
e-customer offer

*How to find valuable problems to solve for
the online customer, more profitably*

THE EXPERIENCE IS BOTH PRODUCT AND SERVICE –
every time.

There is always a natural alternative to being online, so being online
must deliver more of what the customer is seeking in return for his time
(and money).

You need to know the "basic" offer of your products and services is so
that your electronic experience can be aligned to, and strengthen, that
proposition. Additionally, you need to know what your electronic offer is
– why should the online customer pull himself away from the real world,
and other online distractions, to spend his 30 minutes a day with you?

❝ Why should the online customer
pull himself away from the **real world**, and
other **online distractions**, to spend his 30
minutes a day with you? **❞**

You are in the business of solving problems and fulfilling needs. Customers pay you to improve their lives in some way. It is in your interest to find problems that are difficult to solve because, once you have managed to solve them, you will find competition less harsh. It is also in your interest (and that of your customers) to only offer value that you can provide profitably.

Of course, this is not an objective that is limited to an electronic environment, but is one that is often missing when electronic services and products are built and launched. Often, just getting the channel to work has been objective enough in the minds of those involved in the project. You should ask the following questions.

- How should you determine the value offer that is best suited to your business and your online customer?
- How does your offer of value relate to actual e-customer needs?
- How can electronic channels be used to improve the way that value is delivered *and* increase the profitability of solving problems?

By first understanding your online customer and learning to think as he does, you are better placed to walk through the needs he has, see how much they are worth to him, and look at how the resources your business has could profitably meet those needs. This much should be obvious, in theory.

You should aim to only deliver what customers really appreciate enough to:

- sway their buying decision;
- pay more;
- come back and purchase again;
- recommend that others buy.

You should aim to remove from the offer anything that does not have an impact on these four value criteria. Don't put in what the online customer does not and will not recognize as valuable because any attempts to do so will reduce profit. If you attempt to make him pay for value that he does not recognize as being valuable to him, many e-customers will not buy the first time and most will stop paying eventually. Equally, if your business delivers value that you are not being paid for, you will reduce your profit margins with no benefit being earned.

Make sure that you understand what is already available to your customers and how much is being charged for it. The growth of free everything on the internet has destroyed many new business plans. Take a look at websites such as bignosebird.com and thefreesite.com and see if your money-earning service or product can be obtained for nothing.

Example? One telecommunications business in Europe launched a multimillion campaign selling voice conferences for a reasonable fee per month that could be set up via the internet. They didn't know that free services were available that did the same thing; their customers did. They sold under a half dozen subscriptions (there is always a handful not in the know) after 12 months of sales activity. So, check out the competition!

Conducting an appreciated value analysis (AVA) should be a regular part of any new product or service initiative and an ongoing part of the way your business refines its online customer proposition. Informally, it should take the form of a question that is constantly asked by all those working for your business.

- Does this improve the life of the e-customer in a way that he will appreciate enough to pay more than it costs to produce and lead to increased sales in the future?

It is possible to reduce this question to "Does this improve the online customer's life at a profit to us?" but it is important not to lose sight of the multiple criteria that must be met by each initiative. Many business efforts are hampered by their mono-vision.

- **Marketing** attempts to promote the amorphous "brand," but does not highlight what the online customer appreciates the most. As a result, the true value is often hidden, the e-customer goes on unaware that what he wants is provided by the business or is not reminded about the real advantages that it brings.

- **Customer services** is limited by at least two contradictory and often directionless objectives. Those working there are asked to improve "customer satisfaction" and reduce "costs." Often these goals are precise in terms of numerical measurements but very vague in tying them to overall business and customer needs.

- **Product and service designers** work to technical and date-driven briefs. They often work out the details in isolation from those who have to sell and those who have to support the customer who will use what they design and build. The e-customer and what he will pay for is not put at the center of the design, so it suffers.

The only way to avoid efforts that are unproductive and counterproductive is for the whole team (and the whole business) to be working around the same model of customer value, need, and behavior.

Take, for example, the creation of Kodak's new experience proposition to their online customer. For the first time, all three divisions of the business are working together to offer a complete electronic "memory-sharing" experience. The new campaign to promote this experience is completely aligned to the needs that the experience has been designed to meet. The "Share moments, share life" campaign shows e-customers how they can strengthen relationships between their family and friend networks. They do not focus on technical detail but, instead, on the role that the Kodak proposition can have in meeting the needs and desires of online customers. This is hitting their value hot spots by highlighting the naturally strong emotional link for consumers between pictures and memories, and showing how the electronic experience can facilitate their desire to share those memories.

One of the aims has been to take the "mystery and complexity out of Kodak's digital imaging products," according to Nancy Carr, worldwide communications director. In this way, they are able to get back to what most people buy cameras for rather than appealing simply to those who see them as a technical toy. The campaign utilizes film advertisements shown on prime time TV, print materials, and even music via a specially commissioned new song by Willy Nile.

Kodak's new approach recognizes that the e-customer expects to have a problem solved completely and holistically whenever he buys into a proposition. It is no fun and very inconvenient when a complete solution is hinted at in the promotional messages but only one part of the requirement to solve it is sold. It leaves the online customer – who expects it all to fit together – searching around for the other parts from a range of providers. His search is often fruitless, much time is wasted, and he is left as a free agent no more likely to buy again from the original provider than before he made his purchase. This may seem obvious, but a look at some of the advertising out there reveals that it is not at the forefront of some companies' minds.

Creating the offer is about innovation *and* differentiation *and* meeting needs *and* taking away reasons not to buy. The ideal online customer proposition will be different from the competition's, it will maximize the characteristics of the channel that is being used, it will meet a genuine need, and it will minimize the barriers to purchase and reorder.

Let's take a look at the steps required to identify a profitable e-customer proposition.

> ❝ **Creating the** offer is about innovation *and* differentiation *and* **meeting needs** *and* **taking away** reasons not to buy. ❞

- **Step 1: complete an e-customer behavior web**

  Put the online customer in the middle of the piece of paper, whiteboard, or whatever it is that you are writing on. Surround the word with his "Locations," his "Senses," his "Channels," his "Roles," his "Tasks," his "Pastimes" and his "Day" (see Chapter 3).

- **Step 2: identify e-customer needs and trouble hot spots**

  Go back over the behavior web and use a red pen to identify his problems and interests. Use some imagination to step through what turns the online customer on and what really stinks about his life. Then extract the list of e-customer needs and put them in order of importance to the online customer.

- **Step 3: complete an online customer needs statement**

  Take the needs and trouble hot spots and write a first-person demand from the e-customer to your organization. Highlight not only the tangible end-product as it will appear on his credit card statement but also the tangible and intangible needs that the online customer wants to be fulfilled. This is e-customer talking to you.

- **Step 4: cross-match needs against business resources and characteristics**

  Your business situation is unique and its resources will be better at solving certain aspects of the online customer's problems than others. You need to look at how the resources and the characteristics that you do have can be used to meet the needs identified in Step 2. What is difficult to do? What can you do now? What can you do best? Which customers are you most closely aligned to in terms of likes, tone, and dislikes?

- **Step 5: analyze current e-customer experience in relation to needs statement**

  This book is not a replacement for general-purpose marketing books and you will find that the online customer experience is not a replacement for all channels and all product development! They are both complimentary to other efforts. You should look at how the e-customer experience that your business offers can support and enhance the proposition to meet real lifestyle needs.

- **Step 6: brainstorm online customer proposition statements to create new ones**

  With a clear idea of what your *existing* proposition is, you are in a position to compare them to what is really demanded to see how many new propositions you can add. What are the gaps between the promise and the delivery? Could you meet more of his pressing needs by rejigging your core proposition or by using electronic channels to better match lifestyle needs?

- **Step 7: assess the strength of the propositions**

  More ideas are all very well, but how strong are they? Will the e-customer really appreciate them? What difference will these enhancements make to the life of the e-customer and the way that your proposition is valued? Consider the online customer needs statement again and again. Put your propositions in the context of your e-customer behavior web and see how many problems it solves and how likely it is to be used. If it cannot be seen as part of the customer's natural lifestyle, then it will simply not be used.

- **Step 8: identify counterarguments to your proposition**

  Now is the time to try and destroy the best ideas that you have had to date. You need to find out why your ideas will not work. The online customer will be at least as harsh on your propositions as you can be, so don't hold any punches. Destroy your ideas. Blow them up and write each objection down. Then start to modify the propositions or the experience criteria to overcome the objections. Come back to the objections during all phases so that you know what is lurking in the background if you get it wrong.

- **Step 9: prioritize winning online customer propositions**

  Even if your ideas are the best of the best, you should be very wary of doing them all. Why? First, because there is a limit to how many changes and features your organization can effectively implement in any project scope and in any particular timeframe. Second, because the e-customer will not always appreciate everything all at once. He may be overawed by it or simply want constant improvement that you will find hard to deliver if all your good ideas are brought out together.

- **Step 10: complete an e-customer proposition statement sheet**

  Now it's time to give your own organization its own voice. In answer to the online customer's demands, you will write down what the organization intends to do about them. Write it in the first person, as if talking directly with the e-customer. Make it clear what you are offering, how it will help, and even deal with the objections that the online customer will make to your offer. Include in it a list of criteria that the experience will have to satisfy if it is to speak the language of the e-customer and be appreciated by him as a life-enhancing thing.

At all times, you and your team – whether 5, 50, or 50 thousand people strong – should remember that the electronic experience is only valuable if it enhances real life by doing something better than the real world. The two worlds are not equal and if they are treated as if they are merely the same then the key selling points of both will be missed.

The result? If you are a player solely in one or the other world, those who look for both sets of advantages will abandon you. If you are a multichannel player, you will have multiple channels doing nothing but duplicating and wasting each other's efforts. The key is to understand the strengths, characteristics, and attractions of each channel. Why does a customer use one rather than another? How should they work together effectively? What are the natural disincentives to using each one?

Customer alchemists?

The better you understand the mind of the customer as well as the characteristics of the channel, the more wildly successful you can be. You can turn the unfulfilled needs of customers into wealth by building an experience to meet those needs – you become a customer alchemist.

> **66** **The better** you understand the mind of the customer as **well as the** characteristics of **the channel,** the more wildly successful you can be. **99**

Amazon, Yahoo! and eBay have become unmistakable brands in the virtual and real worlds. How did they do it? By creating something for their customers to do with their time that was difficult for them to gain fulfilment from in the past. That's it. That's all. However, as we have a book to fill, let's spend some time explaining how this works in practice.

Now, it is not clear if they will be great businesses in the future, but they will if they don't forget why they have been successful so far. Some have claimed that it is essentially about efficiency,[1] but it's not really about efficiency and it's not got that much to do with brand recognition or at least not the kind that comes from advertising spend. What is the secret, then? It has everything to do with effectively filling voids in customers' lives. That's the secret.

What void did Yahoo! fill? It started by letting customers know where to find the "best" stuff on the net and, in so doing, sold both a reduction in confusion and the comfort that comes from knowing that the customer is not wasting a moment of his precious time with less important sites. It knew, too, that there were other voids left to fill, so it added the famous or infamous chat rooms that allow customers to waste the time that they saved by using the recommended sites in the directory. In return for saving and then wasting time, its customers helped it to revenues of more than $1 billion and profit margins of 32 percent!

Is eBay in the hunger-feeding business? Sure it is. It feeds the need to buy, haggle, barter, and make excruciating (but often unimportant) decisions for millions of customers. Just feel the thrill of knowing that the bid process is going on all the way through the day. It's the hobbyist enjoyment of the buy/sell ads without the effort of buying a newspaper and without the premature ending of the process, because the first guy to call up for an item was able to buy it. Every year (in its very short history) 90 percent more value is sold through eBay, and the pleasure of the game itself has been recognized in its advertising where otherwise decent folk take delight in winning bidding wars with their nearest and dearest.

Amazon has, thus far, most successfully built on the diversity, color, and discussability of books and music and the connection that its customers have with them. Customers love books because books are about content that is as varied as the customers themselves. Suddenly we could talk (share comments) about books with people who shared our interests without boring them or spooking them in bookstores. The lower prices were a bonus. It was the book discussion group experience, wrapped up and put on the customer's desk, that really did it. That's what built Amazon all the way up to sales of $3 billion a year and the brink of profitability.

Is it possible that these three could forget the reasons for their own successes? Of course it is. If they stop using their own services and focusing on interconnection and that all-important save/waste time equation, it could all fall apart.

So, think carefully about the differences between each channel. How does the e-customer relate to each? Consider the main eight categories and how you feel about them personally. What drives you to use them? What disappoints you about them? Does your business make the most of the differences between them? Draw lines between needs and channel characteristics in your mind until you find real customer gold.

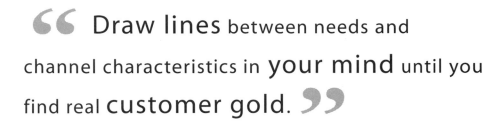

❝ Draw lines between needs and channel characteristics in **your mind** until you find real **customer gold. ❞**

Gloves off: content versus connectivity?

When creating your own customer offer, it's worth considering the great debate between those such as ScreamingMedia CEO Kevin Clark[2] who argue that "Content is the DNA of the internet" and those such as Andrew Odlyzko, senior researcher at AT&T Labs, who claim that "it is connectivity and not content that really matters to people."[3]

Of course both are right and wrong in equal measure. Extreme positions such as these lead to a very limited understanding of what customers want. They want to be connected *and* they want useful content, so the distinction is an artificial one. Your offer should be smart enough to avoid making it. Where they are combined, as in Yahoo!, AOL, and MSN's electronic offers, content *amid* connectivity increases the amount of time that customers spend online (in the examples given, to more than 90 minutes a day[4]).

This is still not the answer, though! Simply encouraging the customer to stay with you is not an automatic source of increased revenue and profits. It has to be combined with useful services, organized in a sales-effective manner, so that the connected, content rich customer can pay you back for all that enriching entertainment and free communication.

Consider why customers are communicating, what are they saying, what are they talking about, what value does it bring to them? Then put your brain to work finding ways in which appropriately positioned content and services can enhance the communication. When you find out that fishermen in the southern state of Kerala, India,[5] are using mobile phones to check which port has the best price for fish before landing, ask yourself what could our experience provide that they would pay more for?

Decisions, decisions
This is a useful starting point, but it cannot capture the depth and diversity of feeling that real people have when trying to navigate the various channels. It is valuable to listen and read as many real people's opinions as possible and frame your proposition as an offer to those people, imagining them dealing with your world and figuring out where they see the value and costs.

Every waking moment, people are moving towards what they feel will give them what they feel that they need. This movement may not be based on a thoughtful analysis of the alternatives. Each purchase is not the result of a formal cost–benefit analysis. It is based on gut feeling, perhaps, a loose combination of wide-ranging buying prompts or impulses.

It is important to consider not only the criteria for making a decision to buy from your business, but the shape, pattern, and timing of that decision. Sometimes, the online customer will sit down and formally consider the benefits of your proposition versus a competitor, but this is not always the case. How, when, where, and by whom is the purchase decision made?

For an advert to attract, to bring the customer to your experience, it will need to grab attention and offer not only something that is useful, but also something that speaks to the needs of the customer at exactly that moment. Don't go for some kind of teaser campaign in the electronic world – so far they just don't work as the more often a customer sees an advert without following it the less likely they are ever to use it. Instead, work out messages that provoke immediate action.

As an example of this, consider the offers made by the top ten banner ads in one month in the US.[6] Two were false system messages (Colonize, "you have 1 message waiting," and Bonzi, "Your net connection is not optimized") that play on the assumption the customer makes that his system is telling him to do something now. Three sold reductions in price (AA, "web-only spring sale," Chase, "earn free gas," and Ebates, "employee discounts at your favorite stores") that suggest offers are on for a limited time.

Two suggested a way out of debt (Consumer Counselling "Erase your debt" and "Consolidate your bills") and another two focused on rapidity of credit (Chase, "Get approved instantly" and Providian, "30-second decision," both of which are playing on the minds of millions of customers. On its own was Classmates, which offered to let people find their, "old friends again." It got to the number two spot in the top ten by offering something good that supports that periodic desire many people have to just get in touch by selecting from photos of real people.

FIGURE 4.1 Classmates.com: "Find old friends again."

Some customers will want more guidance to tell them exactly what they need, but, equally, there are people who want to decide exactly what they want. If they choose a car, they want to decide on the color or any combination of anything. However, both of these require essentially the same layer of technology that provides a link between you and the manufacturing options or the service manufacturing facility that can put all the options together and provide a price (including a profit margin) for you. Make it. Deliver it – mass customization.

The difference between these two groups of customers is not that great. In one case the artificial intelligence (AI) should direct you, because you wish to be directed. In the other case, the AI integrated with the personalization layer should allow you to make those choices because you would prefer to. That is like an electronic chess game when you decide that you, as the player, would like hints about the best move from the computer, your opponent, in order to compete with it. With chess systems, we have become accustomed to making that basic decision (hints or no hints). In a shop, we make the same decision when we are asked if we want any help (yes or no). Some of us say, "Yes, certainly – could you tell me the best video camera to buy for X?" Others would say, "Could you just tell me the technical characteristics of the two cameras?" Some of us would like to say, "I know exactly what I want. Make me a camera like that. How much would that cost?" So, we like to start from different points. The business that understands customers has already recognized these differences so that its sales and service process can cope with them – particularly the two or three basic types.

Already you see such stunning advances that it cannot be doubted that they will fit together. Those who love the future will tend to assume that it will happen more rapidly than has been the case, but it is happening. In my pocket, as for millions of customers, I carry a computer more powerful than those available 20 years ago – in my *pocket* – that's progress, astonishing.

There have been more advances made in the past 30 years than in the previous 300 years. It is almost frightening to me, and to the customer it often *is* frightening. Things are happening so quickly that it can be difficult for people to adapt. Can they evolve as quickly as the world of technology that inventors are creating? To have everything that we can dream of, to have anything that we want, this is not something that society has taught us to deal with. It is a heavy responsibility, and those who lead customers need to know the way so that they can make of this complexity, simplicity.

> ❝ To have everything that we can dream of, to have anything **that we want**, this is not something that society has taught us to deal with. ❞

The results of your deliberations will be an e-customer proposition that is as different from the competition's as possible. It will be appreciated by the online customer so that he will consider the purchase to be "money well spent." It will include success criteria for the delivery of the proposition so that those involved with designing and delivering it will be able to ensure that their efforts are shaped to meet the needs of the e-customer and strengthen the proposition by being aligned to it.

Experience study

Digimon.com and FoxKids.com

 Again, children bring me to the site and it to me. They are fully aware, of course, of the ever-present web and find web addresses on crisp packets, toy packaging, television programs, and from their friends.

It's fascinating to watch child customers, e-kids, surfing. The differences and similarities are both so striking. The child customer will find the bright, bright colors, and structure very appealing. There is a funky tool bar at the bottom with icons, and a background animation, the same options are laid out with smaller text labels, at the top the same options, and, at the left of the space, similar options.

It's also a noisy site! You will probably want to turn it off, but children only turn it up *louder*. Buttons have their own sound effects, with different types of noise for each different menu bar. The animations and games feature as many explosions as they can.

These include Home, Games, Toons, TV Shows, Hangout, Magazine, Digimon, Win Big, Club, Movie, Digifun, characters, the schedule, and the episode guide. Some of these are menu options for the foxkids.com site that digimon.com fits into.

FIGURE 4.2

Digivolve!

The digi shouts are popular and allow children to send messages to their friends by e-mail and by leaving notes on the site to be played at random on the homepage. There are e-cards, digitoons, music, digiart, your thoughts, and wallpaper to add to the customer's own computer. The customer can look at digimusic and download or play the main theme song, or "Hey Digimon" or "change into power" sound effects.

A range of animations keeps everything jumping – instant gratification for children whose sensory preferences make this enjoyable. This includes firey meteors and bouncing buttons. The features themselves invite interaction and soon the customer will find that he is entering each zone.

Plenty of kids' polls, including questions such as "Why do my friends admire me?" and "Would you buy a Harry Potter video game?" that are of interest to many children and of great value to the businesses that know how to collate, analyze, and act on their answers.

There are four games (Quest To Save the Net, Digimon, Boom Bubble, and Digisnake) and clicking on one to choose also shows the customer a choice of many other games on other parts of foxkids.com, just in case they thought that Digimon stood alone. The games all encourage the customer to rate the game *and* send it to a friend.

FIGURE 4.3

Boom Bubble
game on the
web.

The games are fun and it is remarkable how good macromedia Flash has
and is becoming. You get the benefit of full motion, fluid and colorful.
The customer is certainly getting his time suitably structured and, while
parents (including myself) would not approve, almost any child will
spend hours in here, if allowed.

In light of child protection legislation and a protective mood among
parents, it is not surprising to see that each ad is identified as such with
a little "paid ad" notice. Even if your national legal system does not
require it, these rules make sense. Under the very noticeable privacy
policy link, it is made clear that data is to be used with the spirit *and*
letter of the law. Take the following excerpt:

> Some areas of FoxKids.com allow kids to send electronic postcards to their
> friends. Participants are asked only to provide their first name and their
> friend's first name and e-mail address, all of which are deleted once the
> postcard is sent.

Fox makes its money from advertising, so here the advertisements are
aimed at children and the parents of children. Naturally this means
plenty of dressing-up and other toys and eight-seat people wagons.
Advertising "holidays away from the children" would work perfectly for
parents busy browsing with their children.

Overall, it's a fantastic example of an experience focused on its
customers that has adapted to provide what they want to see, hear, play,
and do. Serious experiences for big people to take note of.

Experience study

Xmenthemobilegame.com/ – it's a riot!

Want to reach a new market? Want to make sure that your experience becomes a talking point and has customers focusing on you all over the world?

This was exactly what Marvel, the comic book publishers, and Fox, the film and TV business, wanted to do to further extend the X-Men franchise. The X-Men movie was released in 2000 and became one of the most successful films of that year, but the value was in extending interest associated product sales were strong and the sequel would be more successful than the original.

Naturally enough, there were real-world products, comics, toys, figures, and promotions in partnership with the usual range of fast-food companies. There are also two official websites. One is for the movie, featuring clips from the film, the trailers, and electronic postcards. The other is the Marvel website, which supports the comic book itself, complete with fun-to-watch animated comic book stories, complete with advertising on every third page, just like in the real world.

The great innovation, and the focus of this experience study, is the massively successful use of mobile phone games to bring the X-Men world into the daily fun zones of many thousands of customers. As customers want something enjoyable to do with their time, it makes sense to provide something that they can do all day during little pockets of activity. As customers like to interact with other real people, it pays to build multiplayer activity into the game. That is exactly what this experience does.

FIGURE 4.4 Save the world with Prof X.

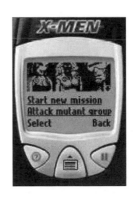

Launched first in 2000 in Italy, Finland, and the Philippines, in 2001 it was extended to include Spain and France with other territories planned. In the first two countries, it attracted more than a million hits.

There are two versions, one of them uses SMS text messaging, and the other is played with WAP, the simplified form of web pages and protocols. The aims of the games differ, reflecting the characteristics of the different technologies and, to a large extent, capturing their individual customer benefits.

- **SMS** is an interactive medium that attracts customers to it because it is so immediate. The game design reflects this. The goal of the customer is to graduate from Xavier's School for Gifted Youngsters and become a part of the X-Men by completing and giving interactive challenges. Duels are played out over four levels of play with other customers.

- **WAP** is a hyperlinked medium that allows the customer to make choices within a predefined world. The game design recognizes this and provides a map of the world in which it is played. The customer takes the role of Professor X, leader of the X-Men. His task is to save the world by advancing from continent to continent, liberating one city after another from the evil clutches of Magneto, the villain with the magnetic powers.

Hyperlink

See Chapter 3. Read about how customers need fun that structures their time to stop them dying of boredom.

The level of interactivity is impressive for such an infant medium. As each city is invaded, the customer must decide which team members to send to which locations and consider carefully how their varying skills are most suited to varying combat situations. By combating with the teams of other customers, he can train his team to be stronger. He can also transfer "mutant ability points" from one team member to another to ensure that the whole team is equally effective. The game moves the action from Europe to America and then to Asia, with the final scene taking place in New York. In the words of the games' creators:

> Choose your side and continue the struggle between good and evil – to the glorious or bitter end!

How many experiences give you that chance? Quite a few in the gaming world, but seldom is this attached to commerce outside of games. How could you use such a feature to bring your business to life outside of the immediate transaction? There will be over a billion mobile phones by 2003, so how many of your customers will be looking for all-encompassing experiences that include their mobiles?

The X-Men games are the creation of a team from Riot Entertainment in Finland. Riot-E was founded in February 2000, as a merger between two content companies. It's worth nothing that Riot-E aims to be a "brilliant storyteller" rather than just a mobile technology company and that it views the mobile device as a "lifestyle enhancer rather than a gadget." The company believes that its people need to be "riotous" enough to change conventions and create "positive chaos" via mobile devices all over the world.

On its way from the same team, in a licensing deal with Finnish content developer Small Planet, is an English-language version of the hugely popular Fish Game, which has been available in the UK since May 2001. It is an SMS game that allows customers to pick a style of fishing and then determine what to try and with what technique in order to make catches that range from old boots to great white sharks in a virtual fishing trip that lasts about ten minutes. All of the fish in the game are based on true weight scales and realistic probabilities of their being caught are used. After the game, customers can check out information about their catches, including a picture, on the game's website. On the same site, customers can see the catches of other customers, check out the fish facts pages, and chat in the community forum. In Finland, the game has attracted many thousands of players every day, and each Finnish mobile user who tries it once plays it again.

FIGURE 4.5

Hot Riots!

Stuff to think about

books, articles, TV shows, and websites

Bovet, David, and Martha, Joseph, *Value Nets: Breaking the supply chain to unlock hidden profits* (John Wiley & Sons, 2000)

Value Nets introduces a new form of business design in which customers' choices set in motion an agile, fast, and digital supply chain – delivering superior customer satisfaction and breakthrough financial results. The book's case studies, bridging the worlds of strategy and operations, provide a practical guide to help you create your own value net – and leapfrog the competition.

Bressler, Stacey, *Communities of Commerce* (McGraw-Hill Professional Book Group, 2000)

This book points out that communities are central to successful e-commerce. In its words, "Customer satisfaction is based on values, expectations, product attributes, and customer experience with the transaction process." That's not very inspiring language, but it makes the point well, that all online customer propositions must be set in the context of the family, friend, and community networks.

Business2.0

Using the versioning of software as a guide, this online and print magazine takes as a starting point the view that business has reached a new stage of development. The US version is particularly strong, while the online version is the most useful in delivering e-business news, analysis, and comment.

Cortada, James, *Into the Networked Age* (Oxford University Press, 1999)

He is absolutely right when he says, "What counts with customers is a company that looks outward as prelude to looking inward at what it can deliver" and that, "A firm's self-knowledge must be tied to knowledge of customers and their hierarchy of needs, the leverage point at moments of potential value." He supports the *E-Customer* principles by saying that, for more and more firms, a winning customer experience during each interaction with the business is becoming the value proposition itself.

Davies, Michael, *Who Wants to be a Millionaire?* (ITV, 1998)

An international success, the original format was created by Michael Davies, a 33-year-old former tennis teacher from the UK whose 5-year-old daughter gave him the idea. It is included here because of the highly effective way in which it has been designed to meet the needs of online customers, with a combination of media channels. In its basic structure, it includes television, audience participation, computer involvement, and the telephone to "call a friend." It has expanded the electronic experience by adding interactive television participation, a CD-ROM version, and an internet site with questions set at a level that allows everyone to imagine winning and becoming a millionaire.

De Mol, John, and Römer, Paul, *Big Brother* (Endemol, 1998)

Popular around the world, *Big Brother* meets the needs of the e-customer to have contact with other people and live vicariously. It took the popular pastimes of gossip and TV-only experience of soap operas, and recast them with networked media. It was the first "must-have" content for web media players and broadband net access. The result was to popularize the already flourishing, but perhaps cult, following of web cam soap operas, characterized by **www.jennicam.org**, created by Jennifer Ringley in 1996.

Fahey, Liam, *Competitors* (John Wiley & Sons, 1999)

Fahey examines the nature of competitors, and elements and types of marketplace strategy that, "embodies where, how, and why an organization seeks to attract, win and retain customers." The best way to do all that is to build an online customer experience, which is why you bought this book. Clever you.

Hartman, Amir, *Net Ready* (McGraw-Hill Professional Book Group, 2000)

The addition of value is the nature of business and that is what electronic channels are eminently well-suited to assist. As Amir Hartman puts it, "In the reconception of the ordinary exists the possibility of creating real value." The finest china pottery is still merely the integration of intelligence, customer needs, and clay.

Hope, Jeremy, *Competing in the Third Wave* (Harvard Business School Press, 1997)

The key, of course, to winning during the Third Wave (information) is to match customers' and business' competences to the value proposition. Jeremy Hope believes that managers need to choose which of three propositions to compete on: product leadership, operational excellence, or customer intimacy. My feeling is that all three must still feature in the offer. Which customers want the worst product that is the most efficient, but the most intimate? This book offers a structure for examining all three value propositions.

Rosenhead, Jonathan, *Rational Analysis for a Problematic World* (John Wiley & Sons, 1992)

This is a collection of formal methodologies that, like this book, aim to enrich the decision making process so that human problems can be formulated and reformulated without simply going directly to what may be the most efficient solution to the wrong (or least valuable) problem. These ideas were postulated before the dot com boom, but provide a strong conceptual basis for creating online customer propositions that matter and online customer experiences that deliver amid the complexities of a networked world.

Wheeler, Steven, *Channel Champions* (Jossey-Bass, 1999)

Steven Wheeler explores how to manage channels by offering different benefits via each as, providing "customers with more value than they want or are willing to pay for can make a great channel concept unviable." As this book makes clear, this is to overstretch the capacity of the e-customer to appreciate what is being offered, and if they will not pay for what they do not want, profits are reduced, sometimes to the point of financial disaster.

Activity 4.1

Back to the primitive: the e-customer proposition statement

Don't ever forget why the online customer spends money and why he spends money with your business. It's the most basic of basics, the most fundamental of fundamentals, and you can be more radical by getting back to it than any other way. The shortest path to e-customer profits is by delivering what he wants to spend his money on.

	Financial (£, $, etc.)	Time	Kudos	Fun	Ease

We give the online customer

	Financial (£, $, etc.)	Time	Image	Trust	Hope

The e-customer gives us

Why is this exchange fair?

Proposition statement (*Complete it as if it were a personal offer to a real person.*)   We give you, our e-customer:

How will you know that we kept our promise? (*Give criteria for judging a successfully delivered proposition or experience.*)

Activity 4.2

Thought shocker: something less boring instead?

It is worth remembering that there are billions[7] of places that the online customer could be rather than within your electronic experience. He does not have to be with you and this means that you need to consider how your experience proposition stacks up against the alternatives.

You are in competition with every other place that he likes or needs to be. This activity involves you writing a top five list of such places based on your study of the e-customer. Then, write beside each one why the online customer should spend time within your electronic experience rather than the alternative ones.

Once you have written down your best competing arguments, write down the desirability of the competing experience in the CD (which stands for competing desirability) column as a mark out of ten. Then write down the desirability of your customer experience relative to that of the competing experience, also as a mark out of ten, in the YD (your desirability) column.

Competing experience (place or activity)?	CD	Why should the e-customer spend time within your electronic experience instead?	YD
1			
2			
3			
4			
5			

Competing experience average?	Your experience average?

Calculate the average of your experience desirability scores and the average of the competing experiences' scores.

This is not, of course, a definitive comparison, but it does allow you to consider how well you are doing and all the reasons the online customer has for not using your service. Work on your experience until it overtakes the competition's.

Activity 4.3

E-customer proposition valuation: feed me!

This is a method of assessing the relative merits of online customer propositions. Simply write down the propositions or features of propositions that you have identified during your brainstorming discussions and use of the e-customer behavior web. Then, ask the team members to write down scores (from one to five) for each of the propositions or features in each of the columns.

- **ECA** (e-customer appreciation) is simply how much the online customer is likely to appreciate your new idea or innovation.
- **MCC** (maximization of channel characteristics) is the extent to which you have maximized the characteristics of your electronic channels and justified the e-customer's time spent getting online.
- **IOC** (improvement on competitors) is a measure of how much the proposition improves on what is offered by competitors. If it does not make a big difference, then how are you going to stop the online customer simply going to the competition? Price? Don't try that path if you can help it!
- **CTB** (cost to the business) is the level of investment in terms of money and time that the business will have to make to deliver the proposition.
- **DRB** (difficulty and risk to the business) is the level of risk that the proposition cannot be delivered or will be more expensive or later than planned.
- **TTI** (time to implement) is a measure of how long the proposition will take to deliver.

Describe the proposition or feature	ECA (1–5)	MCC (1–5)	IOC (1–5)	CTB (1–5)	DRB (1–5)	TTI (1–5)
1						
2						
3						
4						
5						

There is no satisfactory way of calculating a total at present because the individual scores are all subjective, relying on the limitations of the team member's knowledge and opinions. Thus, the final ranking is left to the team responsible for the decisions.

Activity 4.4

The lost art of keeping a secret

Always assume that the e-customer will find out any secret that you care to try and keep about your business. This has significance for the way you choose to transact and relate to him. Why keep secret what he will learn later from another (almost invariably) more damaging source?

In this activity, you are invited to consider, first, what you would rather keep secret and away from the online customer, next, what you fear as the worst result of that information being shared, and, last, how you could communicate that information without creating a negative impact.

	Secret	Worst result of sharing or making it clear	Positive communication?
1			
2			
3			
4			
5			

Now decide which secret to positively communicate to your online customers. How will you communicate it and when will you have completed the communication?

Which secret?	Communication approach?	Positive benefits of communication?
Number:		

Activity 4.5

Putting the online customer in rich context

The trouble often with the requirements definition phase of an e-customer project, regardless of channels, is that it inserts a formal process in between a rich, multilayered, diverse online customer and what should ideally be a rich, multilayered, diverse experience.

That's why you are now invited to get out some crayons (or, more likely, whiteboard markers) and draw a picture of the world that the e-customer inhabits and the relationship that the online customer has with your business, your competitors, and electronic channels in general. There are no rules here – you and your team will have to decide how to indicate what the symbols in your picture represent.

The important idea here is to get out on to paper the participant's perceptions of all the complex elements and all the people involved in the relationship between business, world, problems, and the e-customer. The people can be drawn in stick form. Thought or speech "bubbles" can be used to show the needs, dreams, opinions, or fears of the people in the picture. Simple buildings, maps, places or objects can be used to indicate boundaries, locations, movement, or travel. Arrows, words, and any other image can be used to get over the individual's view of the online customer context.

Here are some examples of symbols that you might use.

Customer experience thinkers

I often use the analogy of ducks. To me, marketing is about spreading corn to get the ducks to come. Sales is about taking the gun and shooting a sitting duck. And if the duck is not sitting, it means that marketing has not done its job. Marketing is about making the market want your product. Sales is about closing a deal with a specific customer.

ELI GOLDRATT, AUTHOR OF *PROJECT MANAGEMENT THE TOC WAY*

We've got to kill the assumption that the way to increase profits is through downsizing and cost-cutting. Instead, we've got to learn how to focus on increasing throughput. How can we do that? By learning how to construct and implement "unrefusable" offers, giving customers what they need – something that gives them a real advantage.

ELI GOLDRATT, AUTHOR OF *PROJECT MANAGEMENT THE TOC WAY*

The most important thing to a customer is: did you do what you promised? Keeping your word is worth more than all the empathy, smiles, and chocolates on your pillow in the world.

CARL SEWELL AND PAUL B. BROWN, AUTHORS OF *CUSTOMERS FOR LIFE*
(POCKET BOOKS, 1998)

> **"** Satori City, better known as Virtuopolis was developed in the year 2017 by the Satori group as the world's first VR city. In terms of its actual acreage in Cyber-Space, it is equivalent in physical size to the island of Manhattan. **"**
>
> ALEXANDER BESHER, *RIM: A NOVEL OF VIRTUAL REALITY*

Creating the ultimate e-customer experience

How to create experiences that feed the online customer with recognition, stimulus, and structure he craves

WHY DO YOU GO TO ONE STORE RATHER THAN ANOTHER?
Is it the merchandise? What about when the product is identical? Could it be the experience?

Why do you choose to walk in one park rather than another? Is it the height of the trees? The lengths of the paths? The color of the grass? Could it be the combination of all the features and characteristics of the park, and the way that they are combined? Could it be the experience?

Why do you choose to eat in one restaurant rather than another? Is it the nutritional value of the food? Do you just eat in the one that is nearest to your home or office or are you usually willing to drive a little further to eat at the one that you like best? Isn't the impact of the service, the people, the style, the tastes, the decor, and what we often term "ambiance"? Could it be the experience?

In all these examples, isn't it the experience you are choosing, not the formal list of cold facilities and so on? What is the alternative explanation? Could some law of probability mean that some stores, parks, and restaurants are more visited than others? Is it just fate or is it possible to explain the differences in popularity by how effectively they deliver experiences that feed the shopper, walker, and diner with what they crave?

The overall experience is what determines whether we don't buy, buy, or buy again. The e-customer experience is even more vital because the decision to move into the electronic world is made based on the expectation and desire that things will be better there. What else justifies making the effort to log on? Why *should* the online customer turn away from physical reality to enter a virtual zone? The answer is that the e-customer enters looking for more efficiency, more fun, more control, more sensation, more humanity, more community, more honesty, more advice, more freedom, more information, and more convenience. If your offer effectively communicates these as features wrapped around your e-customer's lifestyle, then he will come looking for you. On the other hand, if he is let down, he will leave as quickly as he came. This is your electronic moment of truth.

The e-customer experience framework

A good online customer experience should never leave him feeling lost, confused, or frustrated. In keeping with these aims, this chapter will make reference to the e-customer experience framework. This will serve as a structure for applying your understanding of your e-customer to creating and delivering experiences that are aligned to the needs of that online customer (see opposite for the framework in detail).

> **❝ A good online** customer experience should never leave him **feeling lost**, confused, or **frustrated. ❞**

The simplest way to look at the framework is in three sections. The outer section is the three-part approach to online customers, then comes the business organization, including the experience interface, and, finally, the inner section, including the core, which is the e-customer, his needs, and characteristics.

The customer experience framework

Finally, a way to remember all the elements that go into creating and delivering an effective online cutomer experience! Use it to increase your understanding of online customers and help create and deliver experiences that are aligned to the needs of your customer. Each layer and ring of the framework represents a set of components, tasks or possibilities that you will need to be aware of so that you can modify the experience to effectively meet your business objectives.

On the outer ring are the three steps to creating a customer experience – understand, create, and deliver. The next set of rings represents the business and all its resources that need to be focused on optimizing the effectiveness of the interface with the customer. The customer's characteristics, abilities, senses, and needs are set out in the inner rings.

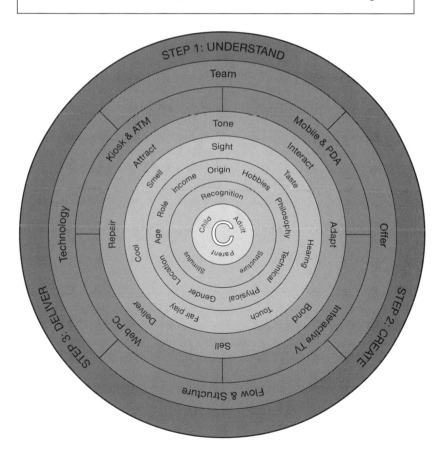

Let's start with the inner section. At the core of the framework is the e-customer – the target, the beneficiary, and the reason for creating the experience. This is the mind and body of the online customer, including everything he is and wants to be.

The survival layer

This layer encapsulates the survival needs of the e-customer or, indeed, any person. These are the most basic of our requirements and are generally the first priority simply because we will not survive without them. The relative economic prosperity of the online customer is such that he is generally confident that his survival needs will be met. He will still need to physically meet them on a regular basis but will look for additional needs to be met at the same time as keeping warm and eating well.

The hunger layer

The hunger of the online customer (also common to all people) is for recognition, stimulus, and time structure. These drive the actions of the e-customer after he is generally confident that his survival needs for sustenance and shelter have been met. He wants to be recognized and appreciated as worthwhile. He wants to have something to do so each waking moment provides interest and stops boredom. He also wants to receive the kind of attention that children receive from loving parents.

The unique personal characteristics (UPC) layer

Here the e-customer is looked at in terms that include age, gender, income, role, age, race, country, politics, interests, technical aptitudes, physical abilities, and intelligence. This list is not all-inclusive, but the layer should invite consideration of all these characteristics as a minimum.

The sensory layer

The sensory layer includes the facilities by means of which the online customer experiences the world, including, of course, hearing, vision, taste, smell, and touch. In addition, there are what can be termed a sense of what is "cool," which he uses to determine whether or not something meets his needs for desirability on subjective fashionable criteria, and a sense of "fair play," which he uses to judge whether or not something is good, right, just, or reasonable. All seven senses are vital.

The middle or organizational layer represents the organization, its resources and its capacity to serve the online customer. Often neglected is the idea that the experience is necessarily the product of every component of the organization and the way that those components fit together. All aspects of the business structure, culture, approach, and expertise are considered here.

The experience layer

Directly adjacent to the online customer sensory layer, the **experience layer** is the point at which the individual e-customer interacts, or experiences, the combination of organizational resources. This is essentially the character of the organization itself as experienced by the online customer. It is here that sales, trust, and satisfaction are determined.

The channel layer

The experience is delivered via the **channel layer**. As this is a book focused on e-customer experiences, electronic channels – namely, web PC, mobile web, kiosks, and enhanced television – dominate it. Also included, though, are face-to-face and voice via telephone channels because online customers live in the real world, too, and the experience they have there is clearly wrapped up with the effectiveness of the total experience.

The business layer

Up against the channel layer, the **business layer** comprises all the resources of the business, their characteristics, and the ways in which they are organized to serve and talk to the online customer via the channel layer. The main components here are the team of people doing the work, and talking the talk and their culture; the structure and flow that connects everything together, including rules, laws, and manuals; the technology applications, systems and infrastructure; and, finally, the offer and promises that are made to e-customers via marketing, advertising, and each member of the team.

Surrounding the middle section is the **e-customer approach**. This gives direction to the activities of the business so that it actively and comprehensively adapts its use of resources to its own needs and the needs, characteristics, and hungers of the online customer.

This book describes the e-customer approach from end to end (see Chapter 1 for an overview). Chapter 3 explains how to understand your e-customer, while this chapter focuses on using the approach to create and design an effective online customer experience. The chapters that follow will focus on delivering the experience as designed and then ensuring that it is kept fresh so that you stay in business.

Feel free to use the framework in a variety of different ways. You can pick and choose sections that are relevant to the role that you have, the stage of the project, the business goals of the business, or a particular emergency. It is also well worth reading through the first half of the book chapter by chapter to ensure that you see the way in which e-customer principles determine how each of the components of the experience need to be designed and fitted together to deliver the desired results.

Now is a good time to look up from the online customer framework and put it into the context of the entire competitive environment. After this, we will return to look at each of the layers in detail, including examples, activities, and case studies.

The online customer universe

Neither your business nor your e-customer exists in a vacuum. Instead, they exist in a universe, or network, in which more than 6 billion other online customers interact, each with their own online customer core. They move from experience to experience, tasting, touching, seeing, hearing, judging, and seeking satisfaction, acceptance, and fulfilment. The natural universe and their friends and family networks deliver most of their experiences, but many more are manufactured deliberately by each of the layers inside organizations.

Organizational experiences – whether charities, governmental bodies, or commercial enterprises – compete for the attention, money, and loyalty of some of the e-customer population.

It is only when your business has the attention of the e-customer that it can stand to gain from his money and hope to build loyalty that increases the likelihood that he will choose to start with your experience next time he feels that he needs what you offer. Let me try three brief analogies to describe the relationship. The experience and the online customer are both a little like jigsaws, looking for another piece to make them complete, or atoms looking for other atoms in order to produce new substances, or planetary bodies moving towards the greatest gravitational pull but disturbed and influenced by the pull of many other objects large and small.

They all indicate the nature of the relationship and, while none is exactly right, the atomic analogy is perhaps the most helpful. Atoms exist as distinct entities, but are pulled in different directions by the activities of other atoms and molecules. They draw closer to some, speed up and slow down, change velocity, and alter direction. They also form bonds with other atoms that form new molecular substances. The collection of atoms that constitutes the business experience molecule is not complete without the correct e-customer atom. Each experience is sent out into the world to find its ideal match and, until it does, the business is not viable, no matter how many temporary bonds it may attempt.

The business molecule is an artificial construct, rather like a plastic. It can therefore be deliberately redesigned to make room for, and be attractive to, more and more online customer atoms. As it does so, its shape, size, and complexity increases and its ability to keep what it has attracted strengthens. Business molecules that have limited adaptability built into their experiences will lose their e-customer atoms more often, for longer, and have to work harder to attract new ones. This requires more use to be made of limited energy resources (sometimes borrowed from venture molecules!) because it is trying to force an attraction and keep a bond with an unwilling atom. The resulting inefficient use of energy will reduce the ability of the business molecule to keep itself together and so it will eventually fall apart.

In the dot com rush, we saw many such business molecules formed using only borrowed energy to force e-customer atoms towards them. No bonds were made, the energy ran out, the e-customer atoms went elsewhere, and the business molecules disintegrated.

The molecular sphere of influence

The other aspect of the online customer universe that should be considered is the influence of other molecules and atoms towards which the e-customer is constantly being attracted or to which the e-customer atom may already be bonded. These others may be competitors, possible partners, or other e-customer atoms.

The effect of competitors is as follows. Where there are fewer competitors in proximity to the online customer, the attraction needed by your business experience will be reduced. Where the e-customer is already bonded to other business molecules, the attraction required of your business experience will be increased.

The effect of friends and family is that individual online customer atoms will either travel in close proximity or bond together to form e-customer molecules that form further relationships and attractions with other molecules and atoms. The lesson for creating experiences is that they should, ideally, attract multiple members of the same friends and family group, network, or molecule. The result can be networked communities of online customer atoms and organizational molecules that form macromolecular polymers that can come in a diverse range of shapes and patterns, including chains, networks, rings, and blobs. The most effective of these will be arranged so that e-customers become almost captive, locked into grooves within their shapes that are so close together that they react as one to the benefit of the whole business molecule.

" The lesson for creating experiences is that they should, ideally, **attract multiple members of the** same friends and family group, **network. "**

Creating the experience: artists and scientists at work

A business cannot expect to bring the entire online customer atomic universe under its control, so should, instead, direct its efforts at adapting the offer and delivered experience to attract and keep the right online customer. All experiences are not equal and, such is the diverse number of possible ways in which a set of organizational atoms can be arranged, if they are left to their own devices, they will not naturally form the experiences that are the most attractive to the e-customer. They will tend, instead, if without direction, to bond around their own more limited needs, reducing the level of adaptation to the online customer.

Visualization is the key to understanding atoms and molecules because they provide an invaluable insight into the behavior that the naked eye cannot discern. This is equally true of organizational atoms and molecules as described above and to being able to adapt them into organizational macromolecules delivering experiences that are attractive to lone e-customer atoms and bonded e-customer molecules. This is why, in Chapters 3 and 4, you and your team were invited to draw pictures and diagrams showing the relationship between the key components, forces, and relationships in your target e-customers' lives. By seeing visually the structure and form of what exists now, you are better placed to design a more effective future experience.

The well-established link between art and chemistry has led to advances in each of them. The three-dimensional models of molecules used in schools – plastic balls joined together by rods – have developed with advances in computer art and animation into the extensive use of animation tools within the chemistry world. Spectacular examples of such work can be found at many online art galleries, including the Online Macromolecular Museum and the Visualization and Animation Laboratory at Scientific Computing Ltd, a center for high-performance computing and networking owned by the Ministry of Education in Finland.

Why is this important? Both chemistry and 3-D animation offer insights into what is required to understand complex networks (including online customer networks) and an effective way to design better-adapted experiences that attract and keep those e-customers. In the next section, the terminology and concepts of both chemistry and animation are used to enrich the design process of an online customer experience.

To illustrate, let's first look briefly at the approach taken to create 3-D animations – from first sketches to wire models to full 3-D animation. It moves through sketched storyboards to capture the flow, structure, and style of the final animation, then to modeling to create 3-D computer models of everything in the film, including the shapes of the objects and the motional controls that animators use to create their movements, then the animation itself begins, where motion is choreographed by defining key positions that the characters will reach, then the shading and lighting are added before the final rendering, during which every little part or pixel of the animation is edited in a process that takes many hours for each frame. Next stop, cinemas or laboratories around the world for excited children and scientists.

Animating the online customer experience: bringing it to life

Of course, the creation of an e-customer experience is not the same as the creation of complex macromolecules or the latest Pixar/Disney extravaganza, but there are some very helpful similarities that can allow the still immature B2C e-commerce industry to create much more effective online customer experiences. The creation process that will be explained next is the result of considerable study into best practice in electronic design, including animation, and adding to it the notion of molecular manipulation. Wow, what a mouthful!

Part A of the animation process involves you animating your online customer character(s) and all his personal characteristics, including age, gender, income, role, race, country he is living in, politics, interests, technical aptitudes, physical abilities, and intelligence. (These are all part of the unique personal characteristics (UPC) layer of the e-customer experience framework that is described throughout this book (a copy of the framework is shown on page 111).

Part B of the animation process is to animate (design and deliver) the props, sets, and characters that will surround the online customer to deliver the desired experience.

	Part A E-customer animation	Part B Experience animation
Step 1 Sketching	By completing the activities in Chapter 3 you will have have a much better understanding of how your e-customer looks and behaves.	List the main characters, actors, and owners involved in delivering the experience. Sketch out their main characteristics so that they are recognizably part of your organization and experience.
Step 2 Storyboards	Time to draw an end-to-end, scene-by-scene view of how the experience and its actors and props interact and how you want them to interact. What is the ending to the story? What are the possible outcomes? What is the pace of the action?	
Step 2 Modelling	A refinement of how your your particular online customer behaves linked to the particular offer that you are making to him. This will allow you to consider in more detail how he will interact with the modeled experience.	Consider changes to direction, timing, prices, features, and content.
Step 3 Animation • **interaction** • **navigation**	First, choreograph the motion and interaction in each scene by defining the different ways in which the parts of the experience will interact with the e-customer. This will include the way a field, game, button, or graphic will behave and the various "states" that it can display, what is happening behind the scenes, and what each of the characters involved are doing at any point and in response to any particular event. The mock-up can be extended to include this information.	
Step 4 Enriching • **colors** • **shading** • **layering**	With the structure, flow, interaction, and navigation complete and included within a storyboard of the experience, it is time to enrich the experience by adding colors, shading, and layers. Layer by providing slide-in panels, pop-up panels, moving buttons, graphics, Flash animation, and other features. Any site can be made usable by making it clear and simple; the task here is to add fun, style, depth, and "stickiness" and still make it usable.	

	Part A E-customer animation	Part B Experience animation
Step 5 Rendering • **build** • **implement** • **training**	This is where you get the experience off paper and simple electronic mock-ups and into a usable, bullet-proof form. Don't let the IT team work in isolation and make sure that the experience remains visible as each part of the organizational layer delivers its element of the experience so that its delivery is harmonious and fully functioning.	
Step 6 Test screening	Time to bring the experience, rendered and ready, in contact with the online customer again. How does the real-life, self-rendered customer fit into your carefully thought-out experience? Do you need more to capture his attention or is the experience storyline unclear? Do you need more alternative endings? Did he laugh, cry, read, and buy at all the right moments?	
Step 7 Distribution	The electronic experience will have to be distributed via a range of channels and channel partners. Are you using affiliates and, if not, why not? Does it fit a gap in the offers delivered by other partners? How does the experience promote itself?	
Step 8 Screening – **go live**	Show the whole world and consider what style of launch will be most effective. Huge parties are not always acceptable or cost-effective, but you need to ensure that the target e-customers know that what they have been waiting for is now here.	
Step 9 Sequel?	The e-customer will continue to change from the point that you first sketch him out at the start of the animation or experience creation process. You may succeed in catching up but can you keep up?	Start preparing your sequel before you release the original. Sketch in what happens next because, if the e-customers like it, you need to be ready to give them more!

This process allows you to progressively flesh out the nature and behavior of the online customer and add that to the context of the offer that your business is making him. You need to use it to experiment while the experience is still on paper, in Steps 1 and 2, because it is simpler and less expensive to make changes at that early stage. Remember, though, that this experience is interactive and likely to demand change more like an electronic game than a one-ended one-sided animation feature.

Back to the framework

The experience framework has been described only at an outline level so far in this book. Hopefully this has left you with a clear understanding of how it represents methodology, the business organization, and the e-customer. You were then introduced to the notion of e-customer atoms and an animation process for designing macromolecular experiences that are ideally shaped to attract and bond with online customers.

This is a good point at which to add considerably more detail to the sections of the framework so that you can continue to modify your online customer experience so that it is better and better adapted to the needs and desires of the e-customer. Each layer introduced earlier in the book will be described, discussed, and considered in turn, including all the key components within each layer and the relationships and interactions between them, other layers, and other online customers and experiences offered by other organizations.

The experience interface (or membrane)

This is the electronic moment of truth, the point at which the e-customer comes into contact with the organization. The experience attracts or repels, it creates the word of mouth buzz or silence or murmuring; the experience satisfies or leaves unfulfilled; the experience fits perfectly around the characteristics of the online customer to provide an empathetic cocoon or acts as a barrier between the objectives of both parties in the transaction.

So, we are going to look at the same model from different angles, including the interface friction idea. As you approach the interface, how do you feel, how do you respond, what is our typical response when we approach something that is inorganic to satisfy a need? How should the organizational layer deal with complex layers of need via the experience membrane? It may appear that it is only filling up the senses, but it is actually dealing with the hungers. There is a fairly rich mix of behaviors, aptitudes, and motivations at play.

The experience needs to be examined from both micro and macro levels. If you look at the background, the environment surrounding the experience, you find billions of inner e-customer cores, millions of organizations seeking to satisfy (or simply do business with) those e-customer cores. They are floating around looking for customers to focus on and are all linked in different ways. Another business being close will alter the way that your experience is perceived because a relative judgement is made that will change the way that the e-customer thinks. Thus, the mere existence of other business offerings will not change the situation very much but if the customer becomes aware of these alternatives, and they move closer to him or one of his network of friends and family, he will become aware of what is offered. At that point, instead of being comfortable and satisfied with the space that you have created for him, he starts to think of, or try out for size or live in, other spaces that have been prepared for him. He may start to skip from your space to others and your business is left without an online customer to deliver an experience to.

How do you get him back? You could try sending him something interactive to play with, such as the viral marketing campaign from LifeFX. The company is selectively sending e-mails out that contain stand-ins. These are virtual personalities that it hopes to sell to web businesses to act as virtual salespeople and site guides. The plan is that recipients will take the time to download the media player to bring the virtual character to life to read the e-mail aloud, moving its lips and assuming facial expressions that match the content. Then, impressed with the player, they will forward it on, with a personalized message to their friends. Will they? Well, LifeFX thinks that about 5 million players will be distributed this way.[1]

If you try out such an approach to attract his attention (and you should!), ensure that you have already prepared the follow-up. Then, you will develop an experience that won't merely amuse or distract him for a moment, but, instead, keep him bonded in. If you don't sell software, what is the payback, what happens next, what keeps the relationship building – will it just be another freebie that the customer consumes and discards?

Is it worth all this trouble to get it right? Yep. Thinking about customers as interconnected atoms leads to marketing communications that are incredibly rapid and effective. Coca-Cola has used this approach to reduce the time required for the launch of a new drink from three years to just four months for Fanta Exotic and to just two months for Burn, a new nighttime energy drink for clubbers that started in Australia.[2]

> **❝ Thinking about** customers as **interconnected** atoms leads to marketing communications that are **incredibly rapid** and **effective. ❞**

Not convinced by soft drinks? Try the world of movies. *The Blair Witch Project* – the film with the highest profit margin ever – was launched as the result of an electronic experience that built on the authenticity and eeriness of the legend. The film became just an obvious part of the experience and, of course, ensured that the customer paid for the ride.

Need another example? How about the internet legend that the founders of Hotmail woke up one morning to find that half the population of Sweden had become members overnight?

Sometimes the online customer is receiving a barrage of different experience offers, which is what happens when he is assailed with many different advertisements or banner ads. Each gives a hint, a promise of what the experience will deliver to him if he enters it. Even within the electronic experience that your business is offering there are usually competing experiences that want his attention and time. Each link is a signpost to a place that he might want to go, a list of many options each saying "Come here. We can give you something you want." You need to phrase all those offers so that he is most likely to accept invitations that lead to the experience that you want him to choose. In such a situation, it is valuable to ask: "Which experiences do we want the e-customer to experience and in what order of priority? Which experiences will be most attractive to the online customer? Which are currently most attractive (first explored, most popular) to the e-customer? How does each experience lead to outcomes advantageous to both the business and the online customer?"

If you choose to offer a game of some sort, then you should know what the link is between the game, which may appeal to his sense of cool and sight and hearing, and his need for structure and your overall offer. Is he left with a dead-end or empty experience, where he is left thinking, when the game finishes, "That was fun! What shall I do next?" If he doesn't see a natural progression from the game, and the next steps are unclear or missing altogether, he will leave to find more to feed his hunger elsewhere. Then your game will become simply part of a set of gaming experiences on the net for which the online customer has paid nothing.

The task is, then, to optimize the experience to deliver what he will pay your business for that it is most profitable for you to provide. Of course the experience is meant to help him because that seems to be what he will appreciate most, but there is no gain to be made from offering him what he will not pay for and you cannot afford to give. Too often, the experience is viewed in bits and there is no flow through from attraction to payday for you and the e-customer, and the relationship that naturally develops from mutual satisfaction. The customer is a multifaceted individual, living in a busy world. There are many experiences waiting for him and he is being pulled one way and another by what he reads, what he sees, and what his friends tell him. Why is this important? Because it leads to payday? Why is this the route to payday? He will not appreciate an experience that delivers only part of a promise or satisfies only one need. He will go looking elsewhere for the rest of the experience that he needs or craves. Know, however, that he would much prefer to have *one* place that delivered the *complete* experience, one that addresses as many of his complete set of needs as possible.

> ❝ **He will not** appreciate an experience that delivers only part **of a promise** or **satisfies only** one need. He will go looking elsewhere for the rest **of the experience.** Know, however, **that he would** much prefer to have *one* place that **delivered the** *complete* **experience.** ❞

In the Kodak example mentioned near the beginning of the previous chapter, the camera is sold, the software comes with it, the software works with the website that already exists, the website links to all the e-mail and communications software used by the e-customer's network of friends and family, so he can share pictures and memories, as the offer indicates. Can your experience deliver on its promise? How many needs does your offer meet? Where are the dead ends? Where are the paths to nowhere?

Adaptive experience membranes

The atomic online customer is ever-changing. An experience that may satisfy today will not necessarily satisfy tomorrow. Satisfaction levels will be altered by the alternatives on offer, and the needs of others in the family and friends network, dependent on the role that the e-customer is currently fulfilling. As a result, the experience interface or membrane will have to change to accommodate this. The time taken to deliver a changed experience to match the new needs or roles of the e-customer can be termed the "adaptive delay." This delay has a cost associated with it that will increase in relation to the size of the gap and the time taken to close it. As the gap between needs and experience grows, the attraction for the online customer to your experience will diminish. This will mean that he is less likely to come looking for the experience, less likely to complete the experience as you would like him to (including buying!), and more likely to be attracted away from you by another experience.

Adapting to these changes may need to be very rapid. Redissue.co.uk – one of the fan sites for the richest soccer club in the world, Manchester United – understands that its customers will be moving between the roles of "fan" and "employee" in a matter of seconds. Its tongue-in-cheek, "Quick the Boss is coming" feature invites its customers to enter a work-relevant web address so that, at a click of a button, they can flip to another less obviously time-wasting site. It not only helps the customer in potentially embarrassing circumstances, but also, more importantly, lets customers know that it understands them and has a sense of humor. This is not a complex feature, but one that is effective in its benefits.

There are many ways in which you can make the adaptive delay as damaging as possible.

- Make only occasional attempts to understand the e-customer.
- Implement only large-scale projects every few years to adapt to large-scale changes in online customer needs.
- Entrust the entire understanding and experience creation process to a third party and let them leave with all the understanding – if you don't know why it worked in the first place, you are unlikely to be able to fix it when it breaks.
- Ensure that there is very little communication between the different parts of the organizational layer and that there is a strict hierarchy and separation of departments – For example, make sure those in the customer services department are the last people listened to in experience design – what would they know? They only serve the customers.

- Avoid using your own electronic experience and those of your competitors.
- Never, ever seek honest, direct, contact with online customers.
- When you do change, do so in a way that confuses all those e-customers who were foolish enough to stay loyal and like what you were offering before.

Closing down the adaptive delay is difficult to do because:

- change to the membrane is relentless;
- it discards what has become precious to our organizational psyche;
- it involves creating an organic model of your organization and its work rather than the mechanistic model that has been the norm.

Fortunately, achieving it means that the payback is considerable. First, you stay in business. You do what most of your competitors will choose not to do (they prefer boom and bust online customer relationships – it keeps things interesting). You determine what the 80:20 rule is for your e-customers, so that you can spend time and money on what *your* online customers want to pay for rather than what someone else decided would look nice or be a good idea.

The channels layer

The experience itself is delivered via one or more channels at any one time. Each different channel has an impact on the nature of what the experience can be because of the differing technical characteristics of each. It is also likely to be used in a variety of different circumstances, but particularly on its home territory, its turf.

The notion of "home turf" is helpful because, as the experience is designed, it should consider as its first priority, and pay most attention to, the place and circumstance it will be most relevant to. The shape of design priorities should fit in with the shape of the likely usage location patterns. All design is compromise and so the compromises that you make on behalf of the online customer should be made with actual usage in mind.

Internet PC at home, school, or office

This is not the place to explain what the internet is! It is the place, though, to explain the particular nature of PC-based internet access, its impact on the relationship with the online customer, and the ways in which design approach, style, and priorities should be adapted to optimize the effectiveness of the experience via a channel that offers the full power of the internet and the greatest number of additional peripherals.

- **Expectation** is probably highest at home. Why? Because our beloved e-customer has spent his own money on all that shiny hardware and so expects someone will deliver complete experiences and really useful features to justify the expenditure.

- **Patience** is the key to understanding the office based e-customer. He may have time to kill – only eight hours until the return commute – because he finds work uninteresting and the internet a potential saviour from death by dullness. In which case, he will need fun, fun, and more fun. Give him opportunities to dream, the ability to communicate, stuff to customize, but nothing to download, and nothing to anger the great god of the firewall. The experienced, patient, furtive office-based online customer is also happy to be anonymous, a fact that explains the lack of interest in anything that requires typing his name into a non-work-related page or cookies. The inexperienced version wants to be anonymous, too, but just assumes he is.

  Alternatively, for the driven – self or otherwise – e-customer, a lack of time leads to a need for more of it, a need for ability-enhancing, time-saving, and reputation-polishing features. How can you make him look good at work or get him home on time or improve the quality or timeliness of what he is doing?

- **Curiosity** at school is most likely to drive students to use the internet. Such e-customers are seeking knowledge to help them complete their school work, look good in front of friends, find out a sports score or where their favorite musician has just had a tattoo, or what is hidden in the dark world that parents and teachers are so concerned about.

Design considerations

The question is really how far do you want to go? This channel offers all the power available to the experience, so the key limitations are the imagination, ability, and budget of the team of creators and implementers. You have a full selection of features to appeal to every sense and hunger that the online customer has. You may rightfully ask at this point "How far can I go? How far can the e-customer experience be taken?"

To answer such a question requires a starting point, so let's start with the screen and chair that your online customer is using. Not an exciting place to begin, but it has been chosen for a reason. Your e-customer may be sat on a stool, the floor, a comfy armchair, lying on a bed, in a wheelchair, or a specially designed orthopedic workstation chair. The chair or other place he uses will affect the way that he is feeling about the general electronic experience and yours in particular.

Where is the computer that he is using? Is it in on a desk, kitchen table, workstation, in a shared office area? The place will also have its own impact on the experience. So, too, will the peripherals that he has available, the noise in the room, the number of people there, and the level and type of light present.

Start with the online customer, as discussed in Chapter 3, but then sketch out the scene and props within his world that have an impact on the way that the e-customer interacts with the electronic world that you have provided. This is not some straightforward retail experience where you have the online customer from toenails to hair follicles totally within your space and influence. Write it down! Always remember that the online customer is in a halfworld and design to reflect that truth.

So, let's walk with the e-customer through the steps he takes into the experience and what he may be feeling at any point along the way. Usually he sits down as a conscious decision to seek a solution to a particular problem or to satisfy a hunger that may or may not be consciously recognized. The first distinction will be between those who still have to dial up using a modem every time that they want to jump in to the virtual internet experience and those who have an "always on" connection. The second distinction to be made relates to the speed of the connection, which could range from 12K a second to more than 12MB per second. Some e-customers will be used to connections that are 1000 times faster than others, and the difference that makes to the experience that you can offer is stunning. What type of connection are you building your experience for?

Enhanced, interactive or internet TV

Enhanced television comes in two distinctive flavors: interactive television, where additional interactive and multimedia services are offered via proprietary technology, and internet television, where the television is used to display the internet itself, with varying levels of sophistication.

The great possibility of internet TV is that it combines two children of the electric revolution into a must-have experience in the same way that electricity originally combined with the lightbulb, then the washing machine, then the vacuum cleaner. Only nine years after electricity became widely available in America in the 1920s, more than 20 million American households were wired and almost half of these had vacuum cleaners, and a third had washing machines.[3] E-mail is the closest equivalent to this of an application attracting high general interest, but it is not yet vital enough compared to the now essential benefit of electric light and household appliances. What happens when the favorite pastime of the Western world is combined with the most interactive technology ever created? Could be an epidemic of remote control RSI?

> ❝ **The great** possibility of internet TV is that it combines **two children** of the electric **revolution into** a must-have experience in the same way that electricity **originally combined** with the lightbulb. ❞

Are you often in a hurry once you are sat back in your favorite chair or cuddled into your settee to watch the television? Nope, and neither is the rest of the population. The only time things get tense is when the film you are watching delivers a stirring moment, complete with a Dolby surround sound scream or explosion. It has often been termed a "lean back" channel and suggests an undemanding, but, at the same time, "come and get me" experience. Online customers want to be entertained principally when they turn on the television, but they do not want to be hassled. They want to be coaxed in and blown away by a range of very clever features. This is not a world where amateur efforts are enjoyed. What does this mean for the design of your e-customer experience?

Interactivity as part of the standard television-viewing experience is usually highlighted by use of one of many icons – a little "i" for information and the use of red to attract attention are popular combinations. The online customer is invited to press the appropriate button on his or her remote control to gain access to a range of super-nifty enhanced services. These might include free offers, the purchase of products, sports scores, news headlines and updated weather, participation in game shows, while continuing to listen to the TV program or watching it in a separate viewing window.

Design considerations here relate to what the core activity is and how the electronic experience relates to that core. Also worth thinking about is the mood and likely objectives of the TV-viewing online customer and the relative size and type of design elements.

Mobile, on the move, internet in the car

The key differences between the requirements of mobile electronic experiences and static ones, regardless of location – on the move, in the park, the car, or jogging – relate to:

- lack of a mouse or hand to provide input;
- physical size of the unit;
- greater need for the experience to be as unobtrusive as possible;
- likelihood that the experience will be enjoyed in the company or the view of others.

As a result, the demands put on design push towards the simple and elegant rather than the complex and ornate – a fact that is borne out by a look at the mobile internet devices themselves.

The mobile user may be utilizing a variety of different devices to interact with your experience. This includes mobile phones with WAP or cut-down HTML browsers, hand-held computers or personal digital assistants (PDA), and a combination of the two that is most often referred to as a "smart phone." The limiting factors to bear in mind include:

- how much information can be shown on the screen;
- whether the experience is in color, uses a gray scale, or two-tone liquid crystal (usually black on green);
- how fast the connection is;
- whether the connection is a dial-up one or always on;
- how many of the standard internet protocols the device supports.

These factors vary remarkably from device to device and movement toward the full always on, fantastically rapid internet is coming fast. It already exists in the UK and is busy turning an irritating and frustrated experience into a must-have blast. However, even working within today's limitations does not mean that your mobile e-customer experience has to be dull and a clone of every other online customer experience. Don't wait for a mature third-generation device base before you experiment.

Simpler mobile phone devices have perhaps 4 text lines with 12 to 16 characters per line. The monitor of a standard PC has perhaps 60 or more text lines with 200 or more characters per line. This means that the mobile phone device holds around 64 characters while a PC holds 12,000. That's more than 187 times more screen space into which you can fit an electronic experience! With such a reduction in space, the first task is to find more of it and the second is to make the very best use of it.

Younger e-customers have overcome reduced room and inefficient input devices by using abbreviations and symbols (or emoticons). They are busy sending text and e-mail messages typed out by clicking on a combination of numeric keys. Your business should consider using them if the age group of target online customers means that they readily understand such messages. Another way to deal with the input speed limitation is to allow the online customer to type in details via another channel that offers a keyboard and then provide it to him on the move. Attention should also be given to the use of the soft keys on the mobile phone screen. These can be reprogramed to provide different options that are appropriate to the various stages of the flow and structure of the experience. This is much easier for the e-customer than scrolling up and down, looking for a link to select. It is also much easier to direct the action and keep to the shape of the storyboard that you have designed.

Ultimately, the most effective method for using a limited area is to ruthlessly cut your service down to the basics. This is a good exercise anyway because it forces you to determine what it is that the online customer cannot do without. For a search engine, this means an icon, a search field, the option to search, then a simplified results screen showing the first few options at a time.

Love of icons, even in a limited range of colors and relatively poor levels of resolution, is something of a fad among the teen group. There are already services that exist simply to provide the budding collector with a full range of logos and, in addition, ring tones. To use such a service usually involves choosing the logo or ring tone, calling a premium order hotline, entering an order code, then watching as your logo or ring tone is sent to you immediately. The delighted recipient can then show off a mobile phone version of whatever track by whichever artist he chooses or a logo of his choice. The Nike swooshes, little cuddly kittens, and Chinese dragons are among the favorites.

Even the "limited" mobile phone, therefore, is capable of having some fun. There are also standard games built into many, including the addictive Snake and a little version of tennis reminiscent of an earlier generation Pong played on the first consoles. The growth area is in online games that bring the online customer the interconnectivity and sense of espionage that is so enjoyable for the audience.

Each location demands a different focus. Consider the car. Do customers really want to browse the net while driving? Nope. While at the wheel, customers want the internet to enhance safety. When they are not in the car, they want it to make it "theft-proof, provide sensors to detect hazardous road conditions, and enable a remote control to start the car and warm it up."[4] As most customers can't tell the difference between most cars from their outward design, it would make sense to add genuinely better safety and security – where are you Volvo?

Kiosk, in the street or in-store internet

This version of the experience does not travel with the e-customer; it is simply there along the way or when he gets to his destination. It can offer, via kiosks, public access, full-strength internet so has the advantage of giving customers location-specific services without reducing the performance or display of those services. So, what does the customer want to use the internet for while travelling about? What benefit can such public space internet provision provide to your business?

The business can find benefits in reducing staff numbers (not advised), increasing customer satisfaction and control, and increasing its reach. It can also become a business in its own right when it provides the customer with essential, location-specific information, entertainment or services. Kiosks can also play a valuable bridging role between the real and virtual worlds by offering assisted usage of the same functionality that exists on the purely electronic channel.

Consider the role of kiosks in the travel industry, where businesses are keen, in principle, to gain greater customer loyalty and avoid horror stories shared by complainers. Airline tickets have become one of the greatest-selling items on the internet. Why? Because, for the customer, it means less time waiting for his call to be answered, more control over the process, and less time queuing at the airport when he gets there because he can use the kiosks available there to print his own ticket out, check himself for his own flight (Northwest), and chat via instant messaging (AlaskaAir).

In return, the airline gains greater loyalty because, once the customer has made the process work, he will be loath to go through the pain of typing in all his details again with another airline or travel company. It can also use the information gained from the customer to personalize the experience to his needs by offering tailor-made deals at convenient moments. It can analyze the traveller's travel history, suggest itineraries, provide maps, suggest taxi firms, and, by judging how long the customer has between checking in and boarding, the kiosk can even decide whether or not there is enough time to try and sell or if it would be better to gently remind the customer that he would be best advised to hurry.

The combination allows savings in marketing and distribution costs (a quarter of total operating expenses). It saves airlines commission expenses and eliminates costs of printing, sending out tickets, and fees for computerized reservation services. It reduces the wait for the customer, who can use alternative identification (code numbers or even credit cards) to board the plane. Then when he boards the airplane, he finds that the kiosk is now airborne and available alongside each seat, providing personalized services, including television and duty free goods billable to the original credit card account.

In the process of designing the experience, you will find that one key difference is that, instead of using the accurate and familiar mouse as an input device, the online customer will be trying to point at what he wants using his fingers via a touch screen. This means that the ideal design will provide larger targets, buttons, and input fields. The hand also tends to obscure the screen as it moves across it, so you will have to ensure that either the interactive elements move around the hand (difficult to figure out) and/or the menu and navigation items are at the bottom of the screen.

The importance that kiosks play is in providing a link between the integrated world of the internet at high speed and in full color to the customer when he most needs it, but accompanying it with corporate "control" and branding that makes the most of each interaction, for the customer and the business.

It can allow you to rethink the purpose of real-world locations. Even a pure play internet-only company can consider putting down roots. Equally, traditional real-world businesses can avoid automatically closing down and shedding staff by considering how to use the real-world and kiosk-based internet services successfully together.

Keep thinking the way that customers think and you may find benefits in doing what innovative banks from Portugal, Japan, Australia, the US, and the United Kingdom have done. They know that the cost of a typical retail branch is high but have chosen to reinvest that cost to radically enrich the experience, delivering a style of banking beyond the norm.

Portugal's biggest bank, Banco Comercial Portugues, bought Banco Portugues do Atlantico and transformed the duplicate branches into what they term "theaters". In these theatres, customers are educated about how to handle their finances by staff known as "retailers" who walk around, in the open, talking to customers and potential customers. The bank has recognized the differences between electronic and real-world locations and created the equivalent of an electronic chat room out in the real-world branch location, which is ideal for building the trust and the relationships necessary to catch additional product sales.

The Portuguese success is echoed by those of Japan's Suruga Bank, the USAs Wells Fargo bank, and the United Kingdom's Abbey National bank that have all experimented with adding coffee shops to their branches. The Abbey National is at the forefront of multichannel experience innovation with its cahoot.com service, yet it has relaunched its branches as quasi-franchises where managers are paid, among a number of parameters, according to the volume of products they sell. As a result, their sales have increased by 20 percent more than fully controlled branches. Managers are able to act according to what they know about the customers and do what humans do best. One such example of this is Alan Thomas, a franchisee in Wales. He sent back posters and leaflets advertising house loans valued at over £200,000 ($285,000) because the area had no houses that cost that much. Then, he created his own marketing material, in Welsh.

In these real-world locations, the internet kiosk is used to provide the powerful assisted and self-service facilities that are available at home in an environment that can educate, build trust, and effectively sell products that can be maintained and supported via the self-service portions of the electronic experience, most of the time post sale. If there are problems, the customer can still use the real-world branch, but, little by little, the trust and confidence of our unconvinced 85 percent is gained.

The organizational layer

It is the combination of organizational efforts that deliver the experience at the membrane. The people working for the organization build, maintain, and change the ways that this experience is delivered, and the ways in which various resources and components are put together. Ultimately, then, commerce is still a relationship between two groups of people: customers and the people who serve them. Sometimes this relationship is so obscured by red tape and firewalls that it is reduced to a transaction at arm's length, rather than a warm, two-way exchange. Shocking that this is particularly true of commerce conducted remotely via communication technologies. You should consider it a terrible waste if the interactive arms of networked technology are not used to bring all those involved in the organizational layer closer to each other *and* to the online customer.

> **❝ Ultimately**, then, commerce is still a relationship between **two group**s of **people: customers** and the people who serve **them. ❞**

Structure and flow

The organization provides structure and flow to the experience. It creates the procedures and processes it operates within. It also delivers the structure and flow the e-customer will have to deal with.

Some questions to start with on organization-side structure and flow. Does the structure and flow of your organization support the creation and delivery of attractive online customer experiences? Are the values included in the offer to the customer the same as the values that guide the rest of the organization? By all means create an advertising campaign that promises to break all the rules, but make sure that you figure out what rules take the place of those that are broken. A brand new world of choice and freedom may be promised by the words and pictures on your website, but do the people who do the work in your business work in that same new world? The organization will find it hard to deliver coherent, substantive, valuable experiences if those who work within it face incoherence, superficiality, and being undervalued!

An organization that is divided by hierarchy and departmentalism will struggle to regroup around the needs of individual customers. Repeatedly it can be shown that businesses that are not radically shaped around responding to customers' lifestyles are ill-prepared for a networked era. This is why they struggle to find a purpose for all that technology – they did not have any particular desire to change the ways things were.

Turning your inquisitiveness toward the experience itself, you might ask these questions. Is it clear at all times what to do next? Does the pace and tone of the flow match the needs of the e-customer and the nature of the offer? Is help offered as a permanent part of the design? Does it cater for the online customer in a hurry by giving him a direct-route, minimal-click process? Can the experience provide entertainment for the online customer who needs to feed some of that structure hunger? Does it inform those seeking knowledge? Does it offer substantive interaction and personalization that allows the e-customer to choose what he wants? Will the happy online e-customer be happy enough to buy only to be dismayed by the after-first-sale experience?

The experience includes everything of which the customer becomes aware, which means that the distinction between business-to-consumer and business-to-business exchanges is artificial. The great interest in it now is merely an admission that the promises made to e-customers demanded off-line *and* online standards that could not be met easily. Let's look at some of those questions in more detail.

What will you do with the feedback that you are receiving? As an "experience" provider, you can use e-mail to track if and when your customers have read promotional offers. You can do as companies like Barnes & Noble and DoubleClick[5] are doing and plant "web bugs" in HTML-based e-mail messages in order to measure the effectiveness of your in-box marketing campaigns. These bugs, buried in the source code as tiny IMG tags, can also tell you the IP address of your customer and match a browser cookie to his e-mail address so that you know exactly who he is if he visits your website. At this point you can vary the structure and flow of the experience to improve its effectiveness and usefulness. Alternatively, you can only use such a device to collect statistics without benefit to the customer or your business. Using such information, if you decide to collect it, only to personalize a few marketing e-mails is a waste, isn't it? It needs to be used to adapt the experience to the characteristics of the customer or it will be resisted and distrusted by him.

Ensure that the structure and flow of your experience does not hide, or appear to hide, from the grievances that your customers have. Your business needs that kind of criticism and honesty. It will be difficult enough to encourage customers to take the time to be both open and clear, even if your business learns how valuable this information (and the process of gathering it) can be.

66 **Ensure your experience does not hide, or appear to hide, from the grievances that your customers have. Your business needs that kind of criticism and honesty.** 99

What does this mean for your electronic experience? First, you need to be very upfront and convincing about motivating customers to take the time to complain. Remember that up to half of your customers will *not* complain, even when they are unhappy, because they simply don't think it will change the way that the business treats them. The rest either are too busy to complain or do not know who to address the complaint to. You will have to repeat and repeat the importance of customers complaining, then make sure that the way that your experience adapts to the complaint makes the effort of the customer takes to do so worthwhile. This may also mean putting real people into the picture because most customers still prefer to talk to someone in the flesh when they have a grievance.[6]

If your culture seeks to avoid responsibility, if your policies invite an adversarial approach to dealing with customer complaints, then your ability to attract and bond with those valuable customer (atoms) will be seriously hampered. To many businesses, the customer is merely an aggravating fact of life rather than the source of all that is good! If this is true of your real-world operations, then this fact will find its way into every part of your electronic experience and the processes that support it.

In business, especially services (and electronic experiences are necessarily services), profits are made by taking responsibility for some of the customer's objectives for payment. That is the essence of the commercial relationship. You will find (if you probe just a little) that your programers have pretty much the same view of customers as your front-line experience delivers and that their attitude is fairly similar to that of your middle management. It is either for or against the customer.

Flow and structure for buying

You don't just want your experience to sit there making people vaguely comfortable. They don't just want to browse; they want to buy. It has become one of the greatest pastimes of the Western twenty-first century, but is often neglected electronically because those designing the experience are not service or sales professionals.

The potential strength of the electronic experience is that it can be a marketer, server, and salesperson, all rolled into one. It can help turn the browser into a buyer, then into a loyal customer by delivering best practice again and again. The strange thing is how these functions, these parts of the same relationship with that all-important customer, are so often found separated, even in the electronic world.

Instead of the team being able to pull together to overcome the deficiencies of the procedures that the business has, it is blocked by the technology that it cannot control. The necessary flexibility is not built into the system and the system is not built to integrate the buying stages together as a matter of course.

Is it any wonder that the conversion rate in electronic experiences is so low so often? Is it surprising that so few return to shop again? Is it a shock that so many decide to buy but give up before the actual payment? Is it amazing that the cost of attracting customers continues to outstrip the revenue that they bring? Of course not! With no integration of flow and structure toward sales and then repeat sales it simply does not happen.

Let's take an example from the real electronic world and look at it in action to see what the experience is doing to act as a perfect combination of sales, service, and friend. We will examine the following as we move through the example.

- Does the experience manage to actively sell?
- Does it do so without being pushy?
- How does it speak to the buyer's psychology?
- How does it use the buyer's feelings to help him to reach a buying decision?
- How does it help him to join in the buying process actively?

Experience curve™ The organization needs to use the interface across the various channels and using all available senses to effectively move the customer through the buying and bonding process. The objective is to increase the repeat purchases, the profitability of each purchase, and the number of customer recommendations, which will reduce the cost of customer acquisition.

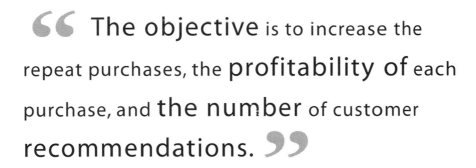

The objective is to increase the repeat purchases, the **profitability of** each purchase, and **the number** of customer recommendations.

The experience curve is a way of picturing the progress of the customer through the experience. Remember that the objective of the business is to move from first attracting the customers through to bonding with them in such a way that there are repeat sales. At various times, the experience may be less or more effective at each main stage of the relationship. We tend to use a five-point scale to indicate the way the customer feels, from appalled to inspired, and over time, from the first attraction of the customer to the point where the customer has bonded with the business.

FIGURE 5.1 Experience curve – from thrilled to appalled.

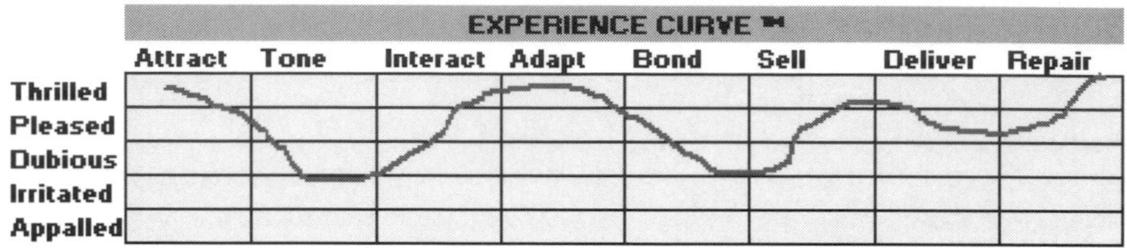

EXPERIENCE CURVE ™								
Attract	**Tone**	**Interact**	**Adapt**	**Bond**	**Sell**	**Deliver**	**Repair**	
Thrilled								
Pleased								
Dubious								
Irritated								
Appalled								

It is self-evidently counterproductive for immense effort at any one stage to be compromised by ineffective flow and structure at any other stage. Spending money on a great electronic experience, but not attracting customers is clearly a waste of money. Selling and then delivering the product or service is great, but failing to repair the relationship when there is a problem is fundamentally damaging to the efforts of the whole experience.

Use tracking technology (discussed on page 246) to identify each stage that your customers pass through and their state of mind as they do. In this way you can redesign the experience to keep the customer at the upper level of satisfaction while ensuring a clean, efficient flow from first attraction to bonding and repeat purchases.

Example

The example that I have chosen to illustrate the experience curve is one from Ebates. It draws the customer's attention to its service via a mixture of great public relations – with the founders Paul Wasserman and Alessandro Isolani often in the news talking about the importance of customer service, customer recommendation, they must be doing something right – and extensive banner advertising.

In this case, let's go from the point of view of a banner advertisement. Ebates uses a range of selling messages that appeal to an urgent, immediate desire to get rebates back from purchases. The following is a good representative example described below with accompanying screen shots.

FIGURE 5.2 Ebates is fighting for ca$h back!

At this point, as the customer, I do not know exactly what ebates.com does, except what is contained in the advertisement. It hits a desire learned from my parents to be careful with money. It talks to my learned behavior, just as the little icon of Moe catches my child-like curiosity. It's a must click advert, and it needs to be to avoid me growing used to it and learning to ignore it.

Next step, I arrive on the first page of my first ebates.com experience. It welcomes me in and gives me a selection of alternative ways to tailor the "sales presentation" to my needs. I can choose to learn more, look around, or register immediately to start saving now. The registration detail option is very clear, simple, and inviting. It also takes up about a third of the screen to prompt my attention.

The offer is simple, sign up, receive $3 immediately and the message is bold, in case I am worried, that there are, "No hidden fees, no strings, no catch," and only "big savings." Each selling point is clearly laid out and I am in no doubt as to the benefits being offered and reassured by the number of big brands on offer.

FIGURE 5.3 Let's start shopping.

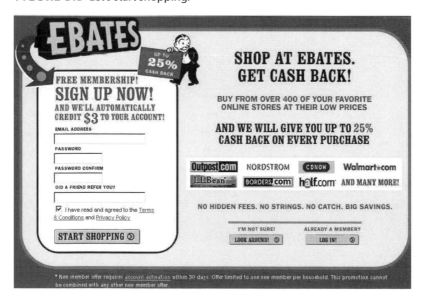

So easy is it that it seems the natural step, and I fill in the details that are requested before continuing. A few moments later, my first e-mail from ebates.com (reproduced below) arrives to welcome me to the service. It confirms my e-mail address given in the registration process and then, in just a few words, explains what I need to do to earn the rebates. It could not be much simpler, as all the customer needs to do is register, then use the shops included on Ebates' list from the ebates.com website. When the purchase order has been confirmed, a rebate of between 25 and 50 percent is paid and, each quarter, a "big fat check" arrives at your address, as long as a minimum of $5 rebate has been paid.

Welcome to ebates.com!
The e-mail address you registered with is: max@maxmckeown.com
OK, now that you've registered you're probably ready to go. So, to get started earning those rebates, here's all you need to do: go to ebates.com, pick from any of our 400+ online merchants and start shopping. It doesn't get much easier than that! But remember, to get that big fat check, you need to go through ebates.com every time you shop.
Once the online merchant lets us know you've made a purchase, we'll post the rebate to your account. How long will that take? Well, it depends. Some online stores take longer to process orders than others, so figure between one and thirty days.
Now go ahead and start shopping at your favorite online stores, and if there's another merchant you'd like to see included here, just let us know by sending an e-mail to: customerservice@ebates.com
Thanks, and happy shopping!
PS: Make your big fat check even fatter by referring new members to ebates.com. Just go to **http://www.ebates.com/member_referrals.go** to find out how.

Duly welcomed, the registration process leaves me on the homepage of the ebates.com site. The promptness of the response has developed a little trust and the experience now knows that I am happy to make rapid decisions and get right down to reaping the benefits of the service. I am amused by the informality of the phrase "big fat check" and know that this service automatically qualifies because only people who buy products become customers of ebates.com.

The next task is to make the buying possible, simple, attractive, and make it happen! Ebates does this by using the brand power of the stores that they work with to pull the customer immediately into the buying process in a main box to the left of the screen space, along with the selling messages that convinced me to sign up in the first place. This draws my attention to the categories underneath each with a maximum rebate value to further interest me.

Below that is a "what's new" area containing new store listings along with the rebate percentages, an advertisement space, and an area that allows me to download the "Moe money maker" and reassure myself that I will never miss another rebate! This was not a particular concern of mine, but it does make me feel an increased urgency to get involved – after all, this is real money, I am reminded.

To the right are three main areas. The "account summary" area lets me know what rebates I have had to date, including the $3 that I have just received. It feels good to have money already in the bank (of course, I will only receive it if I buy something to increase the rebate value past $5, but it still feels like I am nearly there for free). Below this is the "special offers" area containing three brands and three special offers. Below that is the "in the spotlight" area containing two brands that are simply given promotional space.

FIGURE 5.4 Ebates – more than you bargained for?

The overall structure is full of selling messages, but, at the same time, it is clear and simple to navigate. It reassures me because, if saving money will be easy, then it is worth trying for a while. Time is money and I need to have my natural customer skepticism won over by such convincing demonstrations. Again, this step has strengthened my desire for the service while, at the same time, overcoming potential concerns as I quickly figure out the costs of the benefits that are presented.

I decide to shop for computer and electronic goods to feed my desire for gadgets! Ebates is offering maximum rebates of up to 25 percent. I move my pointer over the category option and a floating panel jumps up to tell me about two of the brands in this category, with their rebates, and options to look at others. I choose "more options" from the pop-up and find myself looking at a list of stores. There is the option to select a subcategory to look at a shorter list and an option to hide the logos of the stores for quicker downloading. Helpful little Moe is featured here holding the option to add any of the stores to a favorites list for future reference. The experience is rapid enough to hold my attention and, as I am being helped at every opportunity, I am inclined to want to buy just to try this service out.

I choose buy.com and click on it to enter the buy.com site, but, via a frame, so that the ebates.com colors appear above buy.com. This reminds me that ebates.com is there to reduce the price of each purchase and that the experience itself is being brought to me by ebates.com. At any time, I can access ebates.com help, add the current site to my favorites list, or navigate easily back to the ebates.com homepage.

Usually, a few days after the purchase has been completed, the rebate will appear in the "account summary" area that the customer has already been shown when he first registered at the site. There are no vouchers to lose or post, just reduced cost of shopping and a "big fat check"! It's easier than the real world and more interactive for the customer and the experience provider, who is learning valuable lessons about customer preferences while also building a valued relationship with every rebate.

So, what happens if I want to share the service with my friends and family network? I can earn $5 per registration that leads to a purchase. What happens if I have a question? I can use the customer care options that are constantly at the bottom of the ebates.com web page. It comes as no surprise that ebates.com thinks enough of its customers to offer an e-mail and live chat, powered by egain, from customer care representatives. Once again Moe is featured to add an immediate human face to the customer care team before I have even spoken to them.

The reputation of the customer care is very high. I check it out as a customer on epinions.com and find that 95 percent of those who have written about it highly recommend it, including many who say that they are addicted to it.

The security policies are very clearly explained and the well-publicized involvement of ebates.com founders, two former deputy district attorneys who "take privacy and security very seriously," is very reassuring, as is the repeated commitment to "privacy, security, and integrity." The use of the word "integrity" rings true from the general tone, flow, and structure of the experience, as follows:

> Having represented the people of the State of California collectively for ten years in a never-ending fight for justice, the founders of Ebates know that your word is who you are and integrity is the cornerstone of any enterprise whether public, private or personal. As such, you have our word that we will protect your privacy and safeguard your shopping at all times.

It's impressive, it works, it sells.

Flow and structure for service

When a customer needs help, he really needs help! If your experience can assist the customer in a moment of great need, then it will develop the bonding that your business can use to grow. The reverse is also true if it fails the customer in a moment of stress – at this point there is less logic and more survival instinct. All emotions will be heightened and he will remember an experience that let him down in colorful, negative terms.

Sometimes the "need" is for a convenient way to solve a dilemma that the customer is facing. What appears simply to be a purchase via electronic channels is actually a solution to a pressing problem. The following example illustrates the point because it shows a customer who expects the internet to meet its promises and is left unhappy and compromised when it fails to do so. The important point to note is the emotion, so I will tell the story in the first person.

Example

I was having a very busy week, followed by what was meant to be a relaxing weekend. I had put off buying a roof box for a driving holiday that would start in just a few weeks. In the middle of a lunchtime barbeque, the pressing roof box purchase was mentioned again!

I knew that I had to do something about it, but didn't want to drive to buy the product and abandon my guests. The reassuring thought of internet shopping came into my mind! So, I announced that the "roof box" situation was under control. I would just use the online shop of a well-known brand – Halfords.com in this case. Problem solved, despite a fair amount of disbelief around the garden among friends and relatives.

So, I logon and type in the web address. Within a few seconds, I find myself at the online store, which is light and inviting with white background and light blue highlights. Just a few moments are required to dig down for the information on the roof box. For your typical male customer, this is great because I now feel informed without having had to ask questions from a position of ignorance. It is not the full story, though, because I still have some questions: "How do I fix one to my car?" and, "Which one fits my car?"

Once I decide to think about buying (this is how we customers think), I begin to buy, clicking on the "buy" button, then move into the registration process. Why oh why, though, do I find myself having to sign in again rather than moving directly to the buying point? It's the kind of inconsistent buying flow and structure that comes because someone wanted to save money in the programing effort and did not check via customer testing if the compromise was acceptable.

Unfortunately, this leaves me in a constant loop. Over and over again I find myself at the logon screen. AAARRRGGGGGHHHH!!! So, I click on "help," because I need some. The "help" page assures me that "If you've got questions about the site or your order, you should find the answers here," but, instead, I find no answers to the question "What should I do when your idiot site is not working?"

So, I hit the contacts link and decide not to e-mail or write because I want to order the roof box now. I have invested in the buying process and want to complete it! I choose instead to dial the freephone number and am (naturally enough) greeted by the following message:

> Thank you for calling Halfords Direct. We are unable to take your call at the moment, but please leave a message at the tone. Our customer support line is available from 9am to 4.30pm Monday until Friday. Messages left outside these hours will be replied to as soon as possible.

So, what should the customer do? This is not the attitude of a team that is obsessed with serving the customer. Whose fault is it? What part of the business is responsible for the experience? Did the technical team build it in isolation? Does the customer services team care about or understand the needs of the web customer? The customer couldn't buy, he couldn't tell Halfords, and he wasted his time. Worse, he must announce this sad story to his disbelieving friends and then find some time in the middle of a busy week to buy the roof box. Disaster.

Sometimes the customer need is even more pressing and heartfelt. Think of an insurance claim where the customer has suffered actual theft, damage, loss, or even injury. For the organization it may be simply business as usual, but for the customer it is a period of great stress, pressure, worry, and perhaps hardship.

> **❝ Customers face** problems at any time, day or night, **during the week**, at **weekends**, and on holidays. Why, then, do most customer **support lines** only open Monday to Friday during **office hours? ❞**

Customers face such problems at any time, day or night, during the week, at weekends, and on holidays. Why, then, do most customer support lines only open Monday to Friday during office hours? Why are electronic experiences not used to support the customer with empathy, grace, and efficiency at any time of day or night?

The team Who supports the experience? Who creates the experience? The team. It makes no sense to think that exactly the same ways of organizing teams, exactly the same skills, and exactly the same attitudes are going to be sufficient to deliver new, improved experiences to the customer. If you agree, then your next question might be, "What kind of a team do I need to deliver this experience?" and this book addresses the question in Chapter 6. You might also ask "At what point and in what ways should effective use be made of the team to get personally involved with the delivery of the process? (Where do people fit in?)" Let's look at answering the question in a little more detail.

Humanity, the human touch, will not be felt to its fullest extent if the people in your organization are separated from the customer by barriers or reduced to behaving like just one more component following preordained scripts. Despite advances in artificial intelligence – demonstrated admirably by games such as Black & White and Half-life, and sophisticated natural language expert systems, popularized by search engines such as ask.com – computers continue to lack a range of human characteristics that are necessary to deliver effective service.

This was not helped by the somewhat "antihuman" prejudice of some of those involved in the dot com rush that assumed profits would be automatically higher if real people were reduced to a minimum in the e-commerce transaction. It is a viewpoint that will disappoint some 80 percent of affluent online customers who prefer (like the rest of us) to have some personal support when online. The result has been that many e-customers came on to the net full of expectations that were soon trampled on. They came looking for solutions and found only technology. They desired greater community and found in e-commerce only one-click shopping. They wanted control and found only ambiguity, jargon, and a sinking feeling that maybe they were not "good enough" or "smart enough" to use the net for shopping.

A web-induced inferiority complex is unlikely to encourage your online customer to return, only provoking resentment or even anger toward the cause of that complex. Instead of positive viral, or word-of-mouth, marketing, you are left with an online customer who may wish your business ill. Even as the numbers of net users increase, the percentage of regular e-customers remains below 15 percent. E-commerce sales have increased 70 percent in the past year, fuelled by increased spending by a minority. This still means that the majority are unhappy with what is offered.

From your own experience, you know that only people can understand what other people want. You also know that only people can come up with killer advances capable of solving difficult, ambiguous problems and leap-frogging the competition. The trick is ensuring that the creativity, humanity, and humor of your people are focused on the lifestyle of the online customer.

Only people will care about what other people think and feel. Auravita.com encourages its team to reach out to help beyond the call of duty.[7] One female e-customer ordered a huge amount of slimming products. The people in the company were concerned about the customer's health, so they had their nutritionist contact her, advised her to contact her doctor, and maintained contact with her through a very difficult few months.

Only people will work behind the scenes to create solutions that customers really need. Think about Xerox. The company employed an anthropologist instead of a business process re-engineering (BPR) consultant to look at the work patterns of its field engineers. It was found that the engineers kept two copies of the manual – one pristine, the other dog-eared and annotated with wisdom gained from their experience. It was found that engineers got together informally to swap stories about how to fix problems in better ways. Instead of trying to stop these practices, the company supported them with radio headsets to allow permanent chatter between engineers, leading to more machines being fixed, and happier, profitable online customers.

The e-customer should be able to request personal contact with a real person via your electronic experience. The more rapid and universal this is, the more comforted and reassured the e-customer will be. He will then experiment because he is a little braver as a result. He will take his time to understand because he knows that there is always a real person to help him out. His knowledge that the electronic interface or membrane is simply the face of an organization containing real people who are trying to serve him is comforting and changes the perception that he has of cold, lifeless, electronic windows.

> **Would you** hire an engineer, doctor, accountant, electrician, **marketer without** the requisite **qualifications**? Nope, so why is your business happy to hire **unqualified customer** services people?

Businesses do not take customer services seriously unless they are talking about cutting costs in a downturn. It is not a respected area. Proof? Only 5 percent of those who work in it have qualifications in customer services. Would you hire an engineer, doctor, accountant, electrician, marketer without the requisite qualifications? Nope, so why is your business happy to hire unqualified customer services people?

Customers still prefer to talk to real people rather than technological devices,[8] and 66 percent of them prefer to deal with females. It therefore makes sense to make any attempt at a virtual helper feminine rather than masculine. AOL's choice makes a lot of sense in getting past "techtosterone machismo" to a style of experience that is acceptable to the majority.

It is not always desirable or feasible to have people answering every request in real time. The alternatives are to make non-human assistance as human as possible. This means that the task of deciding on vocabulary, appearance, and behavior of the substitute human should involve the expertise of those who do serve customers. If a mannequin of some sort is chosen, then it should be viewed as the electronic representative of the sales and services teams, using their words, giving their explanations. Why? This will make the substitute human more acceptable to the online customer who will receive the warmth and kind of tone he might expect from a person-to-person exchange, *and* it ensures that the electronic channel is understood and accepted by the business for what it is.

The offer: six "buy" words and one poor alternative   The issue here is not what the offer should be, but how the offer that has been decided on can be best delivered. What is the relationship between the offer and the experience design? Should all websites really look the same regardless of their purpose or their brand or the preferences of the e-customers who need to be attracted to them? Here, it is useful to examine some of the typical selling points of experience offers and look at how the experience can be altered to strengthen or diminish the effectiveness (and ultimate commercial returns) of the offer.

Two out of every three customers prefer out-of-town shopping centers to local, individual shops. This should give you some idea of what the customer seeks from his electronic experience. He wants it to be convenient, complete, to be surrounded by other people, to shop with friends and family, to be able to mix entertainment with provision gathering – he wants an experience with his groceries. Won't two out of every three customers prefer the complete, convenient, electronic experience? It's a bet worth making.

"Do not suffer the problems of the real world," the marketing proclaims, "Enjoy the convenience of our website." Unaware of the danger that awaits, the naïve online customer, who wants very much to believe, trots over to said purveyor of convenience and finds that it takes nearly an hour and two systems crashes to buy one pair of jeans that cannot be worn until they have been delivered, which is confidently predicted to happen within a week. When the jeans arrive, they do not fit, and so must be repacked, postage stamps bought and added, and the parcel returned to the distribution warehouse. That is only the start.

I was appalled, but hardly surprised, to read a survey of European web retailers[9] that showed that more than one in every three orders made by a customer were not fulfilled because of technical or procedural problems. One in four orders was simply not delivered! The retailer's site made all that immense effort to attract the customer to the site and encourage him to place an order but could not manage to deliver the goods. There is nothing convenient about that, it's sloppy, and will not be forgiven. Such poor performance leaves Europe wide open to better offers of convenience from the rest of the world. Retailers should not think that the customer will stay loyal to his country of origin. It may be that "Service from America" becomes more of a selling point than "Made in America" ever was.

"Community" is also promised repeatedly – "Get online and meet other people," newspaper articles suggest and exhort. So, how do you deliver that community feeling the online customer is looking for when he gets to your website? Offer regular, organized chats about your products and how to get the most from them. Provide archived transcripts of the discussions, and two free-to-enter chat rooms at all times (one for registered customers and the other for everyone), complete with a moderator from the business who is there to help with general questions.

Hyperlink

See page 26 for an example of community from Eyestorm.

Be among the early commercial experience creators to recognize the new breed of webwide messaging that can further increase interactivity. Free programs, such as CrowBurst, Cahoots, and uTok can allow your customers to leave notes on any website or chat while cruising through sites. These facilities turn solitary surfing into collective, social, critique, and communication. You can provide downloads of these tools from your site and encourage your team members to use them to answer customers' questions and look at what is being said about your business and your competitors' experiences. As the interactivity increases, the quality of service can increase, and so will your sales.[10]

You can also provide confidential, one-on-one discussion at any point with a business team member who is automatically made available whenever the online customer needs to chat. This need to confess is a product of the seemingly private internet world where e-customers say and do things that they would not feel comfortable doing off-line. Cater for it by making it clear that their information is secure and that you are happy to deal with them anonymously if they wish until they build up confidence in your ability.

There is a lot of "cool" being marketed as an associated offer on the internet. The challenge is that it is not always well received because it is not truly cool in the eyes of the e-customer or the e-customer does not want to buy cool or the experience is nowhere near as cool as the offer. Remember that only a small percentage of the population shares your definition of what is "hot" or "not" and that even the views of that percentage are constantly changing. It is the nature of fashion, and the consequence of promoting the experience as a fashion item is that it will have to change its wardrobe with the seasons.

Of more enduring benefit is the offer of "completeness" – the end-to-end offer, the everything-under-one-roof experience. How can the electronic experience help here? Just to start with, the internet has a virtually infinite roof and its ends have virtually no end! The repeatability of electronic space means that once part of the service has been built, it can keep on working, while the expandability of electronic space means that room to store it should not, typically, be a problem. The most significant feature of electronic space is, naturally, its potential for interconnectivity. Every part and stage of every process and service can be linked to any other part, without gaps, without delays.

"Confusion" is an offer that is made sometimes accidentally or perhaps without thought. It has no particular benefit and is not very attractive, except to those who like mystery. Despite this, many hugely expensive advertising campaigns have attempted to sell confusion to the waiting audience. This has included the rash of vaguely named dot coms and bizarrely renamed traditional businesses. Take the following commentary[11] to heart, which bemoans the way that businesses keep changing their names.

We consumers like names that reflect what the company does. We know, for example, that International Business Machines makes business machines; and Ford Motors makes Fords; and Sara-Lee makes us fat. But we don't know, from the name "Verizon," what Verizon does. As far as I can tell, Verizon consists of some big telephone companies that joined together. So why couldn't they call themselves "An Even Bigger Telephone Company"? And what in the world is "Accenture"? This is a company that buys a *lot* of ads, the overall message of which seems to be: "Accenture – A Company That Buys a *lot* of Ads." I checked the Accenture Internet site, and here's what it says about the name: "Accenture is a coined word that connotes putting an accent or emphasis on the future." Swell! I am all for the future! But what does Accenture *do*? What if it sends me a bill? Should I pay it? What if I don't, and it turns out that "Accenture" is the new name for the organization formerly known as "La Cosa Nostra"? My body parts would be found in nine separate Hefty bags. The police would shake their heads and say, "Looks like he didn't pay his Accenture bill."

A better bet in the post-dot com backlash is to offer to help already confused online customers to deal with something that they do not understand. Your offer could help them understand and productively use the internet itself or subjects that many consider to be inscrutable, such as tax self-assessment, pensions, healthcare, or the dating game.

Not all e-customers will share your notion of objectivity about the relative costs and benefits accruing from a particular experience, but they will make the choice that seems to give them what they crave most at any one time. They may feel that cool, completeness, community, comfort, or reducing confusion are all worth more or less than they would cost. The experience must ensure that it takes only what is valuable to the business and not more than the online customer is prepared to give. Time, energy, and worry are all costs to the customer and he weighs them up when making a decision about the attractiveness or otherwise of any particular experience. Poorly designed payment processes will cost the online customer more, so he will reduce the net benefit to him of your experience and, therefore, his willingness to pay for it. Make sure that your offer is worth more than it costs – to you *and* to him.

Compared to the six offers listed above, "price" is the poor alternative. Why? Because customers don't buy according to the lowest price alone, which means that if they were going to buy from you at one price, they would probably have bought from you at a higher price. Electronic channels may help you to reduce your own expenditure by virtue of better management of stock levels and a reduction in salaries and rent on property. Then again, those benefits may be negated by the increased marketing spend, the additional technology costs, and the efforts of your competitors to also be as efficient as possible. Over any time period, it is difficult to maintain profitability when making low-margin, low-price offers because they demand such large e-customer numbers and such a low margin of error.

Only about half of your potential customers even know whether the internet is really cheaper or not, but nearly 70 percent of potential customers believe that the experience that they have in the real world is worse than the real world. The evidence is strongly behind the conclusion that service, not price, is the pivotal point of competition.[12]

Prices across channels are falling, and the "era of big margins" on products has been declared dead[13] as a result of the efforts of many of your competitors to reduce margins at any cost. The winners will be those who shift from the selling of standalone products based on price (and location) to providing complete services that make the customer's life easier, better, and (in his view) less risky. The recognition by many real-world businesses that product margins are falling explains the increased focus on selling add-on insurance coverage, product health checks, and design services, but it still leaves many questions unanswered: "Why are such services seldom sold as part of the electronic offer? Why are such services sold in such a standalone way? Why is the service that surrounds the sale of the product so bad when the business should be trying to convince the customer that the added services are worth buying?"

> **66** **Why is the** service that surrounds the sale of the product **so bad when** the **business should** be trying to convince the customer that the **added services** are worth **buying**? **99**

Technology Technology provides not only tools for serving the online customer but also the location itself. The experience is housed within electronic space and it is into this that the e-customer is expected to venture. Technology may be neutral, but particular technologies have characteristics and contain design compromises of their own that have implications for the experience that utilizes them. The attitudes of the online customer toward the technologies used will make a significant difference to the optimum technology mix. What impact does the use of technology have on the experience? How should it be used? At which stage of creation should technology be considered? Who should lead its creation and application? When the walls, floors, stairs, carpets, and even the people are created electronically with technologies, the raw material and the methods used should be of interest to everyone. If they are not understood, then someone in the organization needs to ensure that they are explained successfully and continually. Choices, strengths, and weaknesses should be explored in terms that all involved would be able to understand. At the same time, all members of the team should be encouraged and trained to gain a deeper, richer understanding so that they can go beyond the basic, kindergarten explanation.

Back to the online customer (did we ever leave?)

The experience will need to communicate to each of the needs of the e-customer and do so within the capabilities and characteristics of each e-customer. This may be the most basic theory of online customer experience design, but the effort required in terms of the investments of time, mental energy, and resources is high. It is an effort that many business teams are simply not prepared to make. For those involved, it can appear simpler to just roll on completing their own specialty role in isolation from the external e-customer and the overall experience. As the minds behind the online customer experience, those in your team, are the only ones capable of understanding the corresponding mind of the online customer and then intelligently crafting an experience around him.

The survival layer

At the core of the e-customer's concerns is his need or desire to survive. Not all people will do anything to continue living, but many will and, for most of us, it is the most basic of instincts. We need to keep our body alive, so we seek sustenance, providing it with the energy it needs, and shelter, to keep us warm and secure from attack. When we are worried about security, sustenance, survival, or shelter, our attention is turned from other matters.

Sustenance

The great aspect of sustenance for the experience designer is that it is a regular, daily need. You know that issues of food will be on the online customer's mind for at least some time every day. What difference does that make? First, you can set your clock by it because each time period involves meals and so the activity of the online customer can be structured by eating. Breakfast time, lunchtime, dinnertime, supper time, or their equivalents.

> 66 **The great aspect** of sustenance for the experience **designer is** that it is a regular, daily need. You can set your **clock** by it. 99

The times, durations, and approaches to eating differ from person to person, age group to age group, and culture to culture. These differences allow you to plan what should happen in your experience to take full advantage of the e-customer's eating habits. Change the content at different times of the day to feature photos or food subjects. If you can sell the customer food directly, time your advertisements so they are in line with his hunger.

Shelter and security

If the e-customer is without shelter, then it will become his first, nagging desire until the issue is resolved. This explains the stress related to property purchases and renting. This is also the reason behind what can be termed "hotel bed shuffle," where a traveling online customer is not happy or relaxed until he knows where he is sleeping each night.

When designing experiences, you can appeal to these needs by linking your service to ways of locating, buying, or renting shelter. Do not underestimate the lengths – sometimes seemingly irrational ones – that customers will go to to protect and make themselves secure. Experiences that offer increased security, such as net-controlled intruder alarm systems, will be of interest. Anything that your experience can do to reassure him that the experience itself is safe will be a great benefit in opening his mind to the offer you really want him to focus on.

The hunger layer

Once the online customer is confident about survival, shelter, security, and sustenance, he will start to address his hungry psyche, so it is at this point that your experience needs to start attracting its attention and then successfully feed it. In doing so, you will also need to consider the ego states of the e-customer, how these will change through the course of a single set of interactions, and how to respond.

You may have read the explanations and discussion of ego states earlier in this book (see Chapters 3 and 4), but the really challenging part is to work out:

- the relationship between ego states, customer behavior, and the experience;
- the most effective way of designing the experience to respond to the current ego state and make progression toward a mutually beneficial outcome.

These concepts and structures are used, in many variations, as part of many books and approaches to sales. They are used much less in service training, perhaps because of an assumption on the part of management that they are beyond the ability of customer services team members. There has been scant application of such ideas to the field of e-customer experiences as a result, at least in part, of the focus on just "getting things done" and the dislocation that has been grown between the "electronic" team and the rest of the business that know more, often, about selling and service.

How will the experience deliver much-wanted "recognition" to the online customer? He can respond well to personalization at the simple level of being greeted by his name when returning to the electronic experience or being invited in by letter, e-mail, or message. This is a good start because it delivers the electronic pat on the head that he needs to keep happy, but it is seldom enough.

- Many people have an almost insatiable need to be appreciated, respected, and recognized. This is one of the motivations for heading to public spaces, to find other people to give us attention, and this is as true in electronic spaces as anywhere else.

- It is also the case that, as a relationship starts to develop, people want more, not less, attention. They increase, almost without recognizing it, the amount of recognition they deserve for the level of time they have known or been known to you. The demanded level of recognition will also increase in relation to the amount of money that is spent with you.

The first time he comes into your electronic experience, the online customer does not expect you to know his name (it may even unnerve him if you did use it because he doesn't know who you are or why you know him), but he does want to be greeted. He does appreciate the electronic equivalent of the beaming smile or the friendly nod that lets him know that he is important, that you respect his space, and that you are ready to help a valued person like him whenever he requests it. From that point on, each second he spends with you, he will expect slightly more recognition and will feel comfortable as you deliver more personalized content, if you can keep offering reassurances that you are not threatening his ability or security.

> 66 **The online** customer does appreciate the electronic **equivalent of** the beaming **smile or the** friendly nod that lets him know that he is important, **that you respect** his space, **and that** you are ready to help. 99

If you disturb his peace of mind or irritate him, he will be forced into a defensive or potentially hostile mode and want to either run away or attack. As there is rarely anyone to attack, he is most likely to simply act as unhelpfully as he can. This probably means leaving the site with an angry click of the mouse, but can mean sharing the bad news or finding a competitor to act out his revenge by shopping with them. In extreme cases, this might manifest in setting up sites dedicated to the downfall of your business or committing acts of cybervandalism or terrorism. Don't make the mistake of turning clumsy recognition into acts of aggression, as in the following cases.

- When an unwanted e-mail including the e-customer's name is sent. It is immediately viewed with suspicion – perhaps even fear – in these days of virus e-mails. The e-mail will either be viewed as spam, wasting time, or as an intrusion, attacking privacy.

- When too much information is displayed without him requesting it. In the web PC channel, this means an intrusive number of pop-up windows (the number could be as low as one) – the electronic equivalent of a salesperson who is in your face from the first moment you enter the store. For a really good example, take a look at the insurance salesperson in the movie *Groundhog Day* with Bill Murray.

If the online customer arrives and you can avoid scaring him away, well done! The next hunger to address is his desire for "structure." He wants to structure his world and time for two main reasons: first, it stops him losing his mind and, second, it prevents him dying of boredom. You can be pretty sure that once he is fed and housed, he will be looking for structure of time or his world or both.

How do you deal with this? Let him know how your service will meet one of those needs. Pretty simple concept really, but to do so will require some clever thinking and designing. How can you communicate how you will feed this structure hunger? What kinds of words, pictures, and references will you need? To state your intentions clearly will require repeated application of the contents of Chapters 3 and 4 so that you can keep the message resonating with your e-customer. If you can ring his bell, then you have got it covered. The answer is to offer him something at two different levels – something to play with, say, although it doesn't have to be a game, while at the same time giving him something to tidy up his life, although it doesn't have to be a mop.

Not every customer will while away the hours being either organized or entertained. At some point, most of us are prompted to look up from the electronic world by a hunger for "fulfilment" (or stimulus). The ultimate form of this is associated with loving relationships. We want to know that what we are doing is worthwhile, we want someone to tell us so, and we want to be fulfilled. This explains the constant attraction of chat rooms and bulletin boards for those who start to feel fulfilment hunger. It also explains why online customers eventually, and on average, log off after only 30 minutes and go to do something more fulfilling in the real world. Answer? Link your experience to "meaningful" subjects, but make it clear how you don't really need to return to the real world to do anything about them. Find that ideal balance between entertainment and enlightenment.

Note well that there are only three main sources of fulfilment in electronic spaces:

- the ability to create – explaining the popularity of homepages on every subject, however bizarre, obscure, or dull;
- more profound, the interaction with other people;
- that which can be achieved when you link "experience" with – and actively, visibly support – causes that are fulfilling and worthwhile.

With the second source, it is not enough to provide the technology of chat or e-mail addresses or bulletin boards, your electronic experience must offer, organize, and provide interaction that has meaning to its participants. Even the most crowded chat providers on the planet may only have 20 or so in each room, which means that you will have to help the visiting e-customers stop and take part by letting them know continually that there are scheduled chats and special events. Invite visitors to register and send out e-mails to those on your mailing lists so that they can gather and be fulfilled. Include chat transcripts so that the browsing online customer can be attracted to a possible source of human stimulus and look forward to it.

The third will help the world and also help the customer to feel good about himself and the time he is spending within your experience. You could include such services as stoptorture.org, by means of which your customers can send e-mail and mobile phone text messages to put pressure on those governments involved in torture. How about a simple "click to donate" scheme, linking adverts or products or applications with donations to particular charitable causes? The latter is the equivalent of the charity collection box and accompanying thank you letter from the charity in question that are seen in many retail outlets in the real world. The former has not really got a real-world equivalent in commerce because of the delays involved, but, online, the impetus to act, send that e-mail, help defend the weak, leaves your customer in a fine mood with himself and your business.

The ego layer

In offering to feed his hunger, remember that the e-customer will be shifting ego states (or states of mind) from time to time in response to the interaction with the experience or external events. He will move from the rational adult to the learned behavior of the parent to the creative child.

Don't think that any of these states of mind that the e-customer may pass through is necessarily bad or good. Do think about how important it is for the creators of the experience to realize that they will have to deal with each in attracting, managing, and leading the e-customer toward profitable relationships. It is something that we all witness every day, but these states of immense practical value when trying to find the best ways to help the online customer find his way to the useful services and products that you have prepared for him.

Child

Sometimes your electronic offer – or, indeed, the whole electronic world – appeals to the child in every online customer, regardless of age. He responds to it as a fun-packed, wonderland of a toy, seeking novelty, new knowledge. It's a new, new, thing approach that characterizes many of the most innovative web designers.

So much of the advertising during the first dot com generation was designed by ad agencies spending much of their time in a child ego state. Not surprisingly, it also appeals to other adults who spend much of their own time in that creative, not altogether calm and rational, state. This was great as far as it went. The child-adults were happy to play, but were surprised to find relatively dull shopping and banking service experiences at the end of the dot com rainbow. Disappointed with the sign-posted destinations, they went off looking for fun at pleasure parks and side shows throughout the web. Result? The web booms and e-commerce pops.

Adult

When the e-customer comes on board as an adult, he will be coldly critical and rational in determining what benefits the electronic experience is providing. His rationality does not mean that he is right – he may lack the information to base correct choices on or the ability to make accurate decisions. This is not about being right, but it is about consideration and an attempt at open-minded, objective choice.

Parent

The impact of having a parental state of mind when inside your electronic experience will depend very much on the nature, behavior, and generation of the parents in question. It is a very efficient way of responding to situations because the online customer does not consider carefully new reactions, instead responding as he saw his parents behave or assumes his parents would behave.

The characteristics layer

Count them – more than six billion individuals on Earth and over 250 million of them with access to some kind of electronic channel. So, do you build a different electronic experience to appeal to each? Do you segment the offer to appeal to different groups within the population? Will you personalize the experience so that it adapts to an individual's behavior? Does it make sense to allow the e-customer to create his experience in his likeness? Should you instead get people on the team who share the characteristics of particular online customer groups and get them to adapt the offer to suit themselves and their natural constituencies?

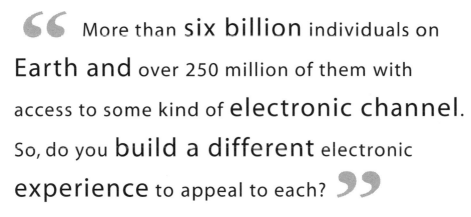

" More than **six billion** individuals on **Earth and** over 250 million of them with access to some kind of **electronic channel**. So, do you **build a different** electronic **experience** to appeal to each? "

No answers yet until we have carried out an examination of the ways in which experiences should be, could be, can, and are altered to meet the needs of a variety of different characteristics that, taken together, form the unique individual. These characteristics mingle and react with ego states and survival needs to produce the responses that our experience will receive. It is this combination that the experience should be designed to accommodate and satisfy profitably. There is a lot to cover here so let's jump in.

Age and generation

When we were born determines our star sign, but, more pertinently perhaps, defines the generation (20 years worth of births) that we will always be part of, regardless of age. There are many fragmented groups within each generation, a trend that continues at accelerated pace (or have we just got better at spotting them?), but what will always differentiate each generation is the level of gap between it and every other generation. It is both the characteristics of each generation and the extent of the generation gap that should be considered in delivering the online customer experience.

Age is a different matter. It starts off defining the generations, but, of course, is merely transitory. The generation about which The Who sang is no longer in its teen years and those who are temporarily teenagers today are served by the defiant, manufactured tones of bands of the likes of Limp Bizkit. Age is what affects your likely outlook, your probable experience, and the chances that you are bored, bald, or bitter about your bank account balance.

Both age and generation affect the way in which the experience should be designed and will be perceived. For instance, age will reduce naturally the typical physical capabilities of the individual, as his sense of smell, taste, hearing, touch, and vision will all be less keen than those of a child. During early childhood, an individual will have great sensory perception but not have added to this the experience to allow him to navigate complex electronic experiences or distinguish between smaller icons and text. You will remember that, as a child, you read large-print books with small vocabularies. After the e-customer reaches about 45, his physical capacities will start to reduce, even while his intellectual capacity continues to increase. This does not mean that he loses it all, but he will reduce in ability at varying speeds, which means that the experience must be capable of adjusting with him, unless it wishes to lose his business.

 ## Usability is not age neutral.

Your electronic experience at first hand must speak to the various needs, interests, and aspirations of the age and generation you are aiming to please. Usability is not age neutral. Take a look at a comic book – something like *Dragonball Z*, the independent fanzine for Pokémon fans. It breaks all the good taste and structure rules for legible magazines, with a lurid, chaotic, brain-jamming layout, but eight-year-olds love it. Don't let the age of your executives or programers determine the way that your experience communicates.

Governments and parents in many countries worry about the impact of advertising on children. In Sweden, TV advertising aimed at children under

12 has been illegal since 1991, and Greece is considering enlarging the current toy advert ban between 7 am and 10 pm to all products aimed at children.[14] How have manufacturers responded? By limiting the selection of new toys sold in Greece, which reduces sales, and avoiding the advertising ban in Sweden by beaming in Swedish-language adverts with offshore broadcasters, which can alienate the parents who are expected to pay.

In such an anti-advertising atmosphere, a less blatant selling message is more likely to reap rewards. Try offering parents what they want for their children via an electronic experience that delivers the messages that you want for their children. Try free computers for schools, like Tesco in the UK, or free TVs to schools, like Channel One in the US.

The reputation of your experience is part of the experience itself. It is the anticipatory layer that speaks to that sense of cool, that sense of wow. Deciding who and what to associate your experience with can be crucial. Take an example from the real world. Rose Marie Bravo is confident that, *"Getting our bikini on Kate Moss cut the average age of our customers by 30 years in one fell swoop,"* and in so doing helped to turn Burberry into a coveted luxury brand. Why mention it here? Because the virtual world needs to learn, learn, and learn from marketing successes elsewhere as the newness of the technology is simply not enough to make business viable.

Interests and hobbies

Without trying to be condescending, there is an obvious benefit in designing an experience for an online customer that has a link with his existing interests and hobbies. This does not explain why so few corporate sites find out what those interests are or build in content that would appeal to what their e-customers are already interested in. It does provide a ready source of inspiration for those will half-open minds, so you will no doubt benefit from the insight the following example brings.

❝ There is an obvious benefit in designing an **experience for** an online **customer that** has a link with his existing interests and **hobbies.** So few corporate sites find out what those **interests** are. ❞

It does explain why the very astute Jaguar car company decided that it could associate itself with the glamour of motor racing not only by sponsoring a team but by creating a hobby-based F1 experience that would pull the customer closer and closer to the racing team and, therefore, to its products. Has it worked? The company has 75,000 signed-up members who have been willing to share registration details and agree to receive marketing material. Customers who would never have considered buying a Jaguar are now so comfortable with its brand that it is an automatic choice. The site has been created to track the movements and interests of every customer so that the content and format of the experience can change to adapt to needs, preferences, and circumstances. If the *experience* fits that well, why not try the *car*?

The world's most successful sports clubs deliver experiences, not simple competitive events. Customers all over the world buy into the Chicago Bulls experience or Manchester United experience although they may never watch the team play in person. They listen to and watch the games on the television, radio, and internet. They buy the merchandise and revel in the history and traditions. Vodafone, the world's largest mobile communications business, has bought some of the attraction of the Manchester United "experience" for more than $40 million over four years.[15] Nike is willing to sell that "experience" branded item at a time to suit customers worldwide. These sporting teams are a great illustration of what experience means. Some of them are managing to translate that into the electronic world, while others know it is important,[16] but struggle to deliver any of that thrill of the goal, of the basket, of the home run.

Gender and sex

It's a chromosome and cultivation (nature and nurture) difference that can be designed into the experience and many different levels. The most basic is to decide whether the electronic experience you are creating is aimed primarily at males, females, or both of them.

Don't assume that your male-dominated, technically obsessed team (or are you the exception?!) is capable of designing naturally for women. Don't assume that they have the least understanding of the differences required for either sex! This is explained in more detail in one of my other books, *E-customer*, but here are some extracts.

> Female customers will favor many color-coded options in one place so that she can find what she is looking for rapidly. The male e-customer may prefer to be led from one task to the next in a very compartmentalized way.
> Men view asking for help as a sign of failure (it's why men insist that they know where they are going and don't ask for directions when they are lost). He wants self-help and for help to be made available in a positive way so he does not have to admit his need.
> The female e-customer wants to talk things through as part of a desirable and necessary part of the shopping (or any other) experience.[17]

How will you reflect these different preferences in the way that the experience is layered and structured? How can you make it appeal to, and feel comfortable for, both or either? Look at magazine content sites directed to either sex and consider how you can create individual tones to attract them.

Consider the efforts of electronic experiences of the likes of carsdirect.com that has created a guide for female customers looking for a car. It is written by female journalists to explore all facets of car buying and ownership. It risks being criticized as condescending, even though it is in pursuit of an experience that more closely adapts itself to the key gender differences between customers.

Role and profession

What we do is what we are. Your experience should be designed to match the particular hat that the online customer is wearing when he walks through those digital doors. Is your experience designed to identify and accommodate an e-customer who could be a bank manager, father, son, husband, and sports captain all in the one day? Have you created tone, content, and services that speak directly to the role that your offer and advertising has spoken to?

> " Is your **experience designed** to **identify and accommodate** an e-customer who **could be a bank** manager, father, son, **husband, and sports** captain all in the **one day**? "

Race, language and heritage

How much do you understand anyone outside of your own race, language, and heritage? Think through how many people you really know with whom you do not share those characteristics. Make a quick estimation of the cultural diversity of your team and compare that with your e-customers' and the world itself. It is surprising to learn how monoculture many organizations have become.

Can you respond in a foreign language to customers who do not share your native tongue? In a survey of 200 international firms, it was found that only 9 percent of e-mails in a foreign language are replied to by top businesses.[18] This may be acceptable, at a push, if we are dealing with unaided customer services people in the flesh, but it is ludicrously bad the technology exists to easily translate between all the main languages in a couple of seconds. The only excuse is incompetence, caused by lack of interest in customers.

Content is still dominated by the English language,[19] but if you plan on being a global service (and what is the point of distance being dead if you don't?) you should take the rest of the world seriously. There is no natural reason for other languages not to catch up – the telephone is popular the world over, so is eating, sleeping, and shopping – why not work on the 80 percent who could use the internet in other languages but are not currently attracted to it. What if Chinese really does become the number 1 language on the web by 2007?[20]

Country of origin and residence

This is a matter, mainly, of geography and the implications for your experience design of the country of residence of the online customer and the likely country of residence of his friends and family. This should have a particularly significant impact if your experience has any connection at all with the real world and, as that includes most of electronic commerce, it is very worthwhile building in such a dimension to your experience design.

It's possible to think, sitting in your offices wherever you are in the world, that everywhere else acts, thinks, talks, and buys in just the same way as your home market. That all you have to do is open up an operation in a new country and success will be automatic. Be careful – cultures enjoy being different, just as they enjoy being the same. This can tend to move in cycles and the one that we are in currently does not bode well for brands that smack of imperialism or attempt to import with no modification. Think of Coca-Cola's experience of crisis in Europe where there is growing disillusion with symbols of globalization in Europe.[21] Think of eBay changing its auction policies to exclude Nazi Ku Klux Klan and other controversial groups because of potential conflict with international laws and standards as it expands outside the US.[22]

Global is possible, but not if "global" just means having values from another culture shoved down customers' throats.

Politics and philosophy

The way your e-customer views life and society will naturally affect the kind of experience that he wants to have and the way he interprets what you have created for him. This much you will probably agree with, but what difference does it make to electronic experience design? Can you tell what approach to life a few popular websites and enhanced TV programs have? Is there any difference between them? How do politics and philosophy alter the priorities of a website?

Have a browse at urban75.com: Its philosophy is distinctly club and direct action with content including, "rave, drug info, stories, photos, and rants," including the enjoyable, if obvious, "slap Eminem" feature. They are also avowedly "no-profit," boasting of the absence of banner adverts and tie-ins. Compare forbes.com, with its emphasis on the most expensive beach homes in the world, great luxury cars, the future of investments, and tie-ins and banner adverts galore. Which group do you want to attract? Do you speak to either?

In 1887, John S. Pemberton, the druggist and inventor of Coca-Cola, said, "If I could get $25,000 I would spend $24,000 on advertising and the remainder making Coca-Cola. Then we'd all be rich." In 2000, Naomi Klein's book *No Logo* (Flamingo, 1999) hit the bestseller lists, and created an anti-brand that has been copied and printed on t-shirts in mock homage of the brand ideal. Which set of beliefs does your experience espouse?

Technical aptitude and attitude

Not everyone feels exactly the same about machines in general and C-O-M-P-U-T-E-R-S in particular, and there is no reason for them to. Early in this chapter, different ways in which the electronic interface or membrane can be viewed by individual e-customers were discussed and explored. A range of these interpretations or reaction types will usually be present in your online customer group. The extent of the range depends on the service that you are offering, so, for example, a website dedicated to Linux junkies will have a narrower range of technical aptitude than an enhanced TV channel offering interactive World Wrestling Federation coverage. Even within a narrow range, there will be differences and these should be considered carefully in the design of the experience.

> ❝ Only a **very** small minority understands (or even wants to **understand**) how the **technology** itself works. ❞

Only a very small minority understands (or even wants to understand) how the technology itself works. The readers of byte.com and register.com may love wiring everything up to everything else. They understand protocols, networking, and know that every operating system has a kernel, but they are not the majority. We all find ourselves somewhere on a continuum between those who love nothing more than designing molecular structures for a new computing material, to those who love to install their own additional hard disks, to those who want the computer to be as easy to use as a television set. In the words of one technology veteran, Ernest Lilley:

> Everything we've been doing with computers is brought to the consumer market without them ever seeing the computer. What struck me most is that while computers were everywhere, they were largely invisible, hidden inside car stereos or on the front of a refrigerator. And everything I saw at CES tells me that marketers have figured that out.
>
> ERNEST LILLEY, "COMPUTATION, CONNECTIVITY, AND CONSUMERS," BYTE.COM, JANUARY 15, 2001

Most customers want to be able to enhance their lives, connect to each other, and communicate with other people, but they do not all want to see the technology itself and, in fact, the majority want the technology to be hidden. They do not talk about the latest gadgets with their friends socially unless it is obvious the gadget has become a fashion item, like the mobile phone. Delivering the experience for the majority will require the best efforts and insights of the marketing people that many technologists love to look down on.

What is good and bad will all depend on your audience: the audience should define the design rules. On one occasion ICQ, instant messaging pioneers, received the "Mud Brick Awards" for being the most ugly site on the web because it had tiny content and lots of it. Did that bother ICQ? Nope, because in the words of its spokesperson:

> We all consider it a badge of honor to get this because the site is a site that only a webhead could love. It's just overwhelming the amount of stuff that's there. But ICQ continues to grow in leaps and bounds. It doesn't stop people from going there every day.

Of course, the range of technical ability may change over time so that the ICQ approach of focusing on "webheads" is no longer sensible given the much wider audience for instant messaging and the fierce competition from less technically exclusive experience providers such as MSN, AOL, and Yahoo!.

Physical capability and health

Are you reading this with your eyes, unaided by glasses? Are you wearing contact lenses or spectacles? Perhaps you are using a brail edition? Clearly, your experience will be different depending on how good your eyesight is. The same is true of hearing, taste, touch, coordination, level of movement, mobility, and pain levels. The experience can be aimed at people of different physical capabilities, either indirectly, by ensuring that the experience accommodates them all, or directly, by using the experience to help solve particular problems that some of them may have. Either way, it's an e-customer win, which means you win, too.

The senses and sensibilities layer

The first five traditional senses are the routes into the online customer's brain and the ways your experience, regardless of channel, will have to travel. The additional two are representatives of the immediate sensibilities that are applied to the signals once they are decoded, but perhaps before they have been considered in detail. Nevertheless, the brain will utilize these senses together to decide what to do next or if it likes what it is being fed within seconds.

Sight

Vision was originally what internet output was designed to accommodate, and it continues to be the starting point for the design of the majority of electronic experiences. Many websites offer no stimulus to the other senses and very little to the default target of the customer's eyes. Enhanced television appeals to more than just sight and it stimulates vision with a slickness that can only be matched by the broadest of broadband.

There is a certain similarity between many corporate experiences that should concern you greatly. If you just buy an off-the-shelf product and deliver an off-the-shelf experience, then you offer no visual choice to the customer. If they all look, feel, and act the same, then the customer will not remember your experience ahead of any other from your competition. Do not listen to the views of anyone who tells you that visuals don't matter because they are clearly out of touch or out of their minds, as with Al Ries in his book with Laura Ries on *The 11 Immutable Laws of Internet Branding* (HarperCollinsBusiness, 2000):

> There are no visual attributes of an internet brand. No yellow flesh that helps identify Perdue chicken. No radiator grills that do the same for Mercedes-Benz automobiles. The only thing your mind needs to remember to log on to a site is the name.

If you follow this logic, then the only thing that your mind needs to remember to buy a Mercedes is the address of the Mercedes dealer, and the only thing your mind needs to remember to buy Perdue chicken is the name so that you can ask for it at the store. If you follow that logic then advertisements for all products should just involve repeating the name of the product and the address of the nearest outlet. Of course, we know that creating a brand involves delivering a set of emotional, rational, and sensual attributes of a product that make sure that its benefits, real and imagined, are at the front and back of each potential customer's mind.

> ❝ **Creating** a brand involves delivering a set of emotional, **rational**, and sensual **attributes** of a product that make sure that its benefits, real and **imagined**, are at the **front and** back of each potential customer's **mind.** ❞

There are, there can be, and there must be visual attributes for the electronic experience. If not, they will simply become bland, faceless terminals that attempt to force customers to become bland, faceless data entry clerks by weight of advertising. This is not the future that we need if the internet is to reach its commercial potential – and it has, thankfully, already passed that particularly dismal scenario by.

Hearing

The growing popularity of digital music has introduced sound to the electronic experience stage direct from the internet. Previously it was either provided in simple sound effects, crackly voice chat, or constantly for some online customers via the real-world radio or sound system. The challenge is that sound, more than sight, is both very personal and very private. Supermarket or elevator muzak in the real world has been proven effective in studies but also inspires fierce reactions among some lovers of music and devotees of the beauty of silence.

Example

Take a look at the very funky (for financial services) bankdirect.co.nz website for an example of adding in sound to the experience mix. The moodscape feature invites the customer to browse while listening to music and news for a "more atmospheric" experience, even if he or she decides to move to other sites. The bonus service uses the latest streaming audio technology to provide music and live radio broadcasts (95Bfm live, Kog, mp3.net.nz, and Flying Nun), while its customers and potential customers are connected to the internet. It's a stylish addition. In the words of one customer, "imagine selecting your groove while sorting your investments and cash."

Listening to the radio while online is a popular pastime for many customers and so online radio has become a natural combination for some. Music can save the day, chase the clouds away, so an old song goes. You should remember that music captures moods as well as anything can and if you can match sounds to the experience that you want to share with the customer, then you will talk straight to his heart. Several studies have shown that Mozart makes children smarter and all the evidence makes it clear that sound goes directly to our brain waves. Make sure, though, that you include a button to turn the sound off for those whose emotional reaction is violent antipathy!

Touch

Generally, the e-customer's hands are on the keyboard, mouse or even the screen. The manufacturers of all these input devices have continued to try and offer better keyboard action, mouse control, and thinner, less fuzzy touch screens. Designers of joysticks and joypads and other gaming peripherals have gone further in exploring the desire of e-customers for sensual input by adding feedback via the devices. Some of them shudder when there is an explosion on screen; others simulate gravity, weight, and earthquakes. What are you expected to build into your experience when you do not have any control over the input devices themselves? Should you get into the input device manufacturers' sector and provide non-gaming equipment that adds touch sensation to the non-gaming electronic experience?

> ** Music captures** moods as well as anything can and if you can **match sounds** to the **experience that** you want to share with the customer, **then you will talk straight to** his heart. **

Consider, Orbit Industries, which has developed a stylus for hand-held computers that slips on to the e-customer's finger to increase accuracy *and* instinctive use of the touch screen. It has been designed carefully with the online customer in mind, to be fully adjustable so it can fit any finger and fit into any pocket.

Think about, the fast-moving developments in electronic cloth that allow keyboards, buttons, and even screen displays to be woven into and formed from the material of our clothing. The e-customer literally wears the experience. The experience can be tailored to fit. No longer merely a concept, like those at Lunar Design,[23] the technology has already turned up in products including the cloth keyboard for the Palm Pilot *and* the five-color displays woven into sweatshirts.

The real world offers touch sensation as part of the package. It is one of the first tests that we apply to products in the real world, as we imagine owning and using them. The electronic experience can use touch to create more accurate, more instinctive, and, above all, more compelling experiences by offering touch sensation beyond the usual real-world experience. So, find as many ways out into the real world as you can, where the customer can feel the texture of the electronic experience. You need to come out into the open.

Consider any person who meets the customer in the flesh as a key representative in the real world. This might be the guy (or gal) that delivers the package. It might be the person who fixes the appliance or the one who meets them to sign the contract. No matter who it is and no matter whether they work for you directly or not, you need to figure out how to make sure that the way they interact in the real world enhances the electronic experience you are offering. Don't just view all delivery partners as equal – some can use technology[24] to fit neatly into your overall experience, enhancing it by letting the customer know what is happening with his package, ensuring that the customer receives what he ordered, when he ordered it for, with politeness, and human warmth – but not all of them can.

Does the packaging matter? Of course, the packaging matters! It's the physical manifestation of all that you mean and offer to the customer. Cool or quaint. Chic or brutal. Never neutral. Why would you want to miss this opportunity?

When the fourth book in the best-selling series about Harry Potter was available on pre-order, the books arrived from Amazon together with a delicious gold envelope that added to the experience, even if the customer did not win the, "fabulous magical trip to Los Angeles" or the ten gift certificates.

FIGURE 5.5

Gold letter from Amazon to announce the new Harry Potter book.

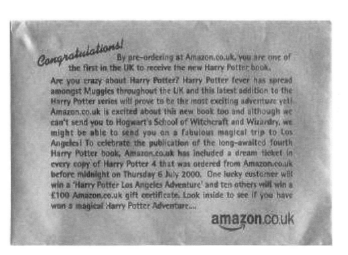

Make sure that the customer thinks about the delivery and the packaging, that it gives him pleasure, that he boasts about it (in passing) to his friends, enemies, and family. Put together a propaganda kit that the customer can touch and play with. Create a collection of stuff and style that reaches into his life and drags him, willingly, into your world, your tent, and your experience. That's the way it needs to work!

> ❝ Create a collection of stuff and style that reaches into his life and drags him, willingly, into your world, your tent, and your experience. ❞

Smell

Our sense of smell may not be as effective as that of some animals – a bloodhound can smell at least a thousand times better than we can – but we can still typically distinguish up to 10,000 different odors. Airborne chemicals float through the air from other substances into our hair-covered nostrils, up to a ceiling area called the nasal cavity, which is about the size of a thumbnail, sink through a yellow mucus until they are trapped in the sensitive hair-like tops of the nerve cells that can recognize each smell. Once recognized, the identity of each smell is sent via the olfactory nerve to the smell center in the brain.

Your online customers have noses, complete with a sense of smell, just like the rest of the population, and it is a fact that this sense has received only limited research and novelty attention. Foremost among those working on how to incorporate smell into the electronic experience has been DigiScents. The company was founded by two successful biotech entrepreneurs and plans on sending customers a dispenser (dubbed ismell), about the size of a computer speaker, full of chemicals that, when mixed, could recreate almost any smell, based on data that would be transmitted over the internet. Not everyone is convinced. Take, for example, the columnist who gently mocks the portal for smells, calling it a "snortal."[25]

In the future, researchers such as neurologist and psychiatrist Alan Hirsch – MD Hirsch at his Smell and Taste Treatment and Research Foundation in Chicago – considers that the use of smells could enrich the electronic experience: "Maybe ten minutes before you wake up in the morning, the alarm clock will spray a scent to make you more alert. You'll go to the kitchen, where an odor will be released to increase or suppress your appetite. Your office may be scented to make you more productive." And at bedtime? "An aroma," he replies, "to make you sleepy – or more amorous."[26]

Taste

What part does the e-customer's tongue play in the electronic experience? How can you employ all those sophisticated taste cells and receptor buds in the great cause of more immersive experiences? The only answer – if we ignore for the short term any developments in taste transmission – is to send something physically that he can taste! There is every reason to send sample food as a way of letting the online customer know the kind of taste sensation that he can expect from the product if he buys it or else simply to invite him to eat the product while using your experience so it is improved for him.

Cool

> We real cool. We
> Left school. We
> Lurk late. We
> Strike straight. We
>
> Sing sin. We
> Thin gin. We
>
> Jazz June. We
> Die soon.
>
> GWENDOLYN BROOKS, "WE REAL COOL," *THE BEAN EATERS* (HARPERS, 1960)

Appealing to your e-customer's sense of what is fashionable, interesting, or stylish is clearly necessary, and this can be done via any of the five physical senses. The question of "cool" starts when the various nerve cells pass signals that reach the cerebral cortex, the outside of the brain, and start moving between its four major divisions. The medial temporal lobe is the bit closest to the center of the brain that contains the amygdala (pronounced a-migdala) that is thought to be important in emotional processing.

Do you really want the online customer experience to be cool? Why? How can it be? What kind of "cool" should you try to be? Allan Liu is one of those fascinated by the obsessive drive toward what he calls, "one of the most single-minded and totalitarian aesthetics ever created" and he has offered categorizations of sites defined as cool by others, including improvized categorizations such as techno-cool, anti-verbal cool, and ordinary cool.

Is the immense interest in personal robots a result of how "cool" they are because they are the "hallmark of the future"?[27] Do customers who are willing to spend around $700 for devices like the Friendly Robotics robot lawn mower buy it instead because it saves time and is many times less likely to chop off careless fingers and toes?

Fair play

To feel comfortable, e-customers judge whether or not the experience they are dealing with is behaving in a way that is "fair" or "right." This is judged by the way they are treated personally, the ways they suspect that they may be treated, and on how they feel that the business treats other people. There are good survival reasons for e-customers being unhappy and unwilling to do business with you if your experience tells them that you are untrustworthy.

 ## Don't lie to your customers.

Don't lie to your customers. Sounds obvious? Consider how all the airlines in one American airport schedule[28] their flights for 8am (the most required morning departure time), knowing that only about 8 of the 40 flights aiming for the slot will take off within 40 minutes of that time. They have invented a term for that, "push-back time," to allow them an excuse. They tell passengers that the plane pushed back from the gate on time and that the delay is due to air traffic control. If a flight leaves the gate within 15 minutes of its scheduled departure time, the department of transportation considers that it has left on time, independently of the time it waits on the tarmac before taking off. They lie to their customers and still expect their customers to trust them. Does that make sense?

Businesses lie about delivery times, they lie about reasons for delay, they lie about warrantee terms, and they lie about the relative performance of their offer. Didn't they learn anything from George Washington and cherry-tree-gate?

Even the slightest hint of a lie matters in the electronic experience because the customer has nothing to hold on to, the sense of substance has nothing physical to back it up and so, even more than in the real world, must depend on trust, fair play, honesty, and openness. Use your honesty to distinguish you from competitors and charlatans that are also sending out e-mail marketing messages that are less than honest or perhaps completely dishonest, like the following electronic con scheme that is regularly distributed as e-mail (spelling mistakes are left intact):

My name is Komani Edula, I was a personal assistance to late Congo president, late Lurent Kabila, who was assassinated early this year. Because of his assassination, I flew to Nigerian for asylum leaving my traveling documents.

However before his death we have secured the sum of US$45,000.00 (Fourty five Millions Dollars) in a security company in Europe, this money is kept in the security company with all the little documents in my name, my reason for writing to you in for your assistance in keeping this money in your personal or company account pending when I am able to get my travelling documents out of Congo so that I can come to your country to invest the money. Please call me on my telephones No:-234-1-7749432 or send me a Fax on my Fax No:-234-1-7593289. But I will prefer you call me so that we discuss what your share will be for your assistance and how I will give you the tittle documents to have the money freely. Send me a urgent email indicating your address, telephone and fax numbers, and the time you will call me.

No wonder customers are made nervous by the legal phrasing in terms and conditions that avoid responsibility for areas that they feel are rightfully those of the business. This is particularly the case with security. Consider, the terms used by Smile, the UK online banking service. It says that it will not be held responsible for money taken in cases where the customer "fails to let us know about any potential breach of security or problem." How much more vague could that be? It sounds like an attempt to try and blame the customer, doesn't it? It certainly fails the test of "fair play" and makes the customer wary.

If you are honest and willing to deal fairly, then it makes sense to say so, clearly. If you do not make your terms and conditions easily available and easy to understand, the customer will sense that you are hiding something. Do anything you can to show the customer that you are playing fair. Join external trusted schemes[29] to show that you are willing to abide by their rules and live with their scrutiny. Let the customer know that all his personal details are well protected by explaining in simple terms the efforts that you have put in place. Get someone to check over the language that you use to ensure that it is as easy to understand as possible.

How "real" can virtual become (and does it improve shopping)?

Since electronic shopping, sales, and service began, there have been attempts to create virtual shopping malls that resemble the real thing. These have generally been failures. They have been too slow, too cumbersome, not easy to use, and found to be a gimmick by customers. Creating the actions and features of the real world is popular but not, so far, the visual appearance. As bandwidth increases, and programing becomes more sophisticated, it is worth a little look at the current exponents of shopping and commerce in virtual worlds.

There is increased competition in this area. Consider 3-D Worlds.com with its focus on celebrity worlds built to showcase the art, images, music, and products of musicians, and promotional worlds created to advertise new brands. We have 3-D Activeworlds.com, offering the ability for customers to create their own objects, homes, and their own digital offspring. There is 3-D Moove.com with actors and scouts to help the customer out. There is also a range of cartoon-like virtual environments that attempt to include shopping, including dobedo.com, hoobahotel.com, and dubit.co.uk, not forgetting the use of 3-D and virtual characters within such well-known examples as the original boo.com.

FIGURE 5.6 Miss Boo returns to London.

Boo.com is back, "simpler and easier" than when it died the first time around. This means a return to some of the animated personality, interaction, community, and 3-D products, and a valuable opportunity to see how the simplified version delivers the customer experience. The new owners are confident enough to gently mock the past excesses via the diary of Miss Boo as in the following excerpt:

> **November 2000** Back in London at last! And thankfully without Troy. After he crashed the rental car en route from Sweden to Copenhagen (via the Oresund fixed link), he inexplicably vanished before the police arrived!
> Luckily, there was no carnage, but I had no qualms about jumping on a plane home sans assistant. (Let's face it: he was only interested in assisting me in the consumption of vast quantities of alcohol, not to mention boo.com's "research" budget.)

Unfortunately, boo.com has been forced to ditch the use of 3-D product images because it no longer stocks its own products. Despite a lot of initial interest, many other websites have also abandoned 3-D for now because of accessibility problems and the cost of production. Some services, such as autobytel.com, used to feature 3-D that could only be seen with special plug-in software that had to be downloaded on to the local PC. This requirement was obstructive for the customers, who had often already seen the car in a showroom anyway or would insist on so doing before a sale as even the 3-D image was insufficient to erase the need to touch before buying.

By contrast with some of the reduction in use of 3-D images of products for retail sites, there has been an increase in the number and complexity of 3-D worlds into which the customer enters to find everything represented in virtual three dimensions.

You could jump into Activeworlds.com and experience a series of 750 virtual worlds larger than California. It's a complex world that allows you to own possessions and build worlds and objects. In one world alone, there are over 82 million objects created for and by customers. There are also automated people, or bots, that walk around and interact with varying levels of sophistication. The words that are spoken float around the tops of the avatars heads like comic book speech bubbles. I enjoyed a great game of chess with a professor from Japan while watching a guy performing back flips across the fields.

Activeworlds.com tries hard to avoid losing the user with its browser-based environment. Help files and other links appear in the right-hand panel, while worlds are listed to the left, and conversations appear below the main resizable 3-D area. There are sometimes as many as 1000 people online, but they are not typically busy shopping in the 3-D shopping mall, despite the following words of welcome:

Welcome to @mart – Where Activeworlds loves to shop!
@mart, designed to resemble a modern shopping mall, is home to a variety of vendors of both traditional and virtual products and services. Taking advantage of the features of the groundbreaking Activeworlds technology, vendors and consumers both have the opportunity to window shop and purchase products online, while chatting, personally, with the shopkeepers.

Why? Probably because 3-D is still in the hand of the techies, the world is too big, and sprawling, and because the fun stuff is not built around the shopping experience. Shopping is built as an afterthought, an aside to the main activities.

There are individual shops such as jcrew.com that sells CDs by being an affiliate of Amazon. This works by displaying pictures of CDs and providing hyperlinks between the 3-D world and the right-hand panel. Clicking on advertising hoardings also presents shopping trolleys and information so that the purchase can be researched or made while continuing the 3-D experience. The shopping works but only really by joining the 3-D world via links to the normal shopping trolley.

FIGURE 5.7

Buying in 3-D at jcrew.com.

In the future, this must change. Already, the bots and avatars are becoming more advanced for the use of businesses. They can send URLs to the web browsers of individual customers to allow them to answer questions by showing the customer an electronic brochure or asking him to fill out an electronic form.

An alternative is the virtual world of Moove.com, which uses a customer browser to give the customer a free virtual home on the internet, complete with walls, doors, and windows, that you can decorate using furniture and pictures. You can entertain from your own house (listen to music, share files, chat) or go visit a friend. It's a combination that is recommended by 96 percent of all those who downloaded it.[30]

Once again, it is surprising how amateur the sales element of these worlds is compared to the sophistication of the environment that is on offer. Trying to buy anything is a challenge apart from the standard upgrade CD-ROM. Why couldn't the attractive 3-D "scouts" who hang around to help lost customers also be employed in virtual stores to provide sales and service?

Why? If you are going to sell something, then make it possible for the customer to buy! Make it as easy as possible to buy or, guess what? They won't buy. They buy for fun and if your experience gives fun without buying, as these sites do, then they will use it without buying. Hopefully your business can still survive on the advertising revenues, and subscription fees,[31] but it makes more sense to bet the future on a variety of income sources.

There are businesses making some use of the ability to create office and store space without leases. Examples, include Atragon, a business finance room, CHATazine the online magazine for chat, Chilli Jam Records, a virtual record label operating from mp3.com and now from Moove.com, Flowing River, a tarot reading room, House of Gifts, with something for every occasion, and Staying Beautiful, with Mary Kay skincare and cosmetic products. They just don't do it very well.

The immense size and number of configuration options of some of these worlds is, to some extent, a problem for those trying to focus them in on sales. Habbohotel.com has overcome this by simply reducing the size of the world to something more manageable. It is Flash "almost" 3-D, rendered in typical cartoon style to create a teen-focused world that takes place in a five-star hotel. This device makes service and sales more natural because of the added structure, with the result that all is clear and all is focused on the payoff for the customer *and* the business.

FIGURE 5.8

Slinky bar at Habbo Hotel.

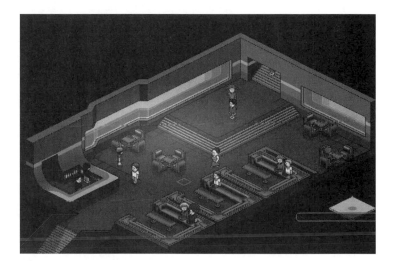

Integral to the design is a wallet system that allows the customer to purchase credits for a nominal amount. Each time I change rooms, an advertisement is flashed past my eyes. In some of the rooms there are information kiosks that further promote products. There is even a tie-in with Splash Plastic, a pay as you go, internet payment-friendly credit card aimed at teens.

Sometimes when businesspeople look at these kinds of creative, fun experiences, they have difficulty seeing how they could ever be applied to dull old commerce. Then, of course, they run off and spend money on building up their brand via "fun" advertising or "creative" gizmos. Is it so hard to imagine customers being happy to use a cartoon environment to buy when one considers the global interest in Disney?

66 **Is it so hard** to imagine customers being happy to **use a cartoon** environment to buy when one **considers the** global interest in **Disney?** 99

Customers bond with three dimensions and become enthusiasts, eager for such features and environments. Talk to any of these customers around the world and you discover that they are hyperusers who spend up to several hours online each day. They are financially well off enough to own their own computers and smart enough to navigate sometimes unclear concepts. They defend the strengths of their 3-D world of choice with vigor, as the following excerpt illustrates:

> Serendipitous: Nope … I don't use other 3-D chats … they don't seem *real*
> <smile>
> Greg G: This is the *only* 3-D chat :)
> Greg G: The others all suck.
> "JA":   Oh this one is VERY real :)

Couldn't your business use such commitment and brand loyalty? The emotional bonds of customers to their experiences suggests strongly that the experience provides a valuable opportunity to differentiate. Use of such worlds by your business could allow your experience to appeal directly to the needs and senses of particular groups so well that they simply would not want an experience of any other kind.

Why not 3-D bank branches to answer financial services questions, record shops where customers could really buy and chat about music? Don't ignore the power of adding that extra dimension just because some early pioneers failed the first time around. The cost is not prohibitive for the large business. Only a lack of imagination and applied customer focus could stop them from exploiting the opportunity to enrich the experience that this provides.

Where do you go from here?

You know it's true, so the only thing left to do is get on and assess your existing e-customer experience (or your plans for one), perform the online customer experience gap analysis and start making some focused improvements. The approach set out in this book has been constructed with great care and thought to ensure that it can be applied at any time in the history of a business and now is a very good time to start. It's too late for yesterday and you will gain no benefits by waiting for tomorrow.

> **❝ Now is a** very good time to start. It's too late for yesterday **and you will** gain no benefits **by waiting** for tomorrow. ❞

Experience study

Worlds.com

So just how immersed can you become in an electronic experience? Can an experience that brings the customer into the internet be more effective at making money than those that let him merely surf on it?

A study of worlds.com will reveal some insights into the sales and service possibilities of 3-D content and technology on the internet. By creating 3-D internet environments, as distinct from websites, Worlds' primary objective is to create an online community of customers to take part in multiuser chat, e-commerce, and advertising forums. In worlds.com's own words:

> Choose your planet, choose your face, unfasten your seatbelt …
> Choose from over 100 different humans, animals, characters and strange
> creatures! You can then walk around the worlds, explore the different
> worlds, see, chat, and interact with people, send e-mail, animate yourself, and
> shop the store – all in 3-D!"

This is an attractive offer to those who like to play, although not to those who are not yet comfortable enough to be adventurous with the internet. The website that accompanies it is not meant to be the main focus for the customer. It is merely meant to provide access to the worlds.com software. Still, it is disappointingly poor at capturing or selling the energy, benefits, and creativity of its offer.

A simple download of the worlds.com software (which, sadly, is more technical than it should be and poorly set out) allows the customer to join for free with a basic level of membership and, a few seconds, later is logged onto the welcome planet. The first task is to choose an animated 3-D character (avatar) from a selection of hundreds. Each avatar can be customized and then used to move about diverse 3-D internet communities.

FIGURE 5.9

Aerosmith at worlds.com

The environments on offer include worlds that are customized for particular music groups, celebrities, sporting events, and brands. These include Aerosmith, Hanson, the World Wrestling Federation, British Telecom, and Road Runner. The customer can use his avatar to travel in and out of these environments and get involved with interactive activities, including entertainment, promotions, and shopping. He can chat to other customers, dance in a nightclub, watch videos, and play games.

In the Aerosmith world, avatars can chat and hang out with fantastical versions of the rockers. The cyberrock venue was launched to coincide with the release of their album *Just Push Play* and is remarkably involving. Despite not featuring truly photo-quality avatars or environments, it is strangely and effectively believable. When you look up at the stars or discover a secret garden complete with exotic goldfish, it can be breathtaking. When you take on wings and start to fly around among the clouds, the impact is immense, even though you know that it is just technology.

The customer can change the viewpoint of the character to the first or third person and look up, down, and side-to-side. He can also chat with other customers publicly or one to one in a private whisper and choose whom to talk with by viewing the personal profiles that others have chosen to share. When he finds a friend, the customer can add that person to a friends list so that he knows in future whether or not they are online. He can join discussion groups to talk about particular subjects or sign up for free anonymous e-mail. It is possible for customers to teleport instantly to new locations via the map or allow a friend to find him instantly.

There is quite a thrill involved in teleporting, moving around the environment instantaneously. What, though, is the shopping like? It has to be understood that this is not your normal, clone-like shopping location. Take the following description as an example.

I chatted to a flying horse as I watched the advertising floating over the hills, towed on the back of a small aircraft. This is hyperlife. As I look around, there are advertising hoardings and posters prominently displayed as part of the space. There is little reason to suppose that this is less effective than those displayed in the real world, with the added bonus that, as a customer, I could simply click on the ad to find out more or buy.

Worlds.com provides official "hosts" to answer questions, keep the conversation going, and make sure that nothing is going horribly wrong. In a shopping scenario, it would not be hard to see the advantages that such a virtual representative would provide. As the customer browses, he can seek help or demonstrations from someone who is recognizably human.

Shopping at Worldsstore.com

The shopping takes place at a separate part of the 3-D world – Worldsstore.com. This allows customers to walk through the "superstar mall" and look at the stores for different artists. The customer can view products in 3-D as they rotate in virtual display cases. To buy, the customer must click for more details and then use the ordering pages on the secure Worldsstore.com site via a new HTML page, where the steps you need to take are set out for you.

1 Walk around the Worlds Store (you can teleport to it via the map or the teleport menu).
2 When you see an item you like, click on it to display its 3-D image.
3 If you want to see more details and/or order info, click OK on the browse, dialog, or cancel to keep looking.
4 If you clicked OK, an HTML page will display at our secured (SSL) store server.
5 If you want to purchase the item, click "Add to shopping basket." You can continue to browse in either 3-D or the web pages, and add or remove items from your basket.
6 When you're done, register your user name, mailing, and credit card information. You can also pay by check or fax.
7 That's that! Most orders will be shipped out within 48 hours. Enjoy!

It's a seven-step process that is overlong and not immediate enough. Once registered, why should the process take so long? The shopping experience cries out to be integrated as part of the 3-D environment, with no pauses or breaks. It is almost the opposite of JCPenney.com, which is presented in the next experience study. It has community gatherings for poetry, birthday rooms, Easter bunny celebrations, comedy, trivia contests, and even organized tours, but it is a challenge to actually buy.

British Telecom (BT) has sponsored a zone to promote its broadband services. It features huge billboards with instructions on how to use the service, reviews from consumer magazines, and the adverts. There is a cyber-parliament, a garden of tranquility, and something called big time.

Let's focus on the potential power of such an environment, but also on its practicalities. Speed? At the moment everything has the tendency to slow down when the rooms are full, but this will get better. Usability? For those who play games, this is natural and enjoyable. The addition of a joystick to full grocery shopping might lead game-playing teens to actually volunteer to do the shopping!

The next stage of development involves adding representations that are as lifelike as possible and as close as possible to the person they are representing. Worlds.com normally only allows customization within set criteria (any avatars outside of the rules are grabbed by a virtual monster and thrown into a locked attic on the site!), but had to change the approach for the development of the Aerosmith world:

> It was an expensive process that required lead singer Steve Tyler and his colleagues to don black Lycra bodysuits covered in more than 40 reflective nubs, including one taped to their chins, while lip-synching and performing. Cameras recorded the light reflecting off their bodies and converted the video data into 3-D figures on a computer screen. Those 3-D figures will form the skeleton for the members' avatars. To create 3-D faces, a special camera, developed by 3Dmetrics, was used.[32]

Worlds.com is not alone in its interest in 3-D avatars. Coca-Cola recently launched an avatar-populated site, in which the avatars mill around and chat in a Coke-sponsored world, aimed at the Hong Kong market. British Telecom (BT) is considering creating a 3-D world for the quarter of a million photo-quality avatars that were created at London's Millennium Dome. Do customers find this appealing? Already, about 20,000 have signed up to have their avatars appear when they play online computer games, such as the ultra-violent Quake III Arena and The Sims, a popular game that simulates everyday life. BT is also figuring out how to provide avatar e-mail, which makes the sender's face appear and speak the message aloud.

Experience sells?

It's pretty clear that costs of avatar creation will have to be reduced. Worlds.com reportedly paid around $50,000 to Atlanta-based Giant Studios Inc. to help make the avatars of Aerosmith's five members, their virtual world cost $250,000 too, and the annual costs for maintaining a single site can range from $100,000 to $200,000 a year. That's $10K for each avatar. Expensive when you consider that the avatars created by British Telecom to replicate a person's face, clothes, and general body shape cost the company a few dollars to produce.

At these costs, worlds.com have had to find ways to gain significant revenues[33] via advertising, sales of music, and other merchandise. This brought in about $1.5 million in 2000, shared between worlds.com and the site headliners. The company also charges customers $1.50 a month for a VIP membership if they want to use an avatar other than a penguin! It claims that it has more than 50,000 users paying for a VIP membership.

Experience study

JCPenney.com – it's all inside

J. C. Penney is cool! At least it is according to two out of every three customers voting in a very unofficial survey set up on freevotes.com. That's pretty good going for a business that was set up a hundred years ago by young James Cash Penney who arrived in Kemmerer, Wyoming, with two revolutionary ideas – cash only and the golden rule: do unto others as you would have them do unto you.

The electronic experience offered by the business that J. C. built is a fine tribute to those ideas. It is designed to fit into a compact area, viewable with scrolling on a 15-inch monitor, allowing the customer's mind to acclimatize itself, then focus on pursuing his wants rather than wasting effort on figuring out what to do next.

Prominent is the J. C. Penney promise – "Service, security, quality" – designed to reassure the nervous and encourage a commercial relationship based on more than low prices. Also frontstage is a photo that changes from time to time in the same washed colors but pertinent to the specific offers and seasons. The images are very family, very soothing, and very simple.

At the left-hand side of the shopping experience is the main departmental categories. These include women, men, children, home items, toys, sports, electronics, and music. It features an option to shop for gifts and allows the customer to check his shopping bag at any time. It features a clearance and auction section, to appeal to the bargain-bidding customer. Also clear and upfront is the option to go to customer services.

FIGURE 5.10 J. C. Penny – it's all inside.

At the bottom of the space is another permanent menu bar that allows the customer to find real-world stores and request a catalog that is the same for all channels – real world, telephone, mail order, and the online store. Customers can also contact J. C. Penney, find out more about it, search for the product by keyword on either the entire site or a specific department. The customer can also save time as it is possible to locate a product by just entering the item number from the catalog.

The customer can shop using a series of logical categories, each one digging towards the purchase. Each stage offers useful additional groupings, all the way down to a simple 2-D photo close-up of the product of interest. There is no 3-D here – a decision that leads to ease of use, but still leaves the browsing customer wanting to see some products in the real world before purchasing. Hopefully this will be a real-world J. C. Penney outlet, but there is a risk in allowing the customer to go without allowing him to buy if he wanted to.

FIGURE 5.11 Karaoke close-up.

The customer services pages are extensive, including the J. C. Penney promise, its membership of the BBBOnline reliability bureau, account services, credit services, order status, and a comforting version of the James Cash history. It is disappointing to find that it is only possible to contact the business by telephone or by filling in an online form. There is no direct e-mail, no discussion boards, no live chat, no possibility of arranging in-store consultations, and no callback facilities. There are no innovations in the field of customer services and little attempt to exploit the advantages of the electronic experience.

Somehow, the overall concern for the customer of those involved comes across, but the experience does very little to bring those people, those experience deliverers out into the open. There are no photos of the real team behind the site, behind the service, and no humor or color are to be seen.

Experience summary

This is an effective experience that delivers more than the sum of its parts. Other experiences – most of which are vastly inferior in overall impact – could learn from an insightful statement by the great man himself:

> It is the service we are not obligated to give that people value the most.

However, it is seriously lacking in emotion, community. The advantage won't last if more innovative experiences start to get the shopping bit right.

Stuff to think about

books, articles, TV shows, and websites

Hurst, Mark, *Goodexperience.com* (Creative Good, 1999)

Another site, very similar in style (plain) and purpose to Nielsen and linked to that other well-known net name of Seth Godin. Lots of free-to-use material that discusses and demonstrates Marks' views on what makes a good customer experience. You may find it useful for background information and for news and views from the industry. Use the knowledge gained within the online customer framework to further enhance your understanding and delivery.

Itvnews.com, The University of Edinburgh

The site is the electronic newsletter from Carat Group/Edinburgh University about Interactive Television. James Stewart and Derek Nicholl of Edinburgh University and Jeremy Swinfen Green from the Carat Group edit it. They define interactive TV as, "a television in a domestic environment which has a back channel (a viewer response medium) as an integral part of the system."

The website offers a selection of international views, a newsletter, and research papers to fill what the editors feel is a gap in information provision.

Nielsen, Jakob, *Designing Web Usability: The practice of simplicity* (New Riders, 2000)

How could he not be mentioned? He is criticized and worshipped by different quarters of the web design fraternity, but is undoubtedly one of the best-known exponents of usability, and in this book, presents the principles he has found from usability studies with 200 users over six years. The key limitation is the way that his designs have usability rather than usefulness as a guiding philosophy. I respect his work, but usability as he defines it is unlikely to get the e-customer excited, grateful or help him to spend more money. What does he say about customers? To save you the trouble of looking for his wisdom yourself, I have reproduced the main words:

> In the networked economy, the website becomes the primary interface to the customer. Indeed, for e-commerce companies, the website is the company. The user interface becomes the marketing materials, storefront, store interior, sales staff, and post-sales support all rolled into one. In many cases, the site even becomes the product itself. Thus, having bad usability is like having a store that is on the 17th floor of a building (so nobody can find it), is only open Wednesdays between 3 and 4 o'clock (so nobody can get in), and has nothing but grumpy salespeople who won't talk to the customers (so people don't buy too much). On the web, users experience usability first and pay later.

The Online Macromolecular Museum
(**www.clunet.edu/BioDev/omm/gallery.htm**)

In its own words, the Online Macromolecular Museum (OMM) is, "a site for the display and study of macromolecules," founded with the belief that, "types of displays represented are invaluable in gaining an appreciation for the details of key biochemical processes." It includes a startling range of 3-D models of complex macromolecules that make extensive use of graphical applications and plug-ins.

Underhill, Paco, *Why We Buy: The science of shopping* (Simon & Schuster, 1999)

It's funny and fascinating. Complete with video equipment, store maps, and customer profile sheets, the author and his team have contributed to the "science of shopping" by observing nearly a thousand aspects of shopper behavior.

Online buying is not a major focus (or perhaps a major area of expertise), but the sophistication of the knowledge gleaned shows how far many electronic experience creators need to progress.

Kraut, Robert, *Internet Paradox: A social technology that reduces social involvement and psychological well-being?* (*American Psychologist* – **www.apa.org/journals/amp**)

This is a paper presenting research into the social and psychological impact of the internet on 169 people in 73 households during their first one to two years online. Not conclusive, but it did show that, as internet use increased, so did depression and loneliness – possibly linked with the corresponding decline in interaction with family, friends, and social circle. If these results are extrapolated to the rest of the online customer population, you can expect to have to feed more recognition and fulfilment hunger!

Liu, Allan, *Voice of the Shuttle: Laws of cool page* (University of California, 2000)

Allan asks, sensibly, why cool, an invention of the "border worlds of the jazz clubs in the 1920s and 1930s and the Beats in the 1950s is now so mainstream-hip that even the major corporations want 'cool' homepages? Who does cool serve?" He produces hundreds of sites that have been nominated as "cool" and categorizes them for his research. Ask yourself the same question, rephrased as "How can cool service our business?"

Process and brainstorming software

The dominant force in diagraming for the past few years, Visio from Microsoft allows you to create flow charts, timelines, and organizational charts. These can be used alone, saved as web pages or used with other documents. It will allow you to add your own icons and arrows to the extensive library already in existence. Create processes that range from the micro level within a single component on a single mobile phone screen to the macro level, end-to-end between multiple organizations.

You could also use a product like MindManager from M-Urge that promotes the use of the style of visual thinking that is described at various places within this book. It offers to turn random thoughts into organized ideas in a structure popularized by writers such as Edward De Bono and the less well-known Tony Buzan.

With both these applications, you will still benefit from the use of real pens and paper to remind you what you have said and what you still need to do, but you may be surprised at how many of your teams' ideas start to flow directly into the software. They can then be communicated to the whole business.

Activity 5.1

Your very own experience curve

In this chapter, we introduced the experience curve as a way of picturing the progress of the customer through the experience. This is your opportunity to create your very own experience curve – lucky you!

Test your own electronic experience first by completing a simple end-to-end task from the point of view of a customer. If you are a retail site, then the task will be a purchase, complaint, and return. If you are a service site, it will be similar, but alter it to meet the specifics of your offering.

It is important for the test to work in such a way that no one within the business is specifically aware that you are testing. To do this you may want to use the credit card, address, and personal details of someone else who does not work for your business.

As you complete the task, look around the experience from the point of view of the customer. Ask yourself the following questions and grade the experience on a scale from one (where you were appalled) to five (where you were thrilled).

- How effectively did the experience attract me to it?
- Were a variety of tones used to speak to me as an individual with my particular characteristics, including interests, gender, role? How about other types of people?
- Was interaction offered? Was it available? How interactive was it? How reliable? How rapid? How varied? How human? Did you enjoy the interaction?
- How well did the experience adapt itself to me once I started to use it?
- Did you feel that you started to build a friendship or relationship with the business and the experience? Were there examples of humor or humanity used?
- Was it easy to buy? Were you encouraged to buy in an effective way? Was it clear how to buy and what the advantages were?
- Once you had bought, was the service or product delivered as promised?
- Choose to complain, regardless of your experience. Can you add your comments to the internet? Was your complaint investigated? Did anyone reply to your e-mail? Could you return your product?

The first time you complete an experience study, don't worry about making it very scientific as the objective here is to get a good feel for the end-to-end experience. It is then possible to start to compare the experiences of your main competitors and test your own experience over time or with more testers.

My customer task and objective

	Date	*Time*	

Started

Completed

Problems?

	Date	*Time*	*Happy?*

E-mail sent

E-mail replied to

Letter sent

Letter replied to

Fax sent

Fax replied to

Live chat

Help files?

	Attract	Tone	Interact	Adapt	Bond	Sell	Deliver	Repair
Thrilled								
Pleased								
Dubious								
Irritated								
Appalled								

Simply mark an "X" in the appropriate box on the experience curve diagram for each stage of the end-to-end experience. Then join the marks with a red pen and discover the shape of your own customer experience.

Activity 5.2

The nuts and bolts of bricks and clicks

Try the following and see how well you measure up to the competition when it comes to the crunch of doing real end-to-end business. The following list includes questions that have appeared in various consumer magazines, TV shows, and websites. They were intended to help the customer select who to do business with, but, if you try them out for your own service and one of your main competitors you will see how well (or how badly) you both

		How well did you both do?	
	Questions	Your experience	Competing experience
1	E-mail the site you intend to shop, asking: "What is your returns policy?" (Advice to customer? If there's no response in 24 hours, buy elsewhere[34])	Response within how many hours?	Response within how many hours?
2	Click on the contact details to ensure that the retailer lists ways to reach the company. Essential details: phone number, address with postcode and an e-mail to solve a product issue.		

3 Choose a site that lets you pay by credit card. Some credit card companies can help resolve problems with e-tailors by halting payment until questions have been answered.

4 Save receipts and packaging – keep all transaction correspondences.

5 Return products if problems arise, and watch the terms policy date.

Activity 5.3

Right to reply

Customers expect and deserve to have their e-mails replied to. If your business expects the customer to use the electronic world in preference to the real world or feel as equal toward it, then it is only right that you can answer e-mails in the same way that you would answer questions in person.

An e-mail is not generally like a written letter, sent physically. With a written letter, the customer knows that there is a delay because the letter must be transported there, sorted, answered, printed, and sent back. With an email, the expectation is that there will be an immediate answer so it is more like asking a person in a shop for help. There may be a little more delay, but not much. Read the following as an example of the customer's attitude,[35] toward e-mail, then answer the questions that follow:

> Many retailers apparently think a website gives them the right to ignore one-to-one communication. It's a problem that retailers should face now rather than later when electronic shopping becomes the preferred method and "word-of-e-mail" complaints could cripple a company's reputation.
> The first communications lesson came in the form of an e-mail from a reader who had ordered a pair of sunglasses from Sunglasses International. More than a month later, not only was he still awaiting his sunglasses, he had yet to receive any response to multiple e-mails he had sent to the company enquiring about his order. I immediately e-mailed the company myself, and got a reply explaining that the glasses had just taken a little longer than expected.

Not to reply before, however, opens a whole new set of fears for the buyer. I wouldn't be surprised if my reader's perception of e-commerce isn't tainted by this experience. Even though this particular episode ended well, he now realizes how helpless one is when there isn't an actual store to march into and verbally express your frustrations face-to-face. If I were a web-based retailer, the last thing I'd want to remind my customers about is the lack of human interaction. Sites that don't respond to e-mails promptly not only do a disservice to themselves, but to all e-commerce."

- How quickly, on average, do you answer e-mails from customers?
- What is your reaction when your e-mails are not answered?
- How good is your reputation with customers regarding e-mail?
- What impact does your e-mail reputation have on the customer relationship?

Customer experience thinkers

As we enter the twenty-first century, there is a pressing need for clear strategies. Because, unless companies have a clear vision about how they are going to be distinctly different and unique, offering something different from their rivals to some different group of customers, they are going to get eaten alive by intensity of competition.

MICHAEL PORTER, EDITOR OF *CAPITAL CHOICES: CHANGING THE WAY AMERICA INVESTS IN INDUSTRY* (MCGRAW-HILL, 1994)

I expect an explosion in entertainment. People will want to be entertained whatever they're doing, whether they're working, shopping or consuming. … I think entertainment will be a guiding principle and it will be factored into many situations. We will want our jobs, our shopping experiences and our consumption experiences to be entertaining. Smart retailers know this.

PHILIP KOTLER, AUTHOR OF *MARKETING MANAGEMENT: ANALYSIS, PLANNING, AND CONTROL* (PRENTICE-HALL, 1967)

When service is poor, shoppers will find another store; bad service undoes good merchandise, prices and location almost every time. Regardless of how practical an activity shopping seems to be, feelings always come first, and good is always better than bad.

PACO UNDERHILL, AUTHOR OF *WHY WE BUY: THE SCIENCE OF SHOPPING* (SIMON & SCHUSTER AND ORION, 1999)

66 It took **300 years** to build and by the time it was **10 percent** built, **everyone** knew it would be a total disaster. But by then the **investment** was so **big they** felt compelled to go on. Since its **completion**, it has cost a **fortune** to maintain and is still in danger of **collapsing**.

There are at **present** no plans to **replace** it, since it was never really needed in the **first** place. 99

K. E. IVERSON, ON THE LEANING TOWER OF PISA

Experience creation teams – the individuals, culture, skills, and the stress

How to create teams that understand e-customers and can design and deliver the ultimate experience without nervous breakdowns, mediocrity, or organizational apathy

IN YOUR OPINION, WHO IS THE MOST IMPORTANT PERSON in your whole business? Who is it in the view of the online customer? Who does your team think that person is? It's too early to come out with an answer now, but let's look at some possible candidates among the team that will create and deliver the e-customer experience. Let's start with some history.

A long, long time ago (back in the mid and late 1990s), web people were viewed (and tended to view themselves) as practitioners of some black art and a class apart from the rest of the poor, slow, real-world organization that just didn't "get it." Cooperation was limited, divisions common, misunderstanding the typical modus operandi. This didn't worry the "techies" and management assumed that they were too out of step with the modern age to understand this brave new web world, and those who knew about the real world were told that it wasn't their place to worry.

The electronic experience was just kind of tagged on to the side of the organization. It was a new shoot of growth or an out-of-place carbuncle, depending on your viewpoint. First, the web designers and then the systems integration companies could get away with a non-integrated approach because the client was confused and it was the easiest way to get on and build what sometimes ended up being separate divisions of the business. Sometimes the e-people were so impatient with the rest of the organization that they even ran off and reinvented their previous employees' services as a dot com without any of the organization to back it up. Sometimes it worked and sometimes it famously didn't.

> " Both the **new kids** on the block and the clicks 'n' **bricks guys** certainly need to fill in the gaping holes in both **structure** and culture **that exist** in their teams' delivery of online customer **experiences**. "

Either way, both the new kids on the block and the clicks 'n' bricks guys certainly need to fill in the gaping holes in both structure and culture that exist in their teams' delivery of online customer experiences. This chapter will look first at the structure and skills and then at the culture needed by an organization that wants to create the ultimate end-to-end customer experience.

Wanted! More believers and fewer workaholics

> Overwhelmingly powerful technologies just happen to have been created by people who are, to a large extent, true believers.
>
> JARON LANIER, COMPUTER SCIENTIST AND MUSICIAN

Let's build the team in the way that makes sense from the perspective of creating the ultimate profitable customer experience. The skills are familiar, but, not surprisingly, each person and the groups involved need to be constructed around the needs of the customer. Each department head should not consider himself as running a department, but, rather as contributing to the overall effectiveness of the service offered and delivered to the customer.

We can identify four main groups of people who will need to work together for the success of the customer experience. Viewing the business organization from this customer orientation provides valuable insights into the role and value of each person in the organization. Typically, these groups can be seen as cross-departmental, to improve the clarity of the customer focus, but if you chose to restructure your business according to these roles, the impact would be radical. Far more radical than BPR (business process re-engineering) because it seeks to adapt organizational shape to human behavior and needs rather than merely streamline existing processes in pursuit of efficiency for its own sake.

The first group is made up of those people who need to know what the customers want. At one level, this means everyone in the organization with the empathy to understand the customer, but here it refers only to those who have the responsibility to know what customers want. We refer to this group as "experience visioneers."

The second group includes those who have to actually draw, sketch, and design the vision, and so are known as "experience designers."

The third group build the components that the experience needs in order to be delivered, so can be termed "experience component makers."

The final group is made up of the "experience deliverers" – those who deliver the vision to the customers.

Group 1: experience visioneers – people who know what customers want

Are these the people at the "top" of the business? Maybe not. Someone has to actually know what the customer wants and lead the business toward that vision. Maybe they are the legal guardians as well; perhaps the CEO is also the experience visionary, but not always, not automatically, and even if he is, there will still need to be additional visioneers on the team.

Take Steve Case as an example. He has always known what he wanted the AOL customer experience to deliver and has pursued it relentlessly, despite criticism that his vision was, "too narrow, too expensive, and too complicated." These criticisms would have remained valid only if the internet had not continued to advance, but it did, and does, and his all-encompassing customer-focused view makes more sense all the time. Now the merger with Times Warner is complete, he has a media empire that can deliver a switched on, integrated, customer-oriented, end-to-end electronic experience. No wonder his rivals wait and worry. Who is your Steve Case? What is his vision and does it take full advantage of the technologies and trends that were explained in the previous chapter? Visions are not meant to make complete sense in the short term. They are meant to deliver superior experiences in the long run by starting on that path now.

> ❝ **Visions are** not meant to make complete sense in the **short term.** They are meant to **deliver superior** experiences in the **long run** by starting on that path now. ❞

Your visioneers must understand the ideas behind the technology. They have to see a reason for the technology to exist from the paying customers' perspective and then lead the business and the customers to that vision.

Some CEOs can be so dense, so uninspired, so focused on anything but the customer. An article in *Computer World* related a conversation with the CEO of a large bank that is typical of so many of the price-obsessed breed:

> We had been discussing the internet's effect on banking. I argued that retail banks in particular are suffering from poor relationships with their customers but that the pain of switching to other banks is what keeps customers from switching. It isn't that customers love their current banks – it's just too difficult to switch. The internet could change all this, I told him. But to keep customers, banks will have to do a better job of understanding customer processes and creating good customer experiences.[1]
> The CEO pushed back. Yes, banks could do a better job of using IT to improve relationships with customers. But in the end, he argued, it was the best interest rates on savings accounts and loans that really attracted customers.
> So much for inspiration, I thought.

So think well on who should lead the vision and don't merely select on the basis of seniority. Instead, you must ensure that the visioneers are given the authority. There are many alternative candidates and the challenge is to ensure that, as a group, visioneers have the characteristics necessary for the successful fulfilment of their responsibility. You will have customer champions, customer services leaders, product experts, and marketing people in the mix.

Even in the fluid structure and culture that is proposed in this chapter there will still need to be "managers" or "leaders." Who should lead the online customer team? "No one who likes sleep," could be the answer from a lot of those who have tried out the role. It has been a rough ride for many of the external and internal program and project managers and the range of net entrepreneurs who have been leading the charge. A discussion of the ways in which traditional businesses and their e-commerce initiatives may be organized will identify those who could be viewed as the online customer experience leader.

On the business side, we will find a hierarchy of some sort with a chief executive at the top, surrounded by a board of directors, supported by a team of senior managers. Each of the directors and managers has a particular responsibility and, in a traditional business, these responsibilities will be based on geography, products, and business functions. Typical of the business functions will be finance, production, operations, marketing, and customer services.

Over on the e-commerce project or program, there will, typically, be a combination of external and internal teams and team members, each will have their own project managers, and will report to an overall program manager who is responsible for the overall e-commerce project and usually reports to a more senior management sponsor.

The typical situation is left without a nominated leader, champion, or manager for the complete online customer experience. Someone needs to believe, someone needs to be able to establish credibility with the disparate specialist functions that will all be required to work cooperatively and creatively together. When you redesign business for any reason, it demands an understanding of multiple disciplines. The more radical the change, the more essential it is to have comprehensive and deep cohesion between each of the elements in the organization.

It is not unusual for good ideas to be delayed for months while business and IT try to understand each other. Each team member, to some extent, is hiding behind his expertise (of his own area) and ignorance (of the other person's area). There are some innovations that can only be created if all elements of the business mix are inside the same head of at least one person in the meeting because people do not tend to innovate in areas they do not understand. They are just about coping with the basic change in the system needed, let alone moving ahead of the current level of thinking.

If your people do not know the way, then they cannot lead the e-customer through electronic channels. The guide must know the way. It doesn't matter one jot whether you or your colleagues find this stuff interesting or not – just think about your online customers, not yourself! They need many guides to get the most out of a networked world. It has crept up around them, without being invited, without being welcome, and so they will need help to overcome reluctance, annoyance, and discomfort with their new surroundings.

> **66** If **your people** do not know the way, then they cannot lead the **e-customer** through **electronic** channels. **99**

An e-customer project manager must be capable of ensuring that the original pure and enjoyable objectives of the project are not hijacked by well-meaning, boring, visionless committees that will translate the thrilling mission of the e-project into gray, soulless, pedantic slop. The e-project manager needs to be so dedicated to the online customer and the principles of experience creation that even when busy with the project, the partnerships and the process, he does not forget to focus on the e-customer.

Day in the life of an experience visioneer

At 7.30am, he wakes up in his hotel room, slumped over his notebook, having worked through most of the night. Shower, interrupted by room service bringing his breakfast. A meeting with the integrators (technology consultancy) at 9am, but, before that, a steering group update at 8.30. Dashes across the road, checking his messages as he goes (already 6), among them the testing boys in India explaining that the connection between the mainframe (big, old-style computer) and the test website is no longer working.

> ## Killer skills checklist
>
> - Fluent translator of e-gibberish.
> - Hybrid skills and aptitudes.
> - Can think big picture strategy and small picture tactics.
> - Works a remote team effectively.
> - Cares about e-customers.
> - Sugar-coated steel personality.
> - Loves and plays with the stuff!
> - Ability to gain trust and backing sufficient to renewal.

The steering group meeting is a chore, with directors explaining how "the internet is just another fad" and "had he heard that another dot com had gone bust?"

By 5pm, he has dealt with graphic designers (to tell them that big photos are not a good idea), customer service teams (to plan the live chat support for the web), security specialists (to get the customer data off an insecure database), eaten lunch on the run, and forgotten his wife's birthday.

That time, 5pm, brings the strategy consultants queuing up in front of his open-plan desk. They want to know why half the product range cannot be available in time for the peak season. "Frankly," they say, "It blows all our ROI figures away."

By the time his eyes close, blearily, in his hotel room, he has (5.42pm) been on to the work flow people to understand why the software he has bought does not seem to exist yet. He has spent time (6.17pm) with the training teams to ensure that 500 members of staff are up to date with the new systems before the launch. He has tried (7.30–8.30pm) to convince the marketing director that TV advertising will reduce the profits of the venture to nothing, and he has been harassed over dinner by an angry reseller who fears that the new channel will cut him out of the buying process.

7.30am he wakes up to face a new day.

Group 2: experience designers – people who design the vision

Vision without detailed design, structure, and flow is what appears in superficial, misleading, and frustrating advertising and marketing. In these self-defeating cases, someone, on behalf of the business, offers the customer the vision but does not ensure that it can be delivered. There is dislocation caused by creative advertising people working without constraint and creative, practical designers choosing to ignore responsibility for delivering a vision that they do not feel they own. These various people are usability consultants, systems architects, graphic artists, systems analysts, and engineers, among others.

This would logically mean that there is a need to create a role of "lead customer experience designer," someone who is directly responsible for ensuring that each of the disparate strands of the experience is woven into a fabric that matches the original vision.

Group 3: experience component makers – people who build the vision

Every experience has to be made of something that can be experienced! Every experience is made, therefore, of components.

This third group is made up of the people who build the components of the experience. Examined from this perspective, the people working in manufacturing, programing, finance, and legal areas, and your suppliers, are equally responsible for building the components that are used to construct the architecture, backdrop, and props of the online customer.

For the visionary, this group can be frustrating. They are too logical, perhaps, too cautious, too wary – or maybe too experienced!

The founder of Big Words, the 23-year-old Matt Johnson, a college dropout with no significant management experience, had vision (and it's a great thing to have). He knew that he wanted Big Words to be the Amazon of college textbooks; he knew that he wanted to sell convenience; he knew that price was not a wise key selling point. He knew enough to create a glossy plan that secured $70 million investment and he knew how to create marketing stunts that really attracted in the customers. However, somewhere in his desire to become the CEO of a multibillion-dollar, multinational corporation, he decided that his vision had no room for dissenting voices and, "never made the fundamental transition from start-up mode run by adrenaline to real mode run by protein."[2]

The "protein" is built by the component guys, the people who know more than you do about stuff you don't want to know about but that matters deeply to the success of any customer experience.

Group 4: experience deliverers – people who deliver the vision to customers

Who in the company deals with your customers most closely? Who interacts with them most on a day-to-day basis? It could be your returns department, complaints, customer services, or the people working for the business who deliver the packages to the doors of your customers. This group includes, apart from customer services and delivery drivers, the warehouse team, billing and accounts team, cleaners – anyone who administers anything.

In a one-person business, the owner-proprietor may be at once, visioneer, designer, component maker, and deliverer. He has the advantage of fulfilling all four roles and responsibilities inside one head. He cannot avoid all the issues because he must answer directly to the customer for the vision, design, components, and delivery. For every person taken on by the organization, the roles become shared out. Functional specialization develops to the extent that entire professions no longer see the customer as a whole person, the experience end-to-end, or their role in improving that experience.

The experience deliverers are usually the least loved and appreciated and rewarded in the business, but, of course, conversely, are the ones doing the toughest job, closest to your customer, and so most in need of motivation! They could all do with the kind of mission statement and prominence given to experience delivery by Sony in the customer service guide that accompanies every new VAIO laptop. It proclaims on the first page:

> We address each individual customer issue with care, attention, and respect and we seek to have every customer feel good about the experience they have had with the VAIO-Link Response Center.

The guide is clear that the value of the experience will "further differentiate our offerings to those of our competitors" and describes how the VAIO team is "highly qualified," and trained and mandated to provide the customer with "the best possible" experience. Mandated! Unusual to see authority aligned to responsibility, but this is essential to allowing the experience deliverers to reap the "customer dividend" – a bonus system based wholly on customer satisfaction feedback rather than some imposed level of time taken for each e-mail or chat response.

Real human impact must be built into the experience design so that it is ready to help whenever help is needed (always) and flexible enough to ease the customer through the experience of dealing with you. Designing real people into the e-customer experience will require the kind of interaction technology that is discussed in the next chapter, so that live help via telephone, video, e-mail, or live text chat can bring that human relationship back into the electronic relationship.

Just as important is the preparation of the customer services representative (a term that is rarely matched by the role) who needs to be trained, educated, and let free to deal with the online customer along any channel he sees fit to use.

Training in communication skills must be expanded to include written as well as verbal skills. The customer services representative (CSR) must also be recognized as being the key to making improvements to the current system and populating the online self-help databases.

The web allows people to do more to help the online customer, not less. Any wise business will seek to give the customer representative the tools needed to help the e-customer rather than reduce the time that they are allowed to spend with him.

> ## " The web allows people to do more to help the online customer, not less. "

Remember, your CSR will have to deal with online customers that have vastly varying experience in using the electronic channel in question. Telephone skills are more likely to be consistent across all of them than are electronic skills. This means that your CSR will sometimes have to be a "net nanny," supporting and educating, and sometimes a "cyber-pal," running fast to keep up with pace of demand. Where e-customers' identities are known, it can be useful to ask them to indicate their level of expertise.

The multiplicity of information systems and service contact points can cause different faces to be presented to the e-customer. If he is to build up his trust in you (necessary to stay loyal, buy more products, and recommend friends), then he needs to feel that he is dealing with a consistent company, no matter which channel or individual he is talking with at any point.

Experience culture

In Gary Hamel's book on innovation, *Leading the Revolution* (Harvard Business School Press, 2000), he says that innovators are the most valuable part of any organization and that the reward system should provide dramatically higher rewards for the innovator than for any other individual. Following this piece of advice will almost certainly lead to a culture of elitism rather than cooperation, however. Ask yourself could the vision of the innovator really survive being designed, built, and delivered by the disenchanted 95 percent of the organization that would not be included in such an elite?

Your business will be more effective at building profitable, lasting relationships with your customers if it is, in every way, bottom-to-top, internally and externally, the kind of business that a real, living person can trust. Anything that your business does that is underhand, mean-spirited, unhelpful, degrading, divisive, or demeaning will damage its ability to form relationships. This is true *even if* the customer does not know about it. It is valid even if you think it is hidden away, not official policy, and perfectly legal.

> **Anything that your business does that is underhand will damage its ability to form relationships. This is true *even if* the customer does not know about it.**

Your people will create and deliver better in a culture that rewards all that is good, no matter who was responsible for that good. Effective innovation is not a solo activity; it requires the best efforts of all those who have a stake in the business. The efforts of each person and each resource owned or used by the organization need to be willingly focused on what the customer wants. This only happens when the sentient, thinking part of the organization is motivated.

Such a culture will have to depend, ultimately, on the needs and characteristics of your customers to shape it, but there are some trends in customer behavior that will demand responding trends in most, if not all, organizational cultures. Some will choose to ignore the obvious requirement to adapt, but such a refusal to change will only increase costs elsewhere that will either reduce profits or shorten the lifecycle of the business.

Buzzing?	Buzz off?
• Emotionally connected	Dispassionate and systems • driven
• Creative (strategic/operational/ practice/tactical)	Tied to routine and past • practice
• Relationship-driven and people-focused	Controlling and negative •
• Trusting with minimal rules	Highly financially focused •
• Positive and highly principled	Remote managers issue edicts •
• Highly focused on people –	Performance freaks •
• unshrink them all!	Excessive denial psychology •
• People identify with leaders	People feel devalued •
• Visionary (forward-looking)	Dismissive of customer needs •
• Obsessed with customer service	Absence of interest in learning •
• Thirst for listening and learning	Cynicism and bad will •
• Valued people like the business	

It does not make sense, nor does experience support, any argument that the treatment of customers can, for very long, not reflect the culture of the business. Miserable service, miserable customers, and miserable team members. That's the way it works and the easiest way to benefit from the link is to recognize it and start working toward a people-friendly, customer-friendly culture.

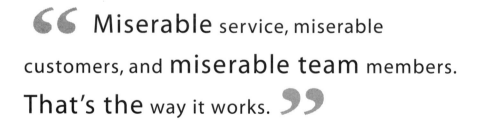

“ Miserable service, miserable customers, and **miserable team** members. **That's the** way it works. **”**

It is easy to believe that powerful technology works without human assistance. It is convenient to look at electronic experiences as something that you can simply purchase and provide to your customers. It's easy and convenient, but not accurate. In the end, people complete everything that is done for the customer. As identified earlier in this chapter, there are people who envision, design it, build it, and deliver the experience.

Let's look in more detail at the necessary characteristics of this culture and the way in which it benefits the effectiveness of the customer experience.

Emotionally connected

The work has to mean more than another task, another hour, another day, and another payslip. Somehow, your team has to invest its own emotions in the individual tasks and chores that deliver the experience so that it communicates that loving attention back to the customer.

It is much more important that the team members are emotionally connected than that they are physically close. The culture should learn from its customers who care little for the location and care *everything* for interconnection. Find the best people wherever in the world they live and then use networks to ensure that they feel like they are working in the same office, the same room, and in harmony with the rest of the team and the customer.

Take as an example, those who deliver the experience and interact with the customer. Doesn't the customer deserve the best? Any business could benefit from a sophisticated and motivated human interface to supplement the electronic one. If technology-literate graduates who are willing to look after valuable customers are impossible to find in your own country, then operate across time zones.

Consider Spectramind,[3] a call center in Delhi, India, that deals with customer requests from the United Kingdom for such well-known brands as Harrods, American Express, and British Airways. Each computer screen in the call center shows Greenwich Mean Time and the temperature in the UK and each member of the team has taken a crash course in British culture. They watch videos of different soup operas to be more familiar with regional accents. They learn about Yorkshire puddings and the Royal family. British tabloids are downloaded for them to know what the customers are reading. They also use the internet to learn more.

The same principle applies to any role within the organization that is supporting the customer experience. Each role needs to be filled to overflowing by people who want to look after each customer and are willing to learn whatever is necessary, including politics, favorite foods, or sports results, to emotionally connect with him.

Allow and encourage your team to use the technology to learn more about and connect with the customer. Let each department or team set up web cams to strengthen the feeling in your culture that you are visible and bonded with the customer. Encourage them to want to answer complaints and requests for help personally. How can your culture understand its responsibilities when it pushes all of the communication between the customer and the business away from the majority of people who do the work? Use chat rooms and instant messaging to get them back into the relationship.

66 Allow and **encourage** your team to use the **technology** to learn more about and connect with the **customer.** 99

That's why IBM provides a facility to find the e-mail address of any person within its business (whois.ibm.com), but what happens when you seek contact with that person? Has the culture prepared its people for direct interaction without warning?

Creative (strategic/operational/tactical)

> Even the best creative team won't succeed without a CEO who creates opportunities for design. Look at Apple: something like the cube would never have happened at Dell or Compaq, because they don't have a leader who, like Steve Jobs, knows that, "If I let these designers go, they're going to bring back something really great."
> RAY RILEY, DESIGNER, *WIRED* (JANUARY 2001)

Creativity must, of course, be set free, but it must not be limited to the traditional creative roles. Leaps of innovation are required along the complete length of the end-to-end process that serves the customer.

66 Leaps of **innovation** are required along the complete length of the **end-to-end** process **that serves** the customer. 99

Who is best placed to judge what a customer wants? Choose from the following:

- the strategist who doesn't serve the customer;
- the designer who doesn't serve the customer;
- the salesperson who sees the look on the face of the customer when he tries to sell a product that just doesn't sell itself;
- the delivery person;
- the aftersales person?

The electronic experience must be capable of adapting not only the style of delivery but also the substance of what is delivered. It should not be used merely to make the unattractive look attractive because, among other reasons, the energy (resources, money, creativity) required to do so is wasted. Someone in or near the customer experience knows the weaknesses in the products and services that are sold and the flaws in the ways in which they are sold and supported. The culture needs to encourage this information out into the open, then actively apply creativity, from wherever it comes, to strengthening the weaknesses and removing the flaws.

Did somebody know that General Motor's car designs were out of step with the preferences of customers in Europe? Yes, three groups knew all about it. The salespeople, who had to try and convince customers to buy. The customers, who were increasingly buying the specialized models from manufacturers such as Volkswagen and the PSA Peugeot Citroën Group.[4] Also, the employees who drove GM cars but secretly knew that their shiny new cars were viewed as dull by their friends and family.

The solution in an online customer culture, where creativity and insight from any source are valued and encouraged, would have been to have asked those groups continually how the cars compared to those of other manufacturers and what could be done to improve them. This would have been (could still be) a daily survey conducted via the internet as part of starting the day process, with results published daily by the same medium. This would have (could still) focus the creativity and knowledge of all those involved to solving the challenges that face customers every single day. It's harder than ever to hide from difficult truths (like "our cars are dull") when the whole business is aware of it. It's hard not to find a solution to those same truths when tens of thousands of minds are working on the problem rather than just a minority of designers shackled by risk-shy management.

Relationship-driven and people-focused

There is no loyalty in a transaction-led business because the focus remains on getting the customer through the transaction as rapidly as possible. At every stage, the culture should instead be confident to allow time and space for relationships to develop naturally.

Don't control how long your team members speak to customers or to each other. Encourage all team members to build relationships by creating enough time and flexibility for it to happen. Experience shows that restricting humanity prevents, not surprisingly, the complete person to emerge. If either customer or team member cannot relax, then they will not start to move beyond superficialities. If they do not learn to move beyond just clock-watching, transaction-driven behavior, they will not be able to create or deliver experiences that bond with customers.

Underpin relationships with time, food, space, and technology. Software that allows teams to work and think together in real time is available, free to download, such as Microsoft's NetMeeting. Suddenly your team can join each other in virtual meetings, using voice, video, and text chat, instantly, in groups. They can even share each other's documents and desktops, editing and viewing at the same time.

Think about that for a moment.

How are you using it? Are you using such software? Every computer in your organization is capable of being connected to the internet or a local network. The software is free that allows such collaboration. You have, with minimal investment of time, the ability to strengthen relationships and working patterns.

When your team thinks about collaboration with customers and each other, they will reach out beyond their own abilities to get others involved. They will ask for help and obtain for your business the benefit of the expertise and time of other people. They will realize that your customers can help, as ezboard.com does, regularly using its relationship with customers to get help with testing and marketing.

> We would like to invite you to come and help us test the newest version of ezboard. This Friday on May 11th, we are releasing ezboard version 6.2 to beta and we need your help. In this release all changes are behind the scenes and features are not visible. We are completing the foundation for our ezSkinz technology.

Every large business in the world has considered, or already has, invested in software designed to "manage the customer relationship," but too few recognize the stumbling block of having transaction-driven cultures that create people who are unable or uninterested in building or managing relationships, with or without the software!

Trusting with minimal rules

> Use your good judgement in all situations, there will be no other rules.
> AWARD-WINNING US RETAILER NORDSTROM'S ENTIRE MANUAL FOR STAFF BEHAVIOR

Doing what the customer needs in every context is too complicated for a master plan to detail. This means, naturally, that there is a need for initiative and improvization wherever the master plan does not mention something. The customer requires flexibility if all his needs are to be met and this will mean a reduction in the number of formal rules, down to a minimum. The business depends on the willingness and ability of team members to make it all work, and these qualities are most likely to be maximized where there is warm trust.

This is not the time for many, many rules about anything because the more rules there are, the more the business team will sit back and feel comfortable about not advancing. It is certainly not a good time to try to ban e-mail, the internet, or place tight restrictions on what we have available to aid the learning or service process. Just make it clear that there are a couple of simple, legally binding rules about content, that this will be tracked for legal reasons via the networks of the business, and that otherwise they should feel free to be as creative and adventurous as they can be.

Take, as a small example of this at work, Linux[5] – a competitor to the Windows operating system in the business environment. It is free to buy or use. It was developed without a business organization to shape or finance it. Programers created it in their spare time because they cared about quality and the experience of the customer. The lesson to be learned here is not whether or not it succeeds in surpassing Microsoft, but that it was created without restrictive rules. It demonstrates what people are capable of when guided towards a motivating goal.

Over at Whole Foods – a nationwide chain of 122 stores in the US with revenues of over $2 billion and profits that are twice the industry average – autonomous teams decide who gets hired and are free to do whatever they feel necessary to serve the customer and achieve the goals of the business in competition with other teams. Achievement brings with it bonuses and a superior customer experience.

The next challenge is to determine how to allow autonomous efforts in the creation and delivery of the electronic experience. At Semco, the Brazilian manufacturing company made famous by its efforts for workplace democracy, no restrictions were placed on who could produce innovations for the use of the internet.[6] The result, Semco.com, is a startlingly bland, uninspiring experience, but it also provided the creation of a successful online exchange to improve the management of commercial construction projects.

People do not need lots of rules to follow.

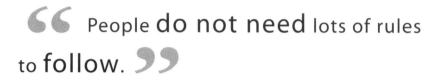

❝ People do not need lots of rules to follow. ❞

Positive and highly principled

> One sticks one's finger into the soil to tell by the smell in what land one is in. I stick my finger into existence – it smells of nothing. Where am I? Who am I? Why should I have an interest in it?
> SØREN KIERKEGAARD

That we need to have a positive outlook is true, but has become a trite thing to say. This need is studiously ignored by the day-to-day activities and attitudes of many businesses. Positive thinking is assisted tremendously by the adherence to abiding morals and principles that keep the conscience of team members clear and their belief strong in the worthwhile nature of their work.

Does your business attempt to cut corners? Does it try to mislead customers? Does it hide behind narrow interpretations of extensive fine print to avoid responsibility? Only when the business is honest and good can everyone believe in the work itself.

There are many opportunities for the business to be dishonest or unprincipled when dealing electronically. It can sell information on when it has suggested that this will never be done. It can track customers when it has not admitted that it is doing so. It can lie about the reasons for internet orders being late. It can use the invisibility of doing business electronically to hide. Every such action will damage trust, not only with the customer but with those who work for the business.

Is it possible for work to play a role in giving team members a "smell" of existence? A purpose? Fulfilment? Each individual is just as complex as the customers the business seeks to serve, they are all looking for fulfilment in what they do, and if they do not get it at work then they will not put their best efforts into what they are being paid to do. In a sense, they are all "moonlighting" if their minds, and best efforts, are elsewhere. The closer work is to our hearts, the more we will create, but this will not happen if work is forced, against our will – that can, and does, lead only to the broken-hearted.

Instead, build work around what the worker believes in, what will bring true peace, and happiness. Family? Service? Choice? Can it deliver to us a sense of wholeness? Can it connect us to the center rather than pushing us to the edge? Too many of those working in the businesses of the world would, in a flash, agree with the following commentary:[7]

> I was part of that strange race of people aptly described as spending their lives doing things they detest to make money they don't want to buy things they don't need to impress people they dislike.

Customer-focused cultures can do better than that. They can create an environment where people can spend their lives doing things that they love to make things that other people need to improve their lives and the lives of the people they like and love.[8]

Highly focused on people – unshrink them all!

The principles discussed in the previous section are necessary for a number of reasons. They are right in themselves, and there is great power in doing what is right. It is also simpler to justify, easier to remember what you are doing, and clearer to create a culture with a widely understood, commonly accepted approach when it is, in effect, the application of natural, moral laws.

In addition, they allow the business to focus on people – the source of growth and the only part of the organization capable of adding value to the products and services that are offered (always remember that fact). Instead of making finance, accounting, or quality the guide to what you do, let the people themselves be the catalyst.

Care about the working conditions of the people who work for your business. Don't do a Nike. Don't wait for campaigns to force you to change unnecessarily poor or mean-spirited conditions. Make sure that their work–life balance always allows them to make their home life succeed – that's not a manifesto for indiscipline, it's the way to ensure that each team member is able to concentrate on work, not home problems, and that he wants to invest his available time and talents to the success of a business that is family.

66 Care about the working conditions of the people who work for your business. 99

Your people are capable of much more than you think. Your customers are capable of much more than you think. Your people can do more than follow directions. Your customers can do more than buy what you make for them. Think of remogeneralstore.com, where the customers become the source of innovation in partnership with the team members who serve them. In its own words:

> From Day One the true substance of REMO has been the collective radiant energy, intelligence, and commitment of its people.

66 Your people are capable of much more than you think. Your customers are capable of much more than you think. 99

The surprise on investigating this bold and proud claim is the extent to which it is genuine. Founded in 1988 by Remo Giuffré, the business was a "general store" in Sydney that is now based in New York. It seeks to be a meeting place, a place to talk, a place where innovative customers seek creative and daring solutions in, 'stationery, skin care, magazines, soaps, shirts, personal items, gifts, information … and entertainment." This role as a meeting place meant that, for Remo, the application of the internet to commerce was a perfect and much-desired tool for which it already had a purpose. Its logo is the head, to represent the mind and soul of the customer, who they serve with quality, intelligence, usefulness, fun, relationships, and entertainment. The focus is on letting people come and build the community that they want. How e-customer is that?

People identify with leaders

❝ The team members will not work hard for leaders they cannot see, do not know, find difficult to respect. ❞

The team members – whether 2 or 200,000 – will not work hard for leaders they cannot see, do not know, find difficult to respect. If the CEO views designers, creators, and deliverers of the electronic experience as just other sources of income to be reported to shareholders, he will fail to ignite the passion for excellence that is so necessary in current times, demanding as they do great flexibility and innovation.

Consider what happened at Apple when the original founder was not at the helm. It became exactly like every other computer manufacturer and stopped meaning anything to its customers who had bought into an electronic experience that *had* to "be different." When Jobs arrived back, the creativity of the team was reinvigorated in pursuit of the excellence that customers expected. They identified that love of excellence with the man Jobs. They do what he does and respond to his attitude to customers, demonstrated when he regularly calls them to try and solve problems personally.

It is difficult to identify with managers who issue remote edicts, lack an appreciation of the expertise of those that they manage, or think that managing in some way confirms their superiority over others in the organization. Columnist Simon Travaglia deftly expresses this in the following statement. He describes how there is nothing worse than:

> A non-technical boss who believes that intellect and experience are obtained at the very same time as a job title – i.e. because he's become IT manager he can now manage IT … Hence the headset. Hence the top-of-the-line brand-spanking new desktop and laptop he demanded as befits an IT Professional. Complete with external consultant-installed virus protection. Hence the smug attitude.[9]

The same statement can be applied to any manager of any area. To look after customers requires focus. This is just not possible if the managers and employees are busy playing internal turf wars and implementing plans based on the knowledge of out-of-touch managers.

Visionary (forward-looking)

Every team member should be encouraged to think ahead in visionary terms. Each should consider how his work could be restructured and rethought to improve his contribution to an effective customer experience. Many will come into your organization more informed and up to date and expectant than their colleagues. They arrive from university, college, or school excited about life, so don't stamp on their "naivety" – instead, encourage their "enthusiasm" and let it feed the business.

As part of your "welcome to the business," find out what their dreams are, how they think that businesses should work for customers, what they hate, and what they like. Ask how they have used technology in the past. They may have had an advanced school featuring wireless laptops, such as at Henrico County Public Schools,[10] which recently bought 23,000 new Apple iBook laptops for every teacher and student in its middle and high schools. How do you know if you don't ask?

Reward, with interest, promotion, respect, and money those who find innovations that improve the customer experience in the way that they do their work and the way that they deliver the experience to the customer.

Obsessed with customer service

> Courtesy is the one coin you can never have too much of or be stingy with.
> JOHN WANAMAKER[11]

The world has done a disservice to the word "service." Its meaning is too often reduced to the niceties of the ritual that surrounds a transaction – the "have a nice day" package – as if, somehow, we could measure the service offered by the width of the smile. You can imagine the manager chiding his staff, "Smile wider, people don't like our service."

Service is the act of helping. Do we serve our customers well – do we help them? Do we leave them happier, wiser, wealthier, more organized, more popular than when we found them? Have we contributed more than we have taken? That's the secret of organic growth. That's the secret of national and global economic growth.

66 Service is the act of helping. Do we serve our customers well – do we help them? 99

It has, typically, a reputation of being at the lower end of the business, something that all those who want to get ahead want to avoid. You can tell what your business feels about customer services by the way they talk about it. Do people in your business talk about their customer services involvement with pride? Is there a customer services position on the board of directors?

Courtesy, kindness, decency, honesty come out of the values that a business espouses and from the way that the team members are treated and rewarded. They make us happy, they reduce wasteful stress, and they improve the bottom line by making customers into repeat buyers and effective, vocal evangelists. Service is so rare as to be the most powerful differentiator available.

Thirst for listening and learning

Leading the customer into a brave new world via your ultimate experience will require a culture that listens to customers and all those involved in delivering the experience. The business should encourage continual learning so that it is capable of producing sufficient new people with skills and knowledge necessary for coping with accelerated change and continual demands from the customer.

Learning should be informal, encouraging inquisitiveness and allowing access to real-world and electronic libraries in the workplace, and formal, associating a member of staff with a particular recognized course of study, for example. So-called "e-learning" provides an effective potential to change the nature of corporate training and is expected to grow ten-fold between 2000 and 2004.[12] Among its advantages is the possibility of a tailored offer to suit individuals' needs and, as a result, reinforcement becomes easier and retention of the learned information lasts longer.

We should have the business learning from the customer about not only what he wants to buy but also how the business should use technology to change the way that it works. So, the company that is trying to serve the online customer should understand that he often knows more about how to use the technology to organize his life than it does. If it uses traditional approaches to organization while the customer goes off at "internet speed," then the organization cannot adapt rapidly enough and will be left behind.

For example, in a chat room, chatters work in different shifts, depending on time zones – the Europeans shift to the Asians who shift to the Americans. The chat is 24/7. Imagine a company organized along chat room lines. No need to book rooms. In an electronic world with no space restrictions, why should you have to look for a physical meeting room? In a world with no travel requirements, why force the team to travel? Team members and customers could create rooms, as they were needed, have individual conversations, organize meetings, anything in fluid actions that would support the needs of the people involved. In a world where time zones can work for you, why force them to work against you? The environment can alter to help.

We are a specialist business that works with a tight core that uses different people with different skills around the world. An English author with assistance from the US, Portugal, Ireland, Mauritius. End to end around the world, with skills that we wanted that are under-utilized because some of them were living in the "wrong" country. Not only should time zones push you to move country effortlessly, so should skills shortage. If the whole organization at every desk is connected to its own private space and to public spaces on the web, then we can invite in colleagues and take e-mail to the next creative level.

There is much to learn.

Valued people like the business

Is your business likeable? Do the people you really need to compete like your business and its approach? I was recently appalled to read a project manager's view of people versus technology. He said: *"Technology is logical and consistent and creates about 20 percent of the problems during the project. People aren't and cause 80 percent of the problem."*[13]

Is the man joking or has he really managed all those projects and not realized that people *are* the project, they are 100 percent of the solution, not the problem? What can you do without the people? If your business thinks like he does, then your best people will not find your business likeable.

When *people* like the business, then there is some chance that *customers* will love the business. Being likeable is the lowest-friction route to attracting customers to become first-time and then lifetime customers. Ask your best people to describe your business as if it was a person. Build up a profile of the human characteristics that typify your culture. Compare these with the electronic experience that you offer.

> ❝ Being likeable is the **lowest-friction** route to **attracting** customers to become **first-time** and then lifetime customers. ❞

Arrogant, self-centered cultures are unlikeable and, our research shows, only produce arrogant, self-centered, incomplete, disinterested electronic experiences. The efforts of web designers are insufficient to overcome the approach and attitude of the team collective.

Experience builders – a summary

The ideal team structure, team members, and team culture described in this chapter rarely exists. Many business organizations have chosen to separate their functions or even their complete internet team rather than figure out how to design culture, structure, skills, and flow around the needs of the customer and the delivery of an effective experience to him.

If your business has done exactly that, then you may have started to bring them back into the main organization. Guard against treating the return as a failure or a demotion or even a loss of freedom. This is a necessary evolution, not a problem. The challenge is not simply to combine clicks and bricks at a company report level, but at a practical and spiritual companywide level.

> ❝ **Each member** of the team must feel that he is part of something **important,** **something right,** good, and worth putting his best **effort** into. ❞

Each member of the team must feel that he is part of something important, something right, good, and worth putting his best effort into. He must also be convinced of the usefulness of each other team member and role in ultimately delivering what customers want and are willing to pay for. The alternative is to allow some extent of dislocation to occur between individual efforts to the detriment of the customer experience and business performance.

Experience study

Google.com

Does the world really need another search engine? Maybe, when it's faster than superman when he's late for a date with Lois Lane. That's 0–1 billion pages in less than half a second. So many customers like it that Google accommodates 70 million searches a day.

FIGURE 6.1

Google – born to search.

The structure – particularly the home (and main) page – is simple, but complete. All that white space focuses the eye on the brand logo and your purpose for being here – the search field. Just one little box offering to be the customer's easy route to more than 1.3 billion web pages. It's not hard to figure out that the guys behind Google – Larry Page and Sergey Brin, two Stanford PhD candidates – are very clear about what is being offered to customers. Are you in any doubt?

Using just 52 words, the experience proclaims all its key virtues. It speaks to the customer as a child by including light-hearted terminology and often playful alterations to the Google logo. The logical adult is offered a list of benefits.

Want to browse pages that are not in your native language? Then you are offered the ability to search in 25 different languages and have the results translated for you into your native language. You are told upfront that this is a feature not yet complete and you are invited to join the testing process.

Awards won, just in 2001? Oh, you'll be talking about the Pandia award for best All-round Search Site, the PC Magazine nomination for Top 100 Websites, the Mobility Award 2001, with an honorable mention for Technical Achievement of the Year, Search Engine Watches award for Outstanding Search Service and most Webmaster Friendly Search Engine – and that's just for starters.

FIGURE 6.2 Letting the people out.

Do you care who delivers the experience to you? Google flaunts the belief that having quality people, in a quality culture, leads to a quality search experience. Choose "About Google," dig just one hyperlink into the site, and the human vibrancy is hitting you in the heart. This is a culture that wants the best and offers free snacks to get them! How Scooby Doo is that?

Google is proud enough of what it does to have created a series of branded Google gear, including baseball caps and sweatshirts. It invites its customers to "help others without saying a word" by pointing at the Google logo whenever that person appears lost or confused. This boosts the value of the service in the mind of the business itself and those who browse through to this point. It creates a bond with fan-customers and lets Google know who they are with the use of the ordering mechanisms.

FIGURE 6.3 Wear Google, think Google.

The Google experience can adapt to the approach of the customer by being usable in a flexible number of ways. It can be added to the customer's Internet Explorer browser via a Google toolbar, and it can be used via wireless devices, including WAP phones and PDAs. Vodafone and I-Mode are both partnering with Google, and both site the objective of delivering the maximum customer experience as the reason for the partnership.

Cap

Item# GO2210 **$8.95**

Order

It does exactly what it says on the tin, only it does *more* than you might expect while keeping the focus (and the speed) at the high levels its customers need.

Stuff to think about

books, articles, TV shows, and websites

Burdman, Jessica, *Collaborative Web Development: Strategies and best practices for web teams* (Longman Higher Education, 1999).

New managers joining website production teams will find useful forms, documentation, and advice specific to the needs of web developers here. The community has recommended it as a good addition to the web team bookshelf. So, if you are in one, you might as well own one.

Gamasutra.com (CMP Media Inc, 2001)

A site dedicated to game development, where the intricacies of the art process, teambuilding, management, and roles are discussed and explored. Not only has it got a clever name, the information on it is first class, so go satisfy structure hunger and have fun.

Activity 6.1

Taking the temperature

So, how appropriate is your culture to creating an electronic experience that is capable of attracting, selling to, and bonding with customers? Take this easy-to-use test to determine the temperature of your culture. First, complete the test yourself, simply according to your own view of whether your own culture is closer to "buzz off" or "buzzing" characteristics. Then, consider taking the test to your team, next to your company via a survey on paper or on the business intranet.

Buzzing?	5	4	3	2	1	Buzz off?
Emotionally connected						Dispassionate and systems-driven
Creative (strategic/operational/tactical)						Tied to routine and past practice
Relationship-driven and people-focused						Controlling and negative
Trusting with minimal rules						Highly financially focused
Positive and highly principled						Remote managers issue edicts
Highly focused on people – unshrink them all!						Performance freaks
People identify with leaders						Excessive denial psychology
Visionary (forward-looking)						People feel devalued
Obsessed with customer service						Dismissive of customer needs
Thirst for listening and learning						Absence of interest in learning
Valued people like the business						Cynicism and bad will

Total score

Activity 6.2

Would this happen in your business?

Read through the following with your team, then discuss the questions that follow it to stoke up some debate. If there is no passion in the room when you have finished, then you did something wrong.

In September 2000, Apple CEO, Steve Jobs, took matters in his own hands earlier this week after receiving a letter from an Apple customer dissatisfied with the service he was getting from the company.

After purchasing one of Apple's stylish Power Mac G4 cubes, public relations executive, Kevin Pedraja, noticed cracks appearing on the new machine. Pedraja contacted Apple but did not receive any help from the computer maker. According to the *Wall Street Journal*, Pedraja then "faxed a strongly worded letter to Mr Jobs that also threatened to spill the beans to the media. The letter yielded immediate results. Apple's executive relations team promptly offered to replace Mr Pedraja's cube with a new one."

Apple's customer relations didn't stop there; Pedraja received a phone call from Jobs himself. "During the five-minute conversation, Mr Jobs didn't exactly offer an apology," Mr Pedraja recalls, "but he did stress that he wanted to come to some sort of resolution. I was pretty impressed that he would call me personally. Not many CEOs would do that."

An Apple spokeswoman told the *WSJ* that "it isn't unusual for Mr Jobs or other Apple executives to check in with concerned customers from time to time."

- Has your CEO ever called or e-mailed a concerned customer personally?
- Is it unusual for your senior management to get involved one to one?
- What would your business have done in a similar circumstance (like those that happen every single day of the week!)?
- What do you think Apple should do next with this customer?
- Who should be answering customer complaints? Whose fault are they?

Activity 6.3

Teams checklist

Ponder whether or not your company is empowering everyone responsible for creating and delivering the online customer experience. Empowered and motivated people on every front means loyal, happy customers. You need to truly know your people, use their ability to innovate, and trust in their good sense to guide themselves and, as a consequence, you'll create the unique customer experience.

Completion date: _____

75% done ☐	100% done ☐	Task	Who will do it? (initials)	By when? (date)
		Part A		
		Identify the visioneers in your company.		
		Identify their visions.		
		Ensure the visions take advantages of the technologies and trends (see Chapter 7).		
		Ensure the visioneers understand the ideas behind the technology.		
		Make clear to the team that the focus is the e-customer.		
		Ensure that the visioneers are given authority.		
		Schedule a discussion to identify the e-customer experience leader.		
		Ensure you have people from different areas in the groups.		
		Identify who in your company deals with customers most closely. • Are those people well paid? • Are they in the bottom of your organization?		

228

WHY THEY DON'T BUY

Expand the communication skills
training to written and verbal skills
when training CSR staff.

Give CSR the tools to help
e-customers.

Don't restrict the time a CSR spends
with online customers.

Allow each department or team to
set up web cams.

Encourage the team to answer
complaints and requests for help
personally.

Encourage the team to use chat rooms.

Encourage the team to use instant
messaging.

Encourage the use of the internet and
e-mail.

Make the company's values and goals
clear to the team.

Commit to never mislead customers
(no more hiding behind the fine print).

Part B

Find out what the visioneer's dreams are.

Find out how the visioneers think
your business should be.

List what the visioneers like and hate
about your business.

Find out how the visioneers have
used technology in the past.

Reward those who improve customer
experience by innovating.

Find out what the team thinks about
the way your company serves
customers.
- Do we help them?
- Do we leave them happier, wiser,
wealthier, more organized, and more
popular?

Encourage access to real-world and electronic libraries in the workplace.

Ask your best people to describe your business as if it was a person.

Compare the characteristics resulting from the above task with the experience you offer.

Activity 6.4

Killer skills checklist

You need to find the experience project manager and it might not be you, so here is an activity for you to complete, either by assessing a group of people of your choice or observing the team while team members complete some of the earlier activities. Your boy or gal will be the one who constantly achieves high scores throughout the exercise.

Completion date: _____

	Killer skills for experience project managers and leaders							
Initials	Fluent e-gibberish translator?	Hybrid skills and aptitudes?	Big and small picture?	Effective will remote team?	Cares about e-customers?	Sugar-coated steel?	Loves and plays with the stuff?	Ability to gain trust and support for renewal?
	1–5	1–5	1–5	1–5	1–5	1–5	1–5	1–5

Highest constant scorer?

Customer experience thinkers

We have to realize … that the new source of wealth is intelligence. It's not land or money or raw materials or technology. It's brains and the skills of the people. For years, corporate chairmen have been talking about their people as their primary assets. It's time they woke up to the fact that it's actually true, because their only hope for future security lies in the brains of those people.

CHARLES HANDY, AUTHOR OF *GODS OF MANAGEMENT: THE CHANGING WORK OF ORGANIZATIONS* (SOUVENIR, 1986)

When you bring new people in, you say to them: "we want you to join us but you'd better analyze what you're coming into. You'd better be prepared to live by these principles or your future will be jeopardized." In other words, they have to buy in, and if the culture is a high-trust culture, they get socialized into it. They come to realize that it isn't just words and slogans on the wall. This is the veritable constitution by which every person is evaluated, and by which their future, career in the organization is governed.

STEPHEN COVEY, AUTHOR OF *THE SEVEN HABITS OF HIGHLY EFFECTIVE PEOPLE: RESTORING THE CHARACTER ETHIC* (SIMON & SCHUSTER, 1992)

Since the process can't always be performed by single individuals, we revert to the idea of a team. No longer is it an assembly line, it's a collection of individuals. A group of people with collective responsibility for creating the end result. For performing the whole process, not bits of it. And for getting their outcome to the customer. So it is a customer-driven, a customer-focused environment, in which teams of professionals, with autonomy and responsibility, create a result.

Every individual on the team is focused on the objective, which involves cooperating with others while carrying out your own particular set of duties.

MICHAEL HAMMER, AUTHOR OF *BEYOND REENGINEERING: HOW THE PROCESS-CENTERED ORGANIZATION IS CHANGING OUR WORK AND OUR LIVES* (HARPERCOLLINSBUSINESS, 1996)

The learning organization will be fundamentally characterized by dramatic enhancements in productivity and by people who feel like the work environment they are operating in is closer to what they truly value. And I think we are getting enough evidence that both are possible: that these statements are not hyperbole.

PETER SENGE, AUTHOR OF *THE FIFTH DISCIPLINE* (DOUBLEDAY/CURRENCY, 1990)

What leaders must learn to do is develop a social architecture that encourages incredibly bright people, most of whom have big egos, to work together successfully and to deploy their own creativity.

WARREN BENNIS, AUTHOR, WITH PATRICIA BIEDERMAN, OF *ORGANIZING GENIUS: THE SECRETS OF CREATIVE COLLABORATION* (NICHOLAS BREALEY, 1997)

Make these people the company heroes – by paying them well; training them "excessively" in class and on job; providing them with outstanding tools; giving them the opportunity to participate in the structuring of their jobs and support systems; and listening to them. The customer game is ultimately won or lost on the frontlines – where the customer comes in contact with any member of the firm. The frontlines team is the firm in the customer's eyes. Therefore, the frontline team must be treated as the heroes they genuinely are – and supported with tools (training, systems) that allow them to regularly serve the customer heroically. Surprisingly, all too few firms understand this.

TOM PETERS, AUTHOR OF *THRIVING ON CHAOS* (MACMILLAN, 1998)

The single greatest challenge facing managers in the developed countries of the world is to raise the productivity of knowledge and service workers.

PETER DRUCKER, AUTHOR OF *MANAGEMENT: TASKS, RESPONSIBILITIES, PRACTICES* (HEINEMANN, 1974)

The reason why Microsoft is such a talented company is the executives. They not only have a half-dozen people at the top of the company who are among the best executives in the world, they've got 40 people underneath them who are among the best executives in the world, and then a couple-hundred people under them who are among the best executives in the world. Executive bandwidth is so important that if they really focus on something and decide to be aggressive about it, they can do just about anything they want.

JEFF BEZOS, FOUNDER OF AMAZON.COM

"" Bill [Gates] is one of the most brilliant programers I **have ever worked with**, and I have worked with some great ones. So, the **real myth** is that we aren't "**tremendously** technically **sophisticated**." As soon as **Microsoft** got off the ground, we focused more and **more on management**, but our technical backgrounds have **served us extremely** well over the years in evaluating **projects** and products. **""**

PAUL ALLEN, MICROSOFT CO-FOUNDER,

"MAKING A POINT," *WIRED* (APRIL 2001)

Trends and technologies for creating experiences

Top ten trends and technologies to create e-customer experiences that sparkle, slip, and slide into his brain without letting him down, destroying his trust, or losing his order

This is a world made out of technology instead of a world that is merely assisted by technology. That is where you entertain and serve the online customer. The technology is not merely the delicious topping on the cake, it is the cake and the bakery that baked it. Ignoring it is not a rational choice and should not be considered as a sensible survival strategy. Nor is it enough to love technology for its own sake. Effective business use of technology involves both:

- viewing it as a tool for creating better customer experiences;
- viewing it as a catalyst that changes the behavior of your customers.

> **" Technology is not merely the delicious topping on the cake, it is the cake. Ignoring it is not a rational choice. "**

In this chapter, I will set out an explanation of the technologies used in a customer experience architecture – not because you need to love the technology, but so that you know:

- what each key component does;
- if you have it already;
- what advantage/disadvantage it has for the customer;
- how to exploit it and what to look for when you buy or implement it.

First, we take a look at the types of technology components that you may choose from in building the experience. These are categorized and put into context so that the non-technical and technical readers can both understand what the technology does and what relevance it has to the overall experience.

Next, we examine the top ten trends in technology that will impact the potential of the experience that can be offered to the customer. The consequences of the trend and its benefits (and potential pitfalls) for the customer are included. The trend is as important as the specific example or application because it is based on trends we have identified as having held constant for decades, if not centuries.

People living in a world of technology should not throw stones of anti-technology skepticism. The electronic experience's creator must lead the customer in to experiences that take advantage of those trends and the customer behavior that they provoke.

Online customer technology architecture – putting it all together

There are numerous bits and pieces of technology to be fitted together to construct and support the experience. No one vendor provides the best of everything and it is often difficult to see what it all does, what it should do, and how it all could fit together eventually. Businesses large and small struggle to see the big picture with so many projects, initiatives, deadlines, and investments competing for time.[1]

Experience has taught us that many businesses choose to reduce the mental effort required to look after the holistic electronic experience by focusing on individual, specialized projects, even if this approach ignores many essential decisions, design options, and opportunities to improve and simplify the complete e-customer technology architecture.

- They may, for example, build the web frontend without preparing a database to support all the much-needed personalization.

- They have, on occasion, not included intelligent search facilities on sites of many thousands of pages.

- They turn away from the need for an overarching multichannel architecture because time constraints mean that such an effort would prevent the launch of channel 1, even though it will all take much longer, in the medium term alone, to launch channels 2, 3, and so on.

- Often there is no overall systems vision, much less an understandable diagram and explanation that every team member can understand and to which each can contribute.

What does it all do?

Let's start with what it can't do because sometimes technology vendors' emphasize their own technology disproportionately and this leads to businesses that fail to appreciate, train or motivate their team members sufficiently. Over $500 million was spent on CRM (customer relationship management) software in just one year, but even its supporters concede that it cannot consider the customer's feelings, share a joke or vary the pitch in response to the customer's tone. It is not within the power of software to empathize – people will have to do that. Now we have restored perspective, back to the technology.

> 66 It is not **within** the power of software to **empathize** – people will have to do that. 99

The bedrock of the technology architecture really has to be the "database." It is not chance that the world's most successful database vendor is named Oracle. It is the database that stores all the customer data. It is from this that information, and potentially even knowledge, can be created to help inform decisions and actions operationally, tactically, and strategically.

Unfortunately for customers, many of the businesses that they deal with have databases that have bred and multiplied energetically and relentlessly through the years. The result is that businesses have many, often conflicting, and seldom integrated, customer files.

> **❝ Customers** want to be treated as a customer with a **relationship** with one **organization,** not as a number of different **files. ❞**

Customers hate being transferred by phone or from site to site and they hate having to type in their details again and again. They want to be treated as a customer with a relationship with one organization, not as a number of different files used by different departments and subsidiaries. It is the database that can make it possible to deliver what the customer wants in terms of service. It is also the database that is at the heart of personalization and cross-selling efforts. If you have a database that is not customer-focused, then all your attempts to deliver an anytime, anywhere, adaptive experience will be hampered. Does the left hand know what the right hand is doing?

Next up is the technology that gets the information in the database to where it can be used effectively (or otherwise) to improve the customer experience. This is usually referred to as "middle ware" or the "glue" that joins the various channel applications together with the data that they need. Middleware, just like a middleman, does all that is necessary to bring the two parties together. Once, the database would have worked with only one frontend application, but for more than a decade now (hallelujah!), software has been becoming more open, less restrictive, and multilayered. Technology is busy delivering the off-the-shelf mix-and-match wardrobe rather than the tailor-made one occasion only ensemble.

The part of the architecture that is seen by customers and most of the business is the set of "frontend" applications – that just means the bit that is visible. It is the part that can be typed into, dragged and dropped, clicked on, and admired for its large graphics and subtle font choices.

FIGURE 7.1 Customer experience architecture.

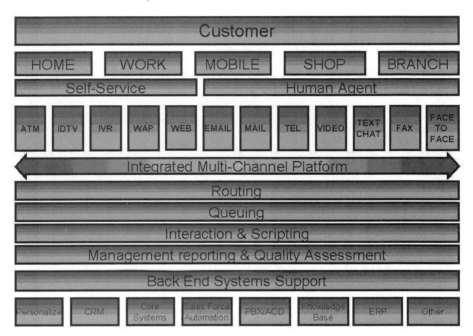

Naturally enough, these three layers provide only the highest-level picture of the architecture because each of the layers consists of many different pieces of hardware (the stuff you can touch) and software (the stuff that you can't touch that tells the hardware what to do). Be patient if this all seems either beneath your understanding or way beyond it! It's an important foundation and one that is needed to build further detail on.

If the layers are inadequately customer-focused and integrated, then the experience is compromised – as I was reminded when making an insurance claim recently.

Example Using the telephone number included in the policy booklet led to me being informed by one part of Lloyds that the telephone number was wrong. Another Lloyd's number was suggested and called, also wrong apparently. I tried the new number, but was told that it would not be supported during the weekend and to try the next day. Finally, I spoke to someone at Lloyds who could confirm that my policy had been placed through them and that she would send out an application form for Zurich immediately. I asked if it was possible to apply more quickly and was told that it was not.

As it happens, there is an online claims application form for Zurich insurance, but it is not possible to get to it directly through the Lloyds TSB website. There is not even a link between the Zurich and the Lloyds TSB sites. To discover the online service required me to move through 14 different pages and 3 different websites, using guesswork to take each logical leap.

Why was it necessary for me as a customer to take so many wrong turns? Because the information that is known about me *and* about the products is not all collected into one place and then distributed in a useful way to each channel, or contact point, as I need it. If the technology layers are used effectively, they can avoid such problems jeopardizing the overall experience and customer interactions.

Interaction technology: from me to thee

FIGURE 7.2 From me to thee – technology for customer interaction.

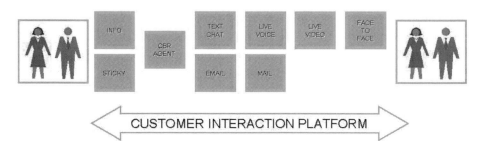

Across the experience interface, the customer interacts with the business in a variety of ways. Each of these has a different level of cost to implement and cost per interaction. Each also has a different level of empathy, humanity, and richness that is naturally supported. These levels are typically as set out in Figure 7.2.

The least costly interaction to support is electronic information that is owned by the business as it has a fixed price to implement and zero cost per interaction. It makes financial sense to put information online because it is cheaper to store and distribute it from here than in the real world. So, why is information online so often incomplete and out of date? Sloppy work and fractured business organizations, that's why.

To help the process, invest in a decent content management system. As soon as you are electronic, you are in publishing. These provide easy-to-use applications that allow people in your business to manage, add, and create the information that is presented to the customer without having to go through a technologist first. It avoids the need for the whole business to learn HTML. It gives the power back to the people.

"Sticky" content is usually more expensive than plain information, but a little of it goes a long way. "Sticky" means anything that can keep the customer coming back for more. It includes information, of course, but specifically means anything that changes or allows interaction or is there for amusement. This could include calculators for working out insurance claims or loan repayments; it might mean games, puzzles, or community features. First, decide what enhances the customer experience, then decide what you can buy off the shelf from a third-party provider and what needs to be built from scratch.

Most standard stuff can be bought or even just rented from a large number of third parties. Save your project money for interactive content that is very, very customized to your business and your customers. A game that allows "fantasy shopping" could be a good idea, as it keeps the customers with you, or a fully functional "banking dashboard," which allows the customer to manage his wealth interactively, smoothly, and stylishly, could also be worth the investment.

The next level of interactivity is the expert system or CBR (case based reasoning) agent that helps the customer by organizing information in a more intelligent way and allowing the customer to ask his questions using natural language. Probably the best-known version of this technology among customers is provided by ask.com on its own website and also to businesses that are keen to improve the efficiency of their support beyond a simple list of frequently asked questions (FAQs).

There are also examples where CBR technology is given a human face so that the illusion of intelligence is increased. The danger with this is that the technology is rarely human enough to meet the expectations that such images give to customers. The cute, cartoon butler at ask.com avoids suggesting that the answers are coming from a real person. It is important to make clear when people are involved and when the customer is dealing with just a relatively smart machine.

Remember that such systems need to be filled up with sufficiently useful information to answer most of the questions that are asked. This information also needs to be kept up to date and tested for accuracy. The team building the system for you will often throw some data in there to complete the project, but cannot maintain and extend it. Instead, turn to the two groups of people who really care about the answers to the questions:

- let customers rate how useful the information provided is;
- let the people who work for the business be responsible for changing and improving the answers that are given.

Next up is a basic split between interaction that is instant and interaction that is delayed.

> ❝ The **online** customer is not really one who likes writing letters. Such **primitive methods** offend him and they should have the same **effect** on you. ❞

The online customer is not really one who likes writing letters that have to use up any of that precious printer ink or require him to do anything like putting a stamp on a letter. Such primitive methods offend him and they should have the same effect on you. Physical paper communication is more costly for you to receive, distribute, store, and reply. If you want to reply to bulk paper mail then it may be worth investigating scanning and barcoding technology that allows the paper to be tracked electronically. It is in your interest to encourage the customer to use an electronic medium while not forcing him to by neglecting to publish the postal address that will only irritate the letter writers and make the rest feel more uncomfortable.

E-mail is a lot less expensive but unfortunately too often it is treated just like, or worse than, paper mail by businesses that receive it. Let me make it clear. You are going to need an e-mail management system if you sell or service anything with more than a few thousand customers. People who expect rapid responses send e-mail and you are in a position to respond rapidly so get it together! Not having a service standard for replying to e-mails is appalling and even the typical 48-hour turnaround time is not impressive.

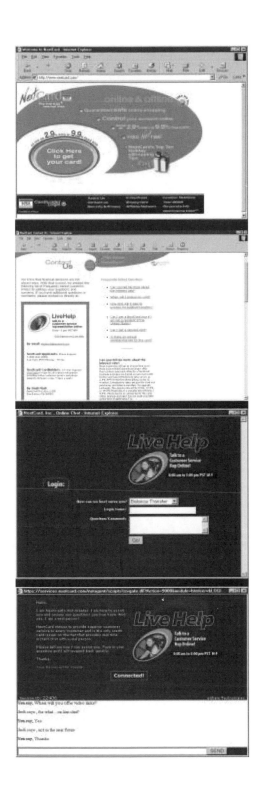

FIGURE 7.3

Live (text message) Help.

A typical e-mail management system works at the side of standard e-mail facilities. All e-mails addressed to the "business" are first stored in a general business in box, just as general postal letters would arrive first to a general business mail room. The e-mail management system then takes a look at the contents of the in box and starts to apply preconfigured rules to them. These rules look at the subject box and the contents of the e-mail before deciding whether they can forward them to particular members of the business or send an automated reply based on a set of standard replies.

When you start e-mail management, it's vital to focus on the rules of that management so that they can cope intelligently and comprehensively with both known requests and exceptions. Make sure that it is clear whether e-mail is being answered by a real person or an automated system. Ensure that the customer cannot end up in a loop of automated answers with no way of communicating with a real person. Test it and test it again, continually, or you will not know if the exceptions or the rules work to anyone's advantage.

> **" Ensure** that the customer cannot end up in a loop of **automated** answers with no way of **communicating** with a real person. Test it and **test it** again **"**

Many online customers will prefer instant interaction. They want to talk now, get answers now, be informed now, and be able to complete their transaction now. The first level of such instant help is text chat. This presents a little window into which the customer can type messages and receive them from a real, live person in the business. The success of instant messaging via the web and text messaging via mobile phones as social media should be enough to convince all but the most closeted that this is a viable form of sales and service technology.

To implement instant interaction can be as simple as adding a few lines of code that allow your customers to use third-party technology as a simple add-on service. Make a little more of an investment and you can allow anyone in the organization to answer customer queries from their desktops in real time. Combine it with routing software and each person will only receive queries that are relevant, but try it out with a small team first to give immediate benefit and start the learning process.

To simple text messaging can be added voice chat or video chat. These normally should be added as options once the customer has chosen to text chat. They both require more equipment and faster connections at both the customer's and business' ends of the communication, so it is best to ensure that all is going well before trying something more complex and expensive.

Finally, the interaction may allow for appointment-making in the real world for face-to-face interaction. This is almost always more expensive and time-consuming, for both customer and business, but can be an effective way of securing business or solving problems that would escalate without the press-the-flesh proximity.

Beware! Appointment-making involves coordinating with electronic organizers and room management systems. You need to check that the right person is available and ensure that there is somewhere for the meeting to take place at a time that the customer can attend. This may be necessary in real time at a variety of different sites. It is entirely feasible and has worked well for some experiences, but the complexities involved should not be taken lightly. Sometimes it will be better to simplify things by just sending an e-mail to the person who needs to attend the appointment that puts him in touch with the customer directly. Weigh the benefits carefully in the short term, but put such a system on the "must haves" for the medium to long term if you make a lot of face-to-face appointments.

Selling technology – banners, offers, personalization, and campaigns

> The key point to consider is that the electronic technology should not be thought of as the end, but rather a means to an end. The technology should be used, then, to mirror the actions of a best salesperson.
> LESTER WANNINGER, CHERI ANDERSON, AND ROBERT HANSEN, "DESIGNING SERVICESCAPES FOR ELECTRONIC COMMERCE: AN EVOLUTIONARY APPROACH," CARLSON-SCHOOL OF MANAGEMENT AND UNIVERSITY OF MINNESOTA

Gotta sell! It's the business of attracting customers to what they want and is a mixture of hitting the right messages to explain why they should buy what you are offering and how to find out what they want so that you can offer it to them.

Advertising is just one way of attracting the customer's attention and relies on the electronic image or "banner" that is hyperlinked to the place that you would like your customer to move to as the next stage in the sales process. At the same time, the banner should be capable of recording interest in it (so you know which adverts were most effective) and transporting the customer to information that directly follows up on what attracted the customer to click in the first place.

Once you have the customer on your site, you can use personalization technology to make offers based on what they have previously bought or looked at or any additional details you know about them. The best-known example of this at work are the "if you liked this, then look at this" lists available at Amazon.

Don't expect the tool that you buy to do all the work, regardless of how it is sold to you! This personalization stuff requires effort in deciding when and where and what the customer will be offered. Use it in conjunction with tracking technology to place offers where they will encourage customers to pursue paths into your electronic experience that are most profitable.

> **❝ Don't expect the tool that you buy to do all the work, regardless of how it is sold to you! This personalization stuff requires effort. ❞**

The other way of making additional offers to your customers and potential customers is to send it via e-mail. First, of course, you will need their e-mail addresses. These can be obtained without their consent by using technology to find them while they are browsing, but this is very unpopular, unproductive, and sometimes against the law. You could buy or rent e-mail addresses, but be careful that they come from a trusted source and customers have really agreed to receive marketing e-mail.

Usually you will capture the e-mail as part of a registration process for a newsletter, contest, or purchase. This naturally improves the chances that the customer is interested before you bother them with additional offers. Ensuring that you have information about how the e-mail has been captured, at what point, looking at what kinds of products, and then using it to make the offer more relevant is good for you and the customer. This demands thinking, considerable technical skills, and preparation. Don't believe anyone who says it will be easy.

Buying technology – carts, trolleys, and stuff like that

Why is it so hard to buy? It doesn't make sense to get the customer all primed to buy with all that selling guile and supportive technology, then make it difficult for the customer to pay you. Some of this is as simple as ensuring that the option to buy is clearly available at every stage of the experience. It also means that the customer should be able to move from wanting to buy to completing the purchase as rapidly as possible, before he changes his mind, before he runs out of time, before he loses all patience and the desire to live.

> ❝ The **customer** should be able to move from wanting to buy to **completing** the **purchase** as rapidly as possible, before he changes his mind, before **he loses** all patience and the **desire** to live. ❞

To avoid death by shopping, bring in technology to make life easier for your wannabe customers. It is possible for the technology to allow one-click shopping. This is a major advantage to the customer and the business, so much so that Amazon tried unsuccessfully to patent the one-click process to prevent rivals, particularly Barnes & Noble from emulating it.

For one-click to work, the customer has to fill in billing information the first time he purchases something and, from then on, merely has to allow himself to be identified by logging on or, preferably, by letting an electronic tag or cookie be left on his own computer that can identify him without logging on.

You could also encourage your customers to make use of software that keeps all personal details safe and then fills in electronic details automatically to save time and effort. Some of these even allow the customer's credit card details to remain private and still allow payment to be made.

Tracking technology – what are they doing out there?

Your business needs to be able to see through a customer's eyes, and technology tools that can help with this objective are rapidly improving. You can measure how many visits are made to each page or how many clicks are made to each link on a page, but, on its own, this information is incomplete and potentially very misleading. A new breed of tool can allow browsing of your website, as a typical customer would do, with the help of algorithms that mimic human behavior. Both require several weeks of customization to ensure that they are reporting what you need to know in a way that you can utilize.

Think of...

- Vividence
- BMC
- Web criteria.

Alternatively, you can use technology that allows customer panels to test your electronic experience by using special browsers that trace the path that is used through the site and the customers' perceptions of it. The combined data can allow you to highlight the most and least profitable paths through the site and who is using the site and why. Such tools can also be used to compare your electronic experience with your competitor's so that your experience is judged on relative competitive measures rather than simply what web designers or senior managers think looks good.

Technology and trends: the world and the tools keep changing

Charles H. Duell, then director of the United States' Patent Office quit his job in 1888 declaring that, "everything that can be invented has been invented." Aren't you glad that he was so very wrong and that, it appears, the future holds no limitations, the e-customer has Star Trek expectations, and one of these days he will have everything that he ever dreamed of?

Read on and then apply the trends to the life needs, style, and desires of your customers. It is possible to understand what they will seek in each new technology innovation and then ensure that it is used to promote the effectiveness of the electronic experience and resulting profitable relationship.

Avoid the repeated failure of large telecommunications businesses to predict what real customers will use the technologies for, technologies their own labs have often created. In the early 1990s, they missed the internet boom (often trying to slow it down) and invested instead in interactive television. Then there was significant investment in simplified internet content via mobile phones, but an underestimation of the rapidity with which European customers would adopt text messaging. In the UK and Germany, messages sent by customers recently exceeded a billion a month. Focusing on TV and the mobile internet was based on a belief that customers would buy access to entertainment and information. The success of mobile phones, e-mail, and instant messaging reveals the truth that people seek connectivity to other people over generic content.

Tech trend 1: transparency, spying, anonymity, and compatibility

Once information is digital, its ability to be manipulated, duplicated, and shared increases. It is simultaneously harder to control and harder to hide. The fantasy of anonymity has proved illusory for many and the greatest hope of the secretive is that the sheer amount of information content and traffic will make their individual contribution and communication less likely to attract the attention of the inquisitive.

Rumour, gossip, and secrets hit the electronic world first and, as they are electronic, the "dirt" travels faster, lasts longer, and is easier to find. This has happened in chat rooms, bulletin boards, and news sites such as register.co.uk that thrive on anonymous tips. It is starting to be formalized with the introduction of services such as repcheck.com, a US site that is creating a massive database of people's reputations based on information from colleagues, associates, and employers. Information is submitted via ratings for character traits such as trustworthiness, honesty, and compassion. Anyone with an interest can logon to the free site and read the entries to obtain a better idea of a person's personality.

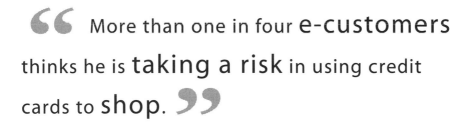

More than one in four e-customers thinks he is taking a risk in using credit cards to shop.

At present, more than one in four e-customers thinks he is taking a risk in using credit cards to shop. The security worries are even greater among those who choose not to shop online. In reality, it's no more risky than handing over a credit card in a restaurant or putting it down to pay for groceries at the checkout, but the perception of the risk is higher, even when the customer is willing to take that risk. The discomfort of not really knowing how these "machines" are using or securing the credit card information is obvious and it is an obstacle to full take-up of e-commerce.

Impact on the customer experience

Trust will have to be maintained as part of the customer experience or customers will stop allowing their data to be used, with the resulting impact that personalization technologies will be unable to provide benefit to the customer or the business.

For businesses, the most effective response to this curious mixture of secrecy and transparency should be don't have any damaging secrets and do act continually as if the customer knew everything already. Encourage customers to ask public questions and make comments. Publish the responses to public questions and assume that the details of private replies may be made public.

Impact on customer behavior

Customers will feel at once more and less secure as a result of these trends. Their reaction will be dependent in large part on their motivations and the ways in which they perceive the involvement of authority. Is the presence of law enforcement officers, cops, or gendarmes on the street corner a comforting source of security or a worrying manifestation of intrusive state control?

As they learn that their data can be kept "safe" but that their actions are not anonymous, they will be more likely to spend less time doing what they would not like to be revealed and more time with trusted businesses that really can keep their data (and actions) private.

Tech trend 2: everything that is wired will become wireless

I am writing this section of the book in bed via a wireless connection to the local area network set up to connect all the computers in my home that is, in turn, connected, via the internet, to all the computers in my office (and the world). As I sit here, I am using wireless headphones to listen to my music system. When I travel, mobile, cellular technology allows me to browse the web, pick up e-mail, listen to digital music and receive directions in real time as I walk or drive. Did I mention that it just happens to let me take phone calls as well?

Imagine, on behalf of your customers, what this technology can do for the experience.

Take, for example, the Sheetz convenience store chain in Altoona, Pennsylvania. The company was an early technology adopter – it was the first convenience chain to adopt satellite credit card authorization at its petrol pumps and was quick to have touch screen order kiosks in its stores. Now the company is exploring the use of wireless or RF (radio frequency) technology by giving its customers a free personal digital assistant, preloaded with the company's software. In this way, the customer becomes permanently bonded with the Sheetz online customer experience. He is more likely to do things like order a sandwich from the store's sandwich ordering machine with a set time for collection or use the PDA to pay at the fuel pumps or inside the store. In the words of the company CEO, Stanton Sheetz, "I've saved the customers' time and I've saved myself time."[2] And that is exactly how to use wireless technology.

In Helsinki, people can use their mobile phones to get soft drinks from vending machines, buy gas, select records on a jukebox or pay for time on parking meters. Bluetooth chips in the latest phones allow them to "talk" to short-range radio transceivers placed in vending machines or at checkouts. Instead of racking up charges to the credit card, people are adding them to the monthly phone bill, with the mobile phone working as a virtual wallet.[3]

Even the power source is becoming wireless. As fuel cell technologies improve, the necessity to continually remember to recharge and the frequent loss of power at inconvenient times will be reduced and eventually removed. Businesses of the likes of Manhattan Scientifics and Motorola are miniaturizing the fuel cell technology developed to create emissions-free vehicles to comply with the legislation of markets, including California. Expect mobile phones and PDAs with six-month battery lives by the end of 2002.

Impact on the customer experience

The result will be an increased need for simplicity and context enhancement. Location increases in importance to the experience and the e-customer learns that he can treat the device like an extension of his body – it doesn't need recharging and it doesn't need wires to provide him with the services, information, and interaction that he requires, whenever he requires it. There is, however, a big question mark over the ability of the telecommunications businesses to create the relationship that they are naturally well placed to exploit.

The value of the early mobile internet is in delivering small amounts of information when the customer is on the move by knowing via your phone exactly where you are and by helping you to find the nearest restaurant, gas station or whatever. Delivering information that is location-specific, time-sensitive, or allows the customer to reach a decision while out that he would otherwise have not been able to make is valuable. Such information includes the latest stock quotes or the football results.

66 Delivering **information** that is **location-specific**, time-sensitive, or allows the customer to reach a **decision** while out that he would **otherwise** have not been able to make is **valuable**. 99

The desire of customers to experience a wire-free existence has already led to volunteer movements setting up free wireless networks in public places in an effort to remove the constraints to interconnection and information. Doesn't the following report tell you something about the way your experience could surround and enfold willing customers?

> In parts of San Francisco's Presidio, a former military base turned vast park, you can sit on a bench and surf wirelessly thanks to Brewster Kahle, a high-tech entrepreneur and founder of SFLan, an experimental internet service provider. He and his friends have put up antennae on several buildings nearby. SFLan and similar efforts such as Consume.net (London), Guerrilla.net (Cambridge, Massachusetts), and Seattle Wireless are reminiscent of the open source movement, whose members contribute to free software such as the operating system Linux. Mr Kahle hopes that his initiative will grow into a citywide wireless LAN (local area network) "from anarchistic cooperation" – meaning an army of volunteers putting up radio beacons on their rooftops.[4]

Impact on customer behavior

There will be strong links between the uptake in wireless devices and the desire of customers to be free. This strong instinct to remove constraints will be frustrated by any complication between the offer and the delivery. Such disappointment will lead to savagely critical reactions to devices that fail to meet expectations. This has already been the case with Bluetooth where reactions have not been favorable to early devices that are too heavy, clunky, and complex.

Expect to see high emotional attachment to the devices. Why? Because they are extensions of the body, a form of bionic enhancement, and people feel strongly about their own bodies and love anything that enhances their abilities without too much difficulty. Having such a device go wrong will provoke emotions similar to those experienced when a person's automobile breaks down or his pet cat falls ill.

The world has been accused of suffering from PDA fever,[5] with the device even being immortalized in a 14 ft-wide painting, "Analysis," by Tom Kemp, composed entirely of a hieroglyphic arrangement of images created on a dull silver Palm Vx. This acceptance of the PDA into popular and artistic culture will continue as it is consciously or subconsciously praised as an extension of the human entity.

Tech trend 3: bigger pipes and concentrated water

There is too much bandwidth in the networks of the world's telecommunications companies and too little in the homes and lives of the customer. It's not that there is a lack of desire on the part of customers for an increase in speed, but the costs and complexities involved are too great and the content too limited.

At the same time, compression and streaming technologies continue to improve radically so that they can transmit better and better pictures, sound, and even more data over the same bandwidth. Likely result? Massive reduction in the real cost of high bandwidth services will lead to huge increases in high bandwidth internet access.

Impact on the customer experience

Any customer who has experienced high-speed access could not be easily dragged back to the electronic experience via a 56K modem. The wait for graphics, the dislike of Flash animation, the frustration with slow-loading intelligent forms all fade away as the customer is able to experience it all as the designer probably first saw it on the corporate network. The use of video and animation will increase, as will customer acceptance of it, even in situations where speed of service is important. This will promote their use to deliver, often significant, advantages.

It is to be hoped that the advertising for electronic experiences will become more inventive with the added power on offer. The boring old banner ad[6] has been with customers since at least 1996 and still accounts for the vast majority of web advertising. With bigger pipes and improved compression, the adverts can become multimedia extravaganzas that make some customers say – as they sometimes do about television – that the advertising is better than the content hosting the advert. If the advert isn't more fun, more personal, and more pertinent than his current surroundings, the customer is not very likely to leave where he is for your place is he?

> ❝ If the **advert** isn't more fun, more personal, and more **pertinent** than his current **surroundings**, the customer is not very likely to leave where **he is for your place** is he? ❞

Impact on customer behavior

The speed increases will open up the range of what is possible to the customer. His potential impact increases and he will be bolder in sharing large files, including video, photos, and audio. Slow and fast access groups will emerge that will regularly forget the preferences of the other group. Fast customers will be disappointed when dealing with businesses that still support slow access customers, who, in turn, will become irritated with the large file attachments and graphic-heavy experiences that they are meant to be enjoying.

It will also change what the customer uses his or her mobile phone for. The next time he upgrades his phone, he may well find that high-speed mobile access is built into the hardware and, within a couple of years, the cost of the high-speed services will decrease. With the massive speed increase, we will find many more than the current 4 or 5 percent using their phones to surf the internet – eventually reaching the 40 percent who use them to receive or send text messages, or even the 70 percent who use them to make calls.[7] The technology is coming, and when it gets fun, expect customers to start playing.

66 The **technology** is coming, and when it gets fun, expect **customers** to start **playing.** 99

Tech trend 4: humanization of technology

The electronic experience has not yet captivated the majority of the Western world's population. The traditional interface of serious keyboard and screen was designed by the technologically apt for their own use, but is a serious hindrance to acceptance for the rest of humanity. Efforts continue to humanize the technology that remains so that the non-technological market will be loved, and comforted, and cajoled, into the loving arms of the experience. As the technology reaches out to those who want its advantages but have neither love nor aptitude for the technology itself in a raw form, the traditional interface of keyboard and screen will sit alongside interfaces that have greater mass acceptance.

66 Efforts **continue** to humanize the **technology** that remains so that the non-technological market will **be loved**, and comforted, and **cajoled**, into the loving arms of the **experience.** 99

In Japan, robotic animals have made a remarkably successful entry into the hearts and homes of the middle aged. Sony was the innovator once again and launched the original AIBO robotic dog in 1999. It was expensive, but still attracted pent-up demand for a more natural, friendly interface. As a range, AIBO has already clocked up 175,000 sales to people who want company and people who like their technology to be hidden from view.

The humanization and hiding of technology is a clear trend in the history of all technologies, particularly computing. The original inventors of these technologies enjoy and understand the innovation, the science, and the complexities for what they are. They have no desire or need to cover them up. The early adopters are also largely able and willing to deal with the raw technology and enjoy fixing, building, playing with it for its own sake. They may fight any movement towards usability that, in their perception, dumbs down the technology. It happened with the transition from DOS to Windows and from Windows 98 to the even friendlier Windows XP.

The internet has been no exception to this trend, we saw the early computer scientists happy with the text-only interface and Boolean search engines. Since then, the creation of the hypertext interface of the web, the addition of graphical elements, and feature after feature have made the internet attractive to the hundreds of millions who are now online. Some of those find themselves being defensive about the future evolution because appealing to the mass market will make the web less exclusive. For business itself, however, it will be important to see this trend clearly, to ride it, and even push it forward. This trend will open the market and free up the spending that is just waiting to start.

Example

AOL has seldom been viewed as the friend of the "serious web user" and complaints about it are common in chat rooms everywhere. Its desire to make the web into a friendly place devoid of mystery but full of Disney-like goodness and light has made it friends in all the right places in growing numbers. Its use of the AOL lady is inspired, and every step of the AOL experience is designed to make the next step understandable and accessible. They have reduced the brainpower and technical aptitude needed to merely survive online. Some may feel unhappy that the bar has been lowered, but not the increasing millions who are willing to pay AOL every month for access to this integrated world.

The anonymity is also being stripped away with the addition of live, personal help on web pages. Customers can type, speak, and wave to real people any time that they need help. Such human assistance goes against the anti-human cost-cutting approach to e-commerce that was so prevalent in the late 1990s, but goes to the heart of making the customer more comfortable, less scared, and more willing to buy.

The quotient of humanity in artificial intelligence will also continue to grow. Computers will not just be expected to get to a given calculation efficiently but also learn to become playful, interact with humor and sensitivity. Virtual helpers across all channels will give a human face to prewritten text and computer-generated responses. Expect to see celebrity faces representing brands online as the full-time face of customer sales and service, not merely as part of a poster or TV advertising campaign.

Take as an example, the 3-D character from Stratumsoft. She recognizes human speech and can answer questions in full sentences. She can remember information about everyone who visits the site and also procure valuable marketing data by asking people about products they have bought previously. Emma can also suggest products to accompany those that the customer has already chosen, such as offering a handbag that matches the expensive shoes the customer has already bought.

It is entirely possible (beware!) to create increased antipathy toward technology that pretends to be human in some way but displays only the more irritating characteristics of our fellows. Think of the general dislike for "Clippy," the animated helper provided in Microsoft Office. It is found to be intrusive by many, who feel he is much like some demented sales assistant, overanxiously and clumsily pushing into their personal space. This was recognized by Microsoft in its $30 million advertising campaign featuring the mock laying off[8] of the long-serving paper-clip. This has shown us that customers can respond emotionally to such characters, but not necessarily as we would like.

Despite these setbacks, little by little, some customers may decide to purchase software that works the internet using artificial intelligence to shop for what they want. This software will adapt rapidly to the needs of just one customer. It will be a "one to many" relationship (rather than "one to one") that learns the needs and preferences of just one customer, its master, and understands the mechanics of many commercial websites.

Some commentators have argued that the coming of personal shoppers will ultimately mean that branding fades in importance compared to the experience. Take, for example, the view of Alan Meckler, CEO of internet.com, who argues:

> There are going to be a series of services and intelligent agents and search bots that people will have, almost like their own dog, that will literally go out and find the information they want. That's why brand isn't going to be important. Ultimately customer service satisfaction for an e-commerce site would be important, but the customers' actual knowledge of the name wouldn't be that important. That's why you should have the best content. The bot will find the best content. If I'm just 50 percent right, and I believe I'm more than 50 percent right, that's further indication of why all the money that's being spent on so-called brand is valueless.[9]

Is Meckler at least 50 percent right? The notion of brand has remained with customers for as long as they have had more than one choice. It is simply the mark that distinguishes one product from another, based on trust, image, past experience, style, and recommendations. Faced with more choices than ever, how will the customer make his decisions? What will he do when faced with a choice of which intelligent agent to use? Brand cannot afford to be superficial – ultimately, it will have to mean something substantial – but it and the experience itself will still determine the customer's choices and purchasing decisions.

Impact on the customer experience

The best experiences will sparkle with humor and humanity. People will be free to communicate in the language, vocabulary, and pace that suits them, and many will not need to interact with a computer via a keyboard or even a remote control in order to communicate.

The best experiences will sparkle with humor and humanity.

There will still be many, many, bad experiences, and they will stand out as dramatically worse than those that include artificial intelligence, virtual personalities, robots, and real, living people as integrated parts of the complete experience.

Impact on customer behavior

Customers will approach the electronic interface and be less conscious of it being a machine. They will begin to act as they would with a real person, for as long as it manages to support the conceit that it is human. This will mean more patience, not less, as a relationship starts to build – to err is human, but an error is the machine's fault.

Tech trend 5: blurring of boundaries between real and virtual worlds

Technology will edge towards a world where electronic tools enhance reality and real-world services and people enhance electronic worlds. Computers and their interfaces will metamorphose and appear in forms that are synonymous with the pre-internet real world.

Paper – the most traditional of information technologies – is undergoing a radical overhaul that will confound usual divisions.

One such example can be found at Anoto, a Swedish company launched in 2000 by Christer Fahraeus to transform sheets of paper into a new frontend for the internet. Anoto's vision is to provide the means to jot down messages on paper that become digitized and capable of being sent and manipulated, just as if they were being typed using a computer.

To send a message, you'll simply put a mark in a box for "Send as e-mail" or "Send as fax" that's printed on the corner of the paper. Marking other boxes will route your message to pagers or mobile phones. A single scribbled note can trigger a cascade of networked events – jotting down a lunch date in your day planner could update your laptop and fire off an e-mail to your assistant.[10]

The very cloth that we surround our bodies with is being digitized and is already used to provide keyboards that can be wrapped up or washed along with your socks. Displays are in the early stages of development, but, even now, simple forms can be created that are rather like the liquid crystal displays (LCD) of the 1970s. It seems unlikely that we will have to wait another 30 years for them to evolve to reach sophisticated levels of clarity and color.

Rolltronics, a California-based company, is developing the ability to print computer components on to thin films of plastic. Such roll-to-roll manufacturing (winding a continuous roll of flexible materials) techniques applied to the production of computers would result in a cheap and a faster way to make electronic devices. More importantly, it will be one more way that computers will become embedded, literally, in the materials that surround us.

The PC still holds many advantages, with its local, private processing power and its ability to keep up with the pace of innovation on the internet. The time will come, however, relentlessly, where varying levels of internet access are built into top-of-the-range appliances and gadgets that have a brand/service/loyalty tie-in, such as the device that allowed customers to order directly from a replica, wired, plastic pizza. The push towards wireless technology will allow networks without cables and powerful PCs to be hidden away as an information furnace,[11] providing local power and connectivity to the wide variety of wireless devices in the home.

Already, a technology enthusiast can add a remote control management system for all appliances and light switches simply by plugging his PC into a specialized socket and then into the electricity supply. Once plugged in, the PC is able to communicate with each appliance in the home via the home electricity cabling.

At the same time, the legal and institutional frameworks of the real world will be extended via technology until they are completely identical in the virtual world. This exchange will also extend in the other direction so that the virtual world "infects" the real world with many elements of its style, culture, and behavior.

Impact on the customer experience

What exactly happens when your customer can interact with your electronic experience using a waterproof digital paperback in the bath? Go jogging in clothes that read heart rate, play favorite music, and provide a permanent link to security services, if there should be a need to call on them? Use the mobile phone that is built into his credit card to speak with customer services representatives at the bank? The relationship will become more personal and the experience that is desired will be delivered.

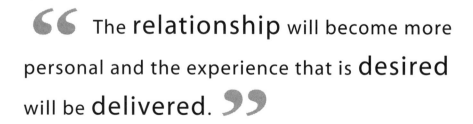

66 The **relationship** will become more personal and the experience that is **desired** will be **delivered.** 99

Impact on customer behavior

Customers will turn more automatically to electronic experiences for help as they will surround them. They will also find it harder to distinguish between what happens in the real and virtual worlds. Eventually, this will allow sophisticated businesses to stay permanently at the customer's side, offering advice and providing services that are location- and context-sensitive.

Tech trend 6: games get serious

People (and would-be customers) go online seeking fun and, at some point while online, begin yearning after serious fulfilment. On the web, commercial sites, or their creators, have understood that games are popular and have added them to their features. These have tended to be added to the side of the site rather than being integral parts of the design. This can leave an unhelpful imbalance or what we term "game lurch," where customer attention is dragged over to the game to the detriment of the commercial offer. When he stops playing, he will turn back to the rest of the site and find that it fails to keep his attention. The result is a rapid exit.

The history of electronic game development gives the experience creator many insights into the future natural development of electronic customer experiences. From the version of tic tac-toe (noughts and crosses) developed on one of the earliest electronic computers, to the simple tennis games on early consoles, to the multiplayer, multicolor games of the moment. One of the most addictive has been Counter-Strike, the popular first-person genre game that allows teams to play together against other teams over the internet in a very social, strategic, brain-involved process. It is the combination of social fulfilment with pure entertainment that encourages players to stay longer and competes more successfully with the real world.

In the real world, the trend is continuing with the development of increasingly extreme experiences in theme parks throughout the world. One of the leaders in what we could call the "adrenaline industry" is Stan Checketts, whose business, S&S Power, competes for the attention of customers and the amusement ride industry. His latest project is the Thrust Air – a rollercoaster that looks like a big exclamation mark. The customer goes up vertically, the train makes a 180-degree turn over the top, and comes vertically down at an incredible speed. The whole ride delivers a unique experience that lasts just 45 seconds. In the words of one of its customers, Robert Coker from thrillride.com, "It's miraculous, incredibly smooth, while all the more remarkable for being just unbelievably violent."[12]

Impact on the customer experience

The best electronic experiences when, for example, paying money into the bank or ordering a new car will be as cleverly thought out and plotted as a multiplayer first-person gaming environment. They will be reviewed as games or films are now in consumer magazines with scores out of ten, star-ranking systems, and percentage scores based almost entirely on subjective judgements as to the enjoyment of the experience.

> ❝ The best **electronic** experiences will be as **cleverly thought** out and plotted as a multiplayer **first-person** gaming environment. ❞

Some of those who think that they can get away with substandard electronic experiences will manage to scrape by, but the future belongs to those who can raise the standard to deliver experiences that make the customer want to tell his family and boast of his membership to friends and colleagues. The branded experience delivered to the customer's enjoyment and satisfaction will be a necessary part of the competitive armory for a consumer-facing business of any size.

Impact on customer behavior

As the electronic experience is more consistently rich, entertaining, and intuitive, the customer will more happily spend his time becoming informed, tell your business what he wants from you, and conducting his financial business with you.

Tech trend 7: distributed computing, virtual grids, and peer-to-peer networking

Letting your customers talk directly to each other, via peer-to-peer networking, and utilizing the power of distributed computing, via virtual grids, are key features of the future. They both start with a networked mindset where the personal computers at either side of the network are more effectively used to power the interaction. Analysts, investors, and technologists (new and old) have shown immense interest (even excitement) in the possibilities for distributed computing in all its guises.

First, a closer look at peer-to-peer networking (P2P), best known to the wider public in its primitive Napster manifestation, which allows the direct exchange of services or data between individual customers' computers, with each peer in the network contributing resources such as storage or processing power to the overall aims of the software. In the case of Napster, this meant that the computers of all those who used the software became, in effect, one giant database of music accessible to anyone else on the network.

A refinement of the principles described above gives the world grid computing. This collects together wasted or spare computing power from each computer on the network and uses the combined power to perform tasks that can ordinarily only be completed by super-computers. Idle computing power on a corporate network can be applied to tasks that require massive calculations, such as film animation or chemical modeling. Idle computing power can also be sold to those who need it by newly opened grid computing exchange companies.

The third part of distributed computing involves the changes that are being made to infrastructure and architecture to encourage the break-up of networks into smaller application-specific parts, with software becoming more intelligent, servers becoming smaller, and the internet transforming into a granular network based on specialized, interacting components rather than documents. All the biggest players are working on this as the future of computing, most notably Microsoft with its .NET initiative, as well as Sun, Intel, and Cisco.

Impact on the customer experience

It started with a network and this trend is simply an enhanced continuation. More and more of the really powerful killer benefits will come from being connected to a network. Some predict that it will transform the internet in the same way the web hyperlink metaphor did from 1989 to the present day.

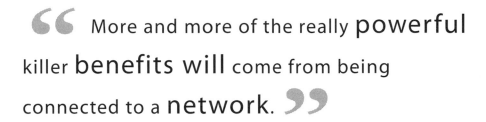

More and more of the really powerful killer benefits will come from being connected to a network.

The software that provides the experience will involve interactions between many machines connected via the internet. Each machine will provide services to the others in the network, such as credit card authentication, airline reservations or English–French translation. These will be paid for on a subscription or a "pay as you go" basis instead of buying a complete package and then deciding whether or not to buy an enhanced model.

Impact on customer behavior

Once the customer experiences the power of Napster, he will be hooked on immediacy and no longer wonder what advantages the electronic medium holds. It's quite a thrill, that first search and downloading of music, and one that customers wanted to share with more than 40 million of their fellow humans, friends, and family. Only the imposition of subscription fees will allow us to see how much the experience has also accustomed them to the heady nectar of "FREE."

Of course, it goes far beyond sharing music and may end up building a stable, adaptive, flexible electronic experience around each individual customer and his computer. It may bring the software, information, and services to his desktop rather than forcing him to go and look for it. Specialized peer-to-peer software may intelligently seek out what the customer wants and, at the same time, reduce the likelihood of system crashes and problems.

Tech trend 8: WYDIWYG and accelerated acceleration

Mass customization – predicted for the past 15 years – promises to deliver customized products to every customer who wants them. The ultimate vision is of sophisticated factories wired into systems that allow the customer to pick from thousands of different possibilities to produce a design for exactly the kind of product that he wants to buy – What You Dream Is What You Get, hence WYDIWYG.

Elsewhere, the technology used in rapid prototyping (RP) machines has developed to the point that it will be used to produce individualized products. Already the customer can buy hearing aids that match his ears, racing drivers have personalized steering wheels, and, in the future, sufficient demand will allow any material to be used to create products one slice at a time. Step by step, over the next 20 years, these technologies will move from the factory, to the specialized high street bureau, to the desktop.

Not only is improvement continuing, but the pace of improvement is increasing. For customers, this acceleration of innovation appears to be the antidote for impatience. Everything gets better before you expect it to!

> **❝ Acceleration** of innovation appears to be the antidote for impatience. **Everything** gets better before you **expect** it to! **❞**

The challenge for customers will be to decide when to invest in this ever-changing world and how to choose between the options. For your business, it will become difficult to ever be certain that anything you have discounted as impossible stays impossible. Worse, you cannot be certain that your rivals will not launch the previously impossible, tomorrow.

Your competitors will focus their communication of new "impossible" innovations on customers rather than you. As a result, you can be in the worst place to know about the state-of-the-art this or state-of-the-art that, far, far worse than are customers. Answer? Get in among your customers and make sure that they tell you (every day) what they want in the future, what is possible now, and what they deem to be essential already. They can tell you if they are on your side. Also, ensure that you are a devoted customer of your competitors – be an enthusiastic buyer at the same time as being a seller and creator.

Impact on the customer experience

> **❝** The **ability** of the organization to push technology to the **limits for** the good of its customers will develop **the skills** and aptitudes most **likely to** cope with the unknown. **❞**

The whole point of accelerated acceleration is that there is no way of knowing what the future will bring, such is the pace of change. So, what does that mean for the customer experience? The ability of the organization to push technology to the limits for the good of its customers will develop the skills and aptitudes most likely to cope with the unknown. It will end up being as good as the vision of the people who determine what the offer should look like. Your business will have to guide the customer so that he continues to see clearly what he should buy and when he should buy it. Timing of decisions will become as important as the purchase itself. Appeal to the sophisticate, but also to the lover of simplicity who does not want to (and cannot) cope with so many choices. Don't let complexity get in the way of a purchase!

Impact on customer behavior

When customers start to believe that everything they could possibly want is just around the corner, expect them to be increasingly unimpressed with what you offer to them, sometimes paralyzed by the possibility of obsolescence, and confused by the level of choices on offer.

If you get it right, there is little reason for the customer to leave for anyone else because you are able to produce exactly what he dreams of as rapidly as he could possibly want it. The ability to guide and advise will become as important as the level of choice itself.

Tech trend 9: interactivity becomes the universal ingredient

Democracy, game shows, banking, medicine, will all throw in interactivity as the enhancement of choice. There are two-way communications facilities built into television, personal computers, personal digital assistants, mobile phones, kiosks, ATMs, and anything else electronic.

New kiosks have been developed that will allow US voters (including those in the state of Florida, which was pivotal to the last US election) to vote electronically in the 2008 elections before reviewing their vote on a printed piece of paper. Enhanced television has shown the way by including buttons to press within much of its broadcasting. For first-time customers, it is a novelty that they either love or cannot figure out how to use. Later, they begin to take it for granted and assimilate it into the accepted benefits of the channel.

The interactive technology continues to become more sophisticated. Take for example, the simple hyperlink that became a straightforward banner advertisement that became a complete video game, played online, that linked the customer to a range of special offers on products of his choice while simultaneously tracking his movements, preferences, and reporting them back to the business that paid for the advertising. Now that's interactive for you!

The development of the XFL format combines the interactivity of the web with the carnival of TV wrestling and competitiveness of American football. It claims a style of football that is rougher, tougher, quicker-paced and more entertaining. Microphones will be everywhere, even on individual players and in the locker room – viewers will be able to hear what the coach has to say to the players at halftime.[13] It's just one more experiment into hybrid interactivity for the customer's benefit, designed to appeal to the customer at every level. It goes where some traditional sports fear to tread, knowing that many customers care more about the interactivity of the "experience" than the competitiveness of the "sport." It gets customers involved, behind the scenes, and that's what they want, whether XFL works or not.

Digital devices are built to connect, they are built to interact, and are fundamentally different – not the same as the products that they seem most to resemble. A digital radio does not merely deliver better sound quality; it is also expected to deliver additional information, have an internet-like browsing capability featuring graphics and services, and the ability to record and then organize the recordings. They are networked to other devices and provide a depth and breadth of flexibility that is a great attraction to so many customers, including those who purchase such interactivity and then fall into "gadget comas" and can speak of nothing else for days following the purchase. Sometimes, as with DVD players, the coma becomes highly infectious and an epidemic ensues. When something is interactive, it invites interaction, whether it's a toy, tool, or pastime.

Impact on the customer experience

Highly interactive experiences will not necessarily be effective ones. The challenge will be for interactivity to serve some valuable purpose within a logical, useful, consistent structure and flow.

Impact on customer behavior

If your experience does not feature interactive technology, it will stick out as inferior and unattractive to a customer who will increasingly make his decision more rapidly, basing it on an assessment of quality interaction.

Tech trend 10: tough tech turns into Lego brick child's play

The task for experience creators will not be to build every component themselves, but to become masters at understanding the new breed of components available that can provide sophisticated, powerful software at low prices, fast deployment times, and on flexible payment terms. These components will be provided direct from software businesses via middlemen integrators; and as complete and ready-to-use services from applications service providers. These developments are about a year behind schedule as profitable businesses but the technology is there and waiting to be used.

Wherever possible, the smart business will try to avoid building any technology from scratch and using anything proprietary. The more complete, out of a box, open, and standardized your components are, the more time you can spend simplifying and enhancing the experience itself from a stable base. Testing effectiveness is more productive than testing for errors and bugs in experimental software.

Impact on the customer experience

The source of uniqueness will become the effectiveness with which components can be fitted together and customized, rather than the creation of the components themselves. Experiences will have a tendency to become feature-rich and, at the same time, indistinguishable from a thousand other sites.

> **"** Experiences will have a **tendency** to become **feature-rich. "**

Impact on customer behavior

Any website can offer live video, chat rooms, voting facilities, news headlines, mobile phone access, translation facilities, and bulletin boards. The customer will not be impressed by their existence, but by how they are combined and made to interact so that their life objectives and minute-to-minute needs are met effectively.

> **"** The **customer** will not be impressed by their existence, but **by how they** are **combined** and made to interact. **"**

A few last words on technology

The electronic experience is technology, as stated at the start of this chapter. A working knowledge of what the main components do and what they can be used to achieve is vital for anyone who wants to translate experience visions into experience reality.

Trends will increase the technology concentration levels that allow businesses to compete electronically. The differences will grow between the experience leaders and the rest, who will be unable to cope with, or afford, the technology required to deliver rich, loyalty-building, relationship-enhancing experiences. This will not all be self-build, but will still require top-notch technologists and hybrid customer experience designers and builders to select from the best available technologies and fit them together into an architecture that makes them useful and free-flowing for customers. Once in place, the technology has to be opened up to customers and team members so that it can continue to change and adapt, applying the best of human craft, warmth, and ingenuity to the needs, wants, and lifestyles of customers.

As technology becomes everything, expect technology-only businesses to consider crowding more and more commercial space. If they continue to see poor implementations of the technology that they sell to others, then they will find their potential competitive advantage too desirable to resist.

Microsoft now runs one of the most popular portals and one of the most usable travel companies in electronic space. Yahoo! and Lycos both have partnerships with banks and thousands of shops. Why would they stop there? If advertising and technology investment dries up, why wouldn't they extend their strong customer relationships to include more and more delivery of non-technology products and services?

> **The advance of technology will mean that everything that has been considered impossible or unprofitable will become possible and then essential in order to compete.**

The advance of technology will mean that everything that has been considered impossible or unprofitable will become possible and then essential in order to compete. There will be no excuses to offer your customers for lack of service or unusable or unattractive or uninspiring electronic experiences when your competitors are already offering what you claim is not possible. Inward-looking businesses will assume that their best is enough and not notice that the standard has leaped forward. Develop your experience in line with trends and technologies and your experience will remain ahead of the pack. Way cool.

Experience study

Ananova.com "it's your news"

Welcome to the world of the virtual news-reading personality. In this case, she has a green tint to her hair, is available from an offshoot of PA News, and is known as Ananova. She launched her career nearly two years ago with the words "Hello world, here's the news – and this time it's personal" to over 30 million potential customers who saw her debut.

Arriving on her website, the customer will find a clean, mainly white design that focuses on the available news stories and Ananova herself. Prominent are requests for customers to get in touch with the team because it is an "interactive news service." To this end, customers can contact them to share new breaking stories via e-mail, telephone, or fax. It is also possible to send SMS text messages from wherever the customer is, giving Ananova up-to-date exclusives from her very own dedicated, unpaid, news reporters, and even to write if the customer insists on being what the site calls "low tech."

We tried the service on your behalf and, sadly, did not get a response back at the time that this book was published.[14] This was disappointing, although it's possible that, had our e-mail been about the latest scoop, it would have been replied to.

Back to the focus of the experience, Ananova is "turned on" by clicking on the video link. This seemed a little impersonal for a feature that is meant to be "human like" and, indeed, likeable. It is a weakness generally that the site does not build up the character of Ananova as would be done if she were a real person. There are no details about her life, interests, or preferences, and no "personality first" language. Even a link with language along the lines of "Watch and Listen to Ananova" would be more friendly.

There are some efforts to flesh out the character, though. Public appearances by Ananova can be arranged. There are a few anecdotes about fans who have been suitably overenthusiastic, including the Dutch couple that named their first child Ananova and the Valentine cards sent every February 14th. There is mention made of the media appearances that she has made in *Vogue* and on Sky and CNN. However, it is very, very little when one considers the possibilities.

The Ananova experience relies heavily on software from RealPlayer. To watch and interact with Ananova's bulletins, you need a RealPlayer version 8 Basic (or higher).

> You can download the Basic version at
> **http://www.real.com/player/index.html** for free. Don't be fooled by the adverts for the one you have to pay for – follow the links to the Basic version that is free.

As I click on this supplied link, I am reminded how immediate and intertwined the net is as I find myself on realplayer.com and am confronted by a pop-up message asking if I want to buy a copy of the latest software. I try to upgrade, but am told that my serial number is invalid. I am left wondering whether the pain of this is really worthwhile to see a moving head deliver the news when I can do that by just turning on the television set or asking a colleague to read the newspaper for me.

Of course in the happy, couch potato world, there is no need to wait for downloads, no incompatibility problems – everything either works, because the business does all the work behind the scenes, or it doesn't, because someone is having problems behind the scenes. Generally, with the exception of some faulty set-top boxes, problems are solved once for every customer. Viva Le Television.

FIGURE 7.4 WAP wisdom from Ananova.

Naturally there is a service (award-winning) for mobile phones. Ananova makes an appearance as a simple picture, but, of course, there is no sound or animation and there is no ability to call up the Ananova voice to read out the news on the move. It does provide personalized news on a WAP page set up to match the customer's preferences and personalized e-mail alerts that are sent out whenever there is a story that would interest the customer.

The help pages are not easy to find, but they do explain what the services do, how to use them, and sell their features. There are step-by-step guides, a WAP emulator to see what the service looks like and a helpline run via SMS. There was also just a glimmer of humanity in one entry on the FAQs. In response to the question, "Why can't I link from the broadcast to the web page relevant to it?" the answer was "good idea, we are working on it."

> You can now choose from more than 3,000 topics to get personal alerts across all platforms. In one year Ananova has brought you 153,000 news stories – the most informative, useful and entertaining out of 4.5 million stories checked by our news spider. And we never fail to put a smile on your faces, with our own brand of popular quirky stories. "Zookeeper mauled to death after defecating on tiger" and "Pigs bite off man's ear, testicle and part of his scalp" were just two of our most talked about offbeat stories.

Why am I looking so hard for the help? Why is the feedback using bullet points and not a simple e-mail with intelligence at the other end to route the inquiry? Why is there no service standard for replies?

This is not the future, yet – especially for those with normal dial-up connections – but it is getting closer. Ananova's team plans on helping her by adding artificial intelligence to her talents. Compression continues to improve and the speed of connections will just keep growing. The need here is for more character, to let the idea of humanity out of the bag as some of the other virtual characters (notably Lara Croft) have done.

Experience study

Firstdirect.com – "Expect the unbelievable"

From the glossy, very rapid animation, to the changing colors on the ".com" part of the logo, to the little man walking happily on the homepage, it is clear that First Direct does not want to be just another bank.

First Direct is already one of the most popular direct banks on the planet. It has fabulously high satisfaction ratings and valuably high recommendation levels. This has been achieved without branches via the telephone since 1989. Its effectiveness, compared to its competition, in looking after customers is not in question. What is is whether or not First Direct is maximizing the benefits of the electronic experience for the bank and its customers.

The people who deliver the experience are mentioned from the first page in a banner that asks, "What's inside?" and answers, "People are inside, friendly and professional." It sets itself high standards, as in the following statement on the website:

Expect the unbelievable.
When you join First Direct you experience something unbelievable. A bank designed around you, which doesn't expect you to fit round it. A bank which recruits people who like to talk and gives them the confidence to do so. A bank which gives its people all the information they need to enable them to help you. A bank which believes in sorting your money out for you without you having to ask.
If you want to feel better about your bank, if you want to feel good about your banking, First Direct is for you. There are over a million customers enjoying a better rapport with their bank, First Direct, 86 percent of them are very or extremely satisfied and 82 percent recommend us to their friends and colleagues.

FIGURE 7.5 The seriously easy way to sort out your financial future?

So, how well does the First Direct experience adapt itself to the customer? Even with expectations set very high, the welcome is impressive in its mixture of animation and simplicity. The customer is then presented with two drop-down menus for navigation in a simple layout of white text on a black background. The menus are part of a frame that stays the same while the content changes to provide fast loading and constant navigation. There is the reproduction of yet more press advertising that proclaims First Direct provides "the seriously easy way to sort out your financial future."

As is fitting for a service that seeks to be a tomorrow's bank, the customer can choose to deal with their money online or via the mobile phone banking service. There are demonstrations of both, complete with friendly instructions and clearly sold benefits that prompt the customer to satisfy his "pioneering spirit."

FIGURE 7.6

Convenience banking.

It has taken many steps that are unusual for a bank in order to support its customers and its relationships with them. One of these is its decision to add independent sources of financial advice to its services. It acts as a broker, giving its customers a choice between the best pension, investment, and life assurance products. It also has a direct insurance service that allows customers to choose from the best quotes from 12 leading insurers. They can also store and retrieve quotes for up to 30 days after the quote has been issued. The insurance can be applied for and paid for online. It provides travel insurance in the same way, with policies bought online and delivered to the customer's home address.

What happens when the customer wants to search for something by keyword, as he has learned to do on every portal? He can't do anything because there is no search facility for the site itself. Even the search facility that is included via a companion site – firstdirect.net – is just a link into a standard web search, provided by a standard portal (Yahoo!).

If the customer wants to communicate with First Direct, his choices are plenteous, but not all-inclusive. He can phone, of course, he can e-mail, fill out an e-mail form, he can write or fax. First Direct is willing to bet that its service is superior to that of its online rivals and confidently quotes a study[15] as indicating that 90 percent of web shoppers want an integrated service offering and 80 percent of them think that good customer service is all about the interpersonal experience. In the words of its Chief Executive,

> In the dot com gold rush, too much attention has been placed on the technology at the expense of the customer experience.

Where did the community go? No bulletin boards. No live chat. No discussion. No articles. The internal culture is rightly proud of its energy and creativity, but it is not given pride of place on this website. It does have real people, but they are not visible. They are hidden, just as they are in the call center itself.

FIGURE 7.7 Net banking at First Direct.

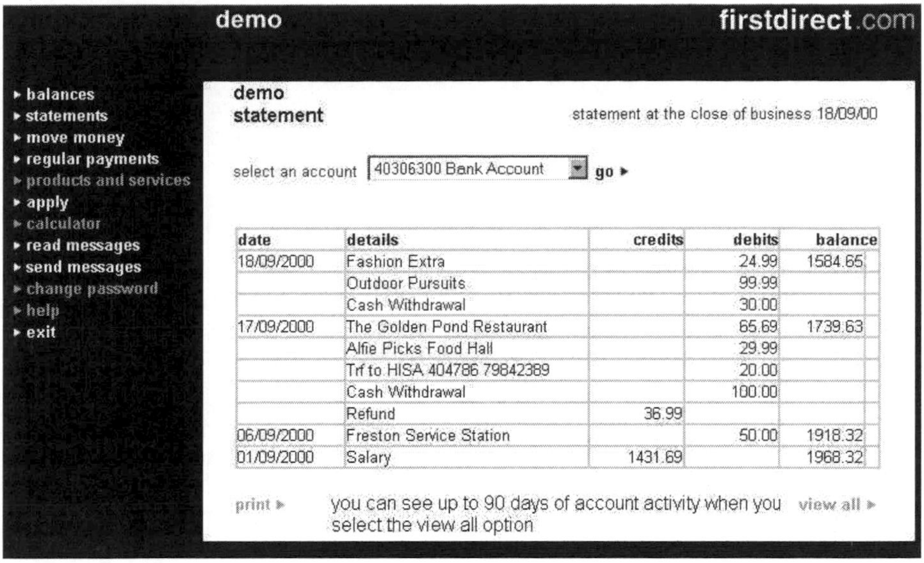

This strange inconsistency continues. Firstdirect.net, the companion site, has a delightful menu built in Flash, and a news and film review service, but there are no screensavers or animations of the little walking man who is so emblematic, or the advertisements.

There is a free e-mail address available with BT's talk21, but why not provide e-mails that are related to the relationship with the bank as well?

A feedback survey is available, tucked away to the side of the experience, but why not ask interesting questions and allow interactive discussion about the answers? A massive opportunity has been missed to bond further with the e-customer.

Stuff to think about

books, articles, TV shows, and websites

AI-CBR.org

Take a look at case based reasoning and artificial intelligence on a site that not only features plenteous details about the subject but is part of a web ring that is also devoted to the field. Find out whether the subject of science fiction films from The Matrix to AI, the latest Spielberg epic, is likely to bring on Armageddon or just might improve your customer service.

http://www.netvalley.com/intval1.html

Make sure to take a look at the entertaining and very informative guide to the history of the web. It is the amusing, accurate, and colourful account of the people, businesses, and technologies that make up the net as we know it today. Obligatory reading unless you like feeling lost all the time.

Search for "cool technology" on google.com

The results will change over time and so you will find out about what is hot and not in the field of technology. Results when I tried it last included Motorola.com (telematics), the cool toys that Lou Gerstner gets to play with, and an article on why you should drag cool technology from work back home with you for the family to play with.

Magazine Rack Trawl

Grab a copy of one of the gadget magazines in your local store.Try a different magazine each month and try to figure out what gadget trends mean for your customers and the services that you offer to them. Browse over to japaninc.net and look at what the kings of gadgetry are buying and selling. Surf to thesector.com and find out what the electronic retailers think will work and not work.

Nerdworld.com

Could do worse that try out the "source for Nerdly culture, life, and work styles since 1995." You got all the usual features and you can learn about why some customers love this stuff. Or just cruise over frontiernet.net/~jbennett/nerd/n500test.html for "The Nerdity Test" to find out how far you are away from them.

ZDNet.com

Owned by CNET Networks, ZDNet aims to offer a "full service" destination for people looking to buy, use, and learn more about technology. It is one of the few destination sites making money from free content provision. It's worth reading *and* learning from.

Activity 7.1

Experience technology rapid check

The electronic experience is technology. A working knowledge of what the main components do and what they can be used to achieve is vital for anyone who wants to translate experience visions into experience reality.

Completion date: _____

75% done ☐	100% done ☐	Tasks	Who will do it? (initials)	By when? (date)
		Don't allow customers to be transferred indefinitely until they get help.		
		Make sure customers type their details only once.		
		Use sticky content adapted to your business to enhance the experience.		
		Use the CRM agent to allow customers to submit questions to the site.		
		Use an e-mail management service.		
		Use a service standard for replying to customer's e-mails.		
		Make it clear who's responsible for answering e-mails (real person or automated system?)		
		Use instant interaction to talk to customers in real time.		
		Use software routing to direct e-mails to the relevant department and person in the company.		
		Allow customers the possibility of using voice chat and video chat when contacting your company.		
		Use personalization technology to make offers based on what you already know of your customers.		

Use one-click shopping.

Encourage customers to make use of software that keeps personal details safe.

Allow customer panels to test your electronic experience.

Track the number of visits made to each page of the company's site.

Track the number of clicks made to each link on a page.

Customer experience thinkers

The curious thing about technology is the way it resolves complexity into simplicity. Let's take a tomato. A tomato is in a very abstract sense a kind of technology – not in the sense of my vocabulary which defines technology as being human made … – but in the sense that a tomato is made up of very complex processes that are all integrated and which work very well. So it's something very parallel to technology. Yet when we look at a tomato, it seems very simple to us. It's easy to pick. We can hold it in our hands. It has a very bounded identity. But, obviously, if we tried to invent a tomato from scratch, it would be impossibly complex. So most of the things that we think of as simple are actually not very simple behind the scenes. They are very complex, but biological "technology," for all its complexity, makes things appear to be simple.

KEVIN KELLY, AUTHOR OF *OUT OF CONTROL: THE NEW BIOLOGY OF MACHINES, SOCIAL SYSTEMS AND THE ECONOMIC WORLD* (FOURTH ESTATE, 1994)

I believe that every company has to master – or at least have the capacity to assimilate – the range of different technologies that are affecting the way it goes about delivering value to its customers. … a sheer scientific breakthrough – or the ability to have the most scientific technological capability in a particular field – does not seem to be that important. It's more the ability to apply technology, that is the source of advantage. And to apply technology you've got to integrate it with a lot other things. So we find over and over again that the first one to market with a new technology is often not the winner in the marketplace. The winner is the one that figures out how to incorporate that technology into the broader system of the company.

MICHAEL PORTER, EDITOR OF *CAPITAL CHOICES: CHANGING THE WAY AMERICA INVESTS IN INDUSTRY* (MCGRAW-HILL, 1994)

The definition of every product and service is changing. Going soft, softer, softest. Going fickle, ephemeral, fashion. An explosion of new competitors, a rising standard of living in the developed world, and ever-present … new technologies are leading the way.

TOM PETERS, AUTHOR OF *THRIVING ON CHAOS* (HARPERCOLLINS, 1989)

You have to have scale in business. This kind of business isn't going to work in small volumes. We have to level the playing field, in terms of purchasing power with the established booksellers, and we have to firmly establish our brand name. Those are expensive things. It's also expensive to develop all the software to continue to improve the customer experience. So that's where our investment dollars go.

JEFF BEZOS, FOUNDER AMAZON.

66 Every man takes the limits of his own field of **vision** for the **limits** of the world. **99**

ARTHUR SCHOPENHAUER

Keeping it fresh, staying in business

Start in the right direction, keep going in the right direction, and avoid mistakes that lose your business money, reputation, and the ability to serve the customer in the future – and remember to have fun!

GUESSING RIGHT ON DAY ONE MAY BE AS SIMPLE AS copying what the competition does or reading the pages of *Wired, Red Herring* or *Financial Times* for ideas about what is cool today. Maybe your business was founded on a legal loophole, the patent-protected genius of its founder or long years of outlasting its competitors. None of this is a guarantee of success tomorrow, and also still being in business today does not prove that your business is also still succeeding.

Your business can no longer rely on size alone to control the pace of technology and innovation. The speed of improvements is so great that businesses have little or no room for determining when to provide an enhancement because a competitor will have already provided it. Worse, the investment that is necessary to keep up with the competition often still has no customer offer associated with it when it comes to market. Result?

The customer is left wondering why he should buy into the new stuff and the business is left without revenues to recoup the cost of investment.

> " Maybe your **business** was founded on a **legal loophole**, the patent-protected genius of its founder or **long years** of outlasting its **competitors.** None of this is a **guarantee** of success tomorrow. "

Bottom line? It is more important to learn what to do with the technology in the service of paying customers than to create the innovation in the first place. If you can't control the timing of entry into the market, then at least you can be the first to figure out how to do something both valuable and profitable with each new technology.

When businesses talk about disaggregation or just "providing one piece of the puzzle,"[1] it is really an admission that it can't see the whole picture and is hoping that someone else can do something profitable with the pieces it can provide. It is what has happened to the financial, computing, and the telecommunications giants[2] who focused on growth more than complete customer experiences. So-called "industry sectors" have not managed to avoid "business cycles" because industry sectors are simply groups of businesses that choose to act like manufacturers, churning out "stuff" and hoping that someone out there will buy it. This applies to Cisco and Intel[3] just as much as it does to Ford and General Motors. Individual businesses that can adjust to what the customer will buy suffer less, and even grow, during downturns and recessions.

> " **Individual** businesses that can adjust to what the **customer** will buy suffer less, and even grow, during **downturns** and **recessions.** "

This customer focus was something that featured more in dot com business plans than their operational realities, but it may still provide hope for many such businesses during the hard times ahead (and there will be always be hard times!) History has shown that maintaining growth of more than 3 percent a year for an economy is difficult – new technology may or may not lead to greater productivity gains year on year than electricity and cars – but individual businesses can grow more than 3 percent a year if you understand the nature of the task.[4]

Your task is to find not only the best way to start, but also the best way to restart each day and week. Renewal, rethinking, and reenergizing the efforts of your organization will be the way to ensure you really succeed. The business is made up of each individual person that works within or for it. The business is the combination of these people, the ways that they work together, and the resources that they can utilize when completing the work. This means that to renew the organization is much like renewing the individual.

Share and grow – the plan, the money, the workload

> Make money your God and it will plague you like the devil.
> HENRY FIELDING

Serving the customer is not easy, and the only way that it is going to work without driving you all mad is if you learn to share and grow. This is a true principle! Sesame Street was part of a largely TV-free educational diet during my early years and it taught me the word as follows:

C-O-O-P-E-R-A-T-I-O-N

It's a great word, but some out there are nervous of it because it threatens to take from them what they prefer not to give. Logically there is no sensible alternative to sharing in the current climate of competition where only the pooling of effort appears sufficient to meet customer needs. This is a principle that works across groups, including customers, resellers, competitors, supplier partners, and team members.

❝ Logically there is no sensible alternative to sharing where only the pooling of effort appears sufficient to meet customer needs. ❞

One way of sharing is to have an "affiliate scheme" that allows others to promote or sell your products, services, and features as part of their experience, in exchange for which you share the revenue from the customer by offering some form of commission. By sharing, you are able to increase the numbers of customers that will become aware of what you offer. If you offer commission only if a customer buys, then you risk nothing (apart from the initial development of the affiliate technology required to process and manage the scheme and its payments) and, as a result, the scheme can be a very cost-effective means to promoting your offer.

It also grows the number of supporters that your business has and benefits from the ingenuity and expertise of the affiliate partners. Of course, you have to make sure that your commission rate does not reduce your margins to a point that is unacceptably low or even makes a loss. Remember, as soon as you offer an affiliate scheme, the users of the scheme become another group of customers who need to have an experience delivered to them that meets their needs and allows them to work effectively on your behalf. The complete experience needs to include adverts, icons, newsletters, customization features, competitions, and tools that allow the customer to be in control of his use of your features, while you know what is happening and can ensure that it is secure.

Example

One example of affiliate schemes is the one offered by Amazon that has around half a million partners advertising its services to particular niche markets. That's a lot of extra brainpower and resources focused on making Amazon bigger and better. Aware of the importance of sharing to its growth plans, Amazon has launched what it calls "Associates Central" to provide what it has promoted as, "a deluxe new self-service area available 24 hours a day for exclusive use by Amazon associates."

It offers a complete range of features, including:

- online reporting;
- fully automated link generation;
- complete account maintenance;
- an extensive graphics library;
- featured associates.

Associates Central achieves two great objectives. First, it puts the affiliate customer in control (where he wants to be) by making the process easier than ever and allowing each customer to get up-to-date figures and customized reports whenever he wants to. Second, it reduces the need for statistics to be e-mailed to affiliates and for direct human assistance, although "skilled and knowledgeable staff" are still available whenever they are needed to provide what Amazon are proud to term their "exceptional service."

It is clear from the tone of the e-mail marketing that Amazon understands the need and desire of its customers to feel important, that they are in "partnership" with big, successful Amazon and that their valuable time is appreciated.

It is essential that you consider the perspective of the customer and the nature of the competition as well as how effectively your product or service fits into such a scheme. Making the scheme profitable in principle is not the same as making a profit from it in real life. If you reward too low or for sales that appear to be more work than they are, then you will find that the target affiliates abandon your scheme, however usable it is. You should weigh up carefully the costs and benefits of a managed program for affiliate payments. Can you differentiate sufficiently if you build your own program to justify the added costs and risks involved?

Staying in business means spending less than you earn – a lesson that BigWords learned too late to keep it afloat. It spent much of its $70 million from investors on marketing, but gained the most from the activities that cost the least and shared the money and the experience with its customers. The marketing for Guerrilla shared the experience by hiring students to stroll along university campuses wearing yellow-orange coveralls, handing out flyers and dropping thousands of yellow superballs with cash and free books. The "tell a friend" program shared the money with customers by paying them for each referral that resulted in a sale, and it reduced the cost of attracting many new customers to only $3.50.[5]

Pull your customers into the same space as your designers and let them work out what they want and how they want it together. Encourage customers to vote for and nominate new enhancements. It works for Microsoft, which has made this a feature of its new operating system and supporting website. If you both get what you want, that's win:win isn't it? In the words of two prominent designers:

> Designing with people, not for them, brings the whole subject of user experience to life. Success will come to organizations with the most creative and committed customers.
>
> JOHN THACKARA

> I would like to see a different relationship between the designer and the consumer, and I think that's very likely to happen. Digital networks will make it happen. We have to disintermediate the production process.
>
> BRUCE STERLING

" Pull your **customers** into the same **space as** your designers and let them work out what they **want and** how they want it together. "

When the benefits, plans, and prestige are shared, then your team (and your customers) can feel confident in sharing their time and knowledge. A "knowledge base" – the internal sharing of information and knowledge – is a very desirable goal, but why should anyone share what they know (and what makes them valuable) if they are not rewarded for it, have to do it in their own time, receive no credit for it, and fear for their job security? Sharing needs to be a consistently applied principle if it is to work effectively.

It also needs creative and thorough use of the technology that exists for the purpose. Think it through from the team member's point of view. Such knowledge bases developed using internet technology are used by many, many large businesses. This includes McKinsey, the management consultants, which has created just such a continuously growing business resource that can be used by any member of the team.[6] Put the technology and the environment of the online customer to use in your own team and across the business.

Change and grow – be radical, not foolish

> Let's innovate and, as a consequence of that, make money.
> PHILIP KAHN, IN INTERVIEW, BOB PARKS, "THE BIG PICTURE," *WIRED*,
> OCTOBER, 2000

This is what I call the principle of "good change." The addition of the adjective "good" to change reminds us that change as a word is neutral, but change in reality can be viewed as somewhere between really, really good and really, really bad for each person affected by it. To assume that all change is good is to miss a serious point that will lead to capriciously thought through, but often dully delivered, change.

Particularly with the chilly breeze of a downturn in the air, it is possible to either swing at change with fear-induced, adrenaline-fed energy or cling to the way that the business has always done it, whether that way has worked or not and whether the company is old or young. To state the obvious, refusal to change in a changing market is courting death, while making all the wrong changes is akin to suicide.

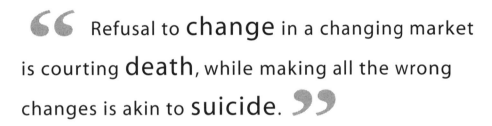

❝ Refusal to **change** in a changing market is courting **death**, while making all the wrong changes is akin to **suicide**. **❞**

It is at times like these that otherwise clever people ignore that age-old advice and, instead, choose to panic, often taking one of two misguided approaches. They either cut back spending on everything, thus killing off the business' capacity for growth and ending the likelihood of recovery, or assume that they "might as well go for broke" and spend all those hard-accumulated investment funds and continue to buy on credit, hoping that the expenditure will save the business before it all runs out.

Let me suggest a better way! The golden rule is to never cut anything that the e-customer appreciates sufficiently to pay for. So, particularly at times like these, you need to know (or find out) what he appreciates. This is where supernormal profits can still be made. If you don't do this, you can't recover. You still need to cut back, but the aim is to divert all available funds to anything that can return your investment with the maximum possible profit. Take the following lists as an example of this process in action.

> **“** The **golden rule** is to never cut **anything** that the e-customer appreciates sufficiently to **pay for. ”**

Cut it	Keep it
• Non-expert externals.	• Your own employees.
• High advertising spend.	• Guerrilla-style marketing.
• In-house server costs.	• Virtual service provision.
• Free and low-margin goods.	• Stuff customers pay for.
• High-rent property.	• High-quality equipment.
• Champagne culture.	• Fun learning culture.
• I am the leader.	• The team creating together.
• Machine fixation.	• E-customer obsession.

When air is in short demand, don't waste your breath but keep breathing! (Think about it.) If you think through these lists, you will see that everything that is profitable or likely to lead to greater profits is worth spending on. The changes have to be improvements, not simple cutbacks. Your customer does not want less help. You do not want fewer resources!

What you need is the growth of production of what the customer is eager to buy from you from a given amount of human effort and money. Increasing productivity is nothing to be pleased about if the customers do not want to buy more stuff! Decreasing production is nothing to be pleased about if it has simply reduced the size of the business. The key to economic growth is useful increases in production of solutions to problems that customers are willing to purchase. The potential value of the "new economy" is the increase in effectiveness in meeting customer needs profitably – not merely producing more, or less. Unfortunately, the post-crash realism[7] that has swept the world will lead many to question the medium and the potential rather than the lack of customer focus (and investor foolishness) that has led to it.

It's simple. Build in the ability to change naturally by taking away all the stuff that stops the change from happening. Remove the fear that prevents team members embracing the change, strip away the policies and procedures that slow down useful change and the work of knowledgeable people, wherever they are in the business. You need your business to be able to recognize the inevitable killer advances before they kill your future success and act to use those advances for the good of the customer, rather than simply try to hide them away to protect the status quo.

- Achieve inbuilt flexibility.
- Never panic.
- Learn and grow.

Sell and grow

> Making money is art and working is art and good business is the best art of all.
>
> ANDY WARHOL, GRAPHIC ARTIST, PAINTER AND FILMMAKER – ONE OF THE MORE CONTROVERSIAL FIGURES IN POP ART.

The point of a commercial electronic experience is to make money, but, sadly, not all electronic experiences have this as the central core of their design. Only spend if the customer will pay.

> ❝ If **everyone** in the business does not think they are in both sales and **service**, then neither **sales nor** service will be delivered consistently or with **excellence**. ❞

If everyone in the business does not think they are in both sales and service, then neither sales nor service will be delivered consistently or with excellence. The technical support person needs to believe in selling and service together or he will simply "do his job" and use his initiative only to get customers off his back – a lot like the technical support man who snarled at me, "I don't work in customer services" when I asked for help. Also a lot like the following example, where a customer who has waited for six months for a broadband connection tries to get some help with wireless networking:

> I wait. And wait. Around 4 pm I crack, and ring the helpline again (Warning: If you value your sanity never ever ring a BT helpline.) The guy who answers is amazed I would even ask. "We don't support wireless networking," he says several times. This is, I point out, hardly the time to tell me after a six-month wait. He's adamant. "WE WILL NOT HELP YOU," he says. Twice. BT calls this using his initiative, presumably.
> In the end I sorted it out myself. It took me two hours, whereupon I (helpfully) e-mailed the settings to BT. The **** didn't even thank me.

The tragedy here for your business is that the goodwill of the customer is lost and the experience is sadly distorted, stunted, deformed, with different parts suiting themselves rather than the customer. The guys in the examples might be worth going to grab a pizza with, but they have lost their ability to sell, serve, or smile by the time they come in contact with the bringers of revenue. Take this recent criticism of Cisco as illustrative of this point:

> Cisco's problems can be traced directly to an arrogant and even lazy salesforce, which is too used to taking orders rather than aggressively selling to and serving customers.[8]

It's a problem that plagues many businesses. Your people need to believe that both sales and service matter and that they are responsible for both! It is the real problem with the new economy – it didn't think it would ever have to sell and somehow believed that it could just lie back and the orders would roll in.

Relax and grow

A paradox? Counterintuitive? I hope so. If your business does not relax and let its metaphorical, and actual, hair down, if it cannot have fun, if it cannot sharpen the saw, then it will be in no mental, physical, or emotional state to create great places for the customer to spend his time and money.

Take a simple example like team members using e-mail at work. There is a backlash in some parts of the corporate world against it. Nestlé Rowntree and Camelot are just two companies that have prohibited the use of e-mail one day a week, to "generate more ideas and improve face-to-face communication."[9] How likely is it that an authoritarian ban of an essential creative medium[10] will promote creativity? Managers who do not understand the way that the technology can be used to promote ideas and healthy communication will naturally blame it whenever they can, but if they just relaxed and let it do its thing, much would be improved. Such draconian measures are misguided and smack of ignorant desperation.

Instead of reducing freedom, use the power of your electronic experience to give back confidence to battered cultures. It is when times are hard that you will need the best that your team members can offer, but, unfortunately, this is often the time that a lack of confidence steals away their creativity. If they are preoccupied with their own job prospects, they will not be occupied with securing those prospects by focusing on improving the customer experience (look at the demoralized faces of team members at Marks & Spencer[11]).

The web can strengthen the business' view of what it stands for, what its brand means, by relaxing the many unnecessary barriers between the team and the customer they serve. Just agree a few simple guidelines (don't defame the business, nothing illegal, racist, pornographic, or sexist – that kind of thing), relax and let the people get on with the jobs that they know best. Create competitions to award web cams to those who come up with the best use of them to communicate with each other and customers. Put up discussion boards and let people chat about what matters to them.

> **❝ Relaxing** makes the brain work better. It presents the **business** as likeable and **approachable** for customers, team members, and potential **recruits. ❞**

Relaxing makes the brain work better. It presents the business as likeable and approachable for customers, team members, and potential recruits. Think party! One French software company did when it needed 250 new engineers. Instead of using the usual recruiting channels, it booked a trendy nightclub and threw a party, hoping that the word-of-mouth method would encourage young talent to come forward.[12]

Moving to a fun fusion of work, life, fun, real, and electronic worlds is more attractive and more effective at solving real-world problems than cutbacks and redundancies. Why pretend life and work are not part of the same continuum? It is exactly this kind of information that is needed if the business is to understand its customer's life:work balance. You are what you do and cannot do – do for your customer what you would like to be able to do for yourself.

Example Gateways' founder is often described something along the lines of, "a normal dude, an everyday guy you'd go out and have pizza with."[13] His team performed miracles in the relaxed culture that he nurtured. Rock music blared, cow spots adorned the packaging, team members would turn up barefoot and drink beer in meetings. It was only when he put the culture into less inspiring, more serious hands, from around 1998, that the energy went into infighting and memo writing rather than improving the customer experience. There were rules that dictated what "employees" could put up in their cubicles and what time they could go to lunch.

Result? Sales fell by 30 percent and customer satisfaction took a nosedive. The policy of putting reducing bonuses on team members who spent longer than 13 minutes talking to a customer meant, naturally, that they began doing just about anything to get customers off the phone. This increased costs and reduced the willingness of customers to recommend Gateway to friends and family, with the result that its referral business fell from 50 percent to about 30 percent.

Anyone want to offer some conclusions? If you get all efficient at doing the wrong (grown-up) things, then you will end up doing a lot less good than being relaxed and doing the right things!

Still reading? Still in business?

Glad to see that you are still reading and thinking along with me. Not every business avoids death. Some are dead and will not realize until every last part has completely decayed. For the rest, renewal is essential – opening up the business to connect the best of its people with the best of its partners and the best that its customers can offer.

In a business environment where Cisco is making losses,[14] Intel and Apple are facing reduced profits and Amazon is hoping to make a profit by the time you read this book, there will be little patience with those who think they can put off the day of viability. This is at the heart of an effective selling customer experience, and this book. Ensure that it also goes to the hearts of your team members and organization.

Experience study

Gateway.com – "You've got a friend"

Unfortunately, at first there are few signs of the character that Gateway has been fond of showing in advertising or the colorful culture for which Gateway is famous. If the browsing e-customer wants to know what kind of people he is dealing with, then he could gain something from the tag line "you've got a friend in business," but not much. Clicking the link "About Gateway" will reveal dull information and language – nothing to inspire here. It all rather saps at your will to live.

On the positive side, the prominent "best site" award from *Computer Shopper* builds trust, as does knowing that Gateway delivers on time, 98 percent of the time – although all the talk in the review about "mind-boggling choice" that goes with the award is a tad disconcerting for a customer looking for answers, a computer, and a little entertainment. An attractive touch is the explanatory text box that appears when the cursor moves over the black-and-white-spotted Gateway box. It explains that:

> Ted Waitt founded Gateway on his family's Iowa cattle farm. Our Holstein cow spots remind us of our Midwestern roots and our company's values: hard work, honesty, friendliness, quality – and putting people first.

FIGURE 8.1 Gateway's cow spot boxes.

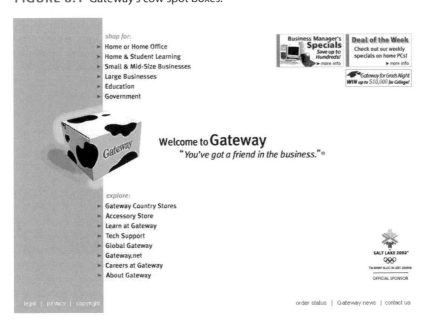

It is a comforting note on which to try the buying flow and structure, and purchase a personal computer for use at home. The options give me the appropriate choices, but they do not give me a choice of tone. Visually, the area for home users is much the same for students as it is for small businesses as it is for corporations, educational institutions, and government bodies. There is variation in content, to provide, for example, case studies relevant to education and government buyers, but it is delivered in a monotonous style. As customer's needs are different, does this make sense?

The technical support and presales facilities were excellent, featuring online order status, a technical support knowledge library, and driver downloads, and the update facility that finds, downloads, and installs the latest drivers for the customer's computer.

The customer can also choose to chat with a "Gateway Co-Pilot" using a remote help software form to allow the co-pilot to share the computer, guiding the mouse and keyboard, viewing the screen, and chatting, all in real time. Are you impressed? Does your electronic experience offer anything as good?

FIGURE 8.2

Let me drive!

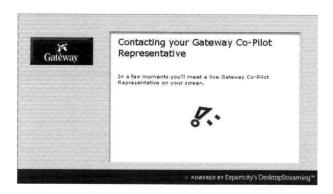

Its just a shame that so much that is so good is so uninspiringly presented. You can sense that Gateway cares about the customer, but that the vigor and humanity of which it is proud has not made it through without being diluted. There is too little of a sense of fun or humor. A great shame.

In its own words

Gateway, Inc. has grown from a two-person start-up in an Iowa farmhouse to a $9.6 billion, Fortune 250 company that employs 21,000 people around the world. Consistent with its vision of "humanizing the digital revolution", Gateway is about relationships, and about treating clients as we would like to be treated ourselves, giving them honest advice, great products and services, the best value and genuinely caring about them.

Stuff to think about

books, articles, TV shows, and websites

Ambler, Tim *Marketing & The Bottom Line* (Prentice Hall 2000)

Some people have called this one of the most important books written about marketing. I don't go that far but it's a good example of how the flakiest of professions can be expected to return serious results. Apply the same demanding criteria to your online work.

Luckedcompany.com

The leading "will they or won't they go out of business" site. The language is far from pretty but the information is very valuable. Find out whether your company is on the list and rumours about others that are instructive in understanding the causes and symptoms of ruined businesses.

Affiliatemarketing.co.uk

This is Neil Durrant's site on affiliate marketing. Just look around at what is on offer and consider how such schemes and their features could be applied to your own business. Bring existing customers closer and new customers onboard.

Opensource.org: Share & Grow

The home site of the Open Source Initiative (OSI). In it's own words, "The basic idea behind open source is very simple: When programers can read, redistribute, and modify the source code for a piece of software, the software evolves. People improve it, people adapt it, and people fix bugs. And this can happen at a speed that, if one is used to the slow pace of conventional software development, seems astonishing." Don't think these ideas belong only to the software world.

Workoptions.com

Understanding what your team members may want more (or as much as money) is a smart way of improving your ability to organize an effective, evolved customer team. This site attempts an aproach to how to negotiate for what both parties want.

Creativityforlife.com

These guys are full of gushing mission statements but it's far from dull. Keep the bottom line on the page but keep the rest blank for a while as you fill it with some of these suggestions and the stuff that they sell. Yep – they are into creativity for the money!

Dunndeals.com

It boasts that it is the greatest brainstorming session on earth. The radio is useful when you are busy with something else but want to keep your brain ticking over. Probably not as good as the hype but then what is? It features interviews, call-ins, and appearances.

Superstats.com

How will you know what they want and therefore what to cut and keep if you don't know what your online customers are doing? This is a pretty effective tool that gives you online, graphical reporting on just about anything that you want. Try it out.

Activity 8.1

Keeping it fresh checklist

Staying in business should mean keeping it fresh by creating value for the online customer. The following tasks for you to check on are part of the four-stage process that keeps your head comfortably above the waterline:

- share and grow;
- change and grow;
- sell and grow;
- relax and grow.

Use it to create your own tasks that are specific to your own unique business situation. In keeping with the principles of this book, involve everyone, then focus in on individual, precise projects, subprojects, and stuff that you have to get finished.

75% done	100% done	Tasks doing this?	Are we When should we start?
☐	☐		
		Find the best way to restart the business every day.	
		Start by renewing individuals when renewing the organization.	

Stress C-O-O-P-E-R-A-T-I-O-N.

Set up an affiliate scheme.

Promote gathering together between customers and designers for them to work out what they want and how they want it together.

Encourage customers to vote for and nominate new enhancements.

Set up a knowledge base.

Reward those who share information and knowledge.

Ensure that there is time to share information and knowledge.

Put the e-customer's technology and environment to use in your team and across the business.

DON'T PANIC! (You can't really measure this.)

Don't take cutbacks for improvements.

Keep
- Your own employees.
- Guerrilla-style marketing.
- Virtual service provision.
- Stuff customers pay for.
- High-quality equipment.
- Fun learning culture.
- The team creating together.
- E-customer obsession.

Cut
- Non-expert externals.
- High advertising spend.
- In-house server costs.
- Free and low-margin goods.
- High-rent property.
- Champagne culture.
- I am the leader.
- Machine fixation.

Remove all that prevents change from happening.

Remove team's fear of embracing change.

Strip away policies and procedures capable of slowing down change.

Develop your ability as a business to recognize killer advances.

Ensure that everyone in the business knows they are in sales.

Use the power of your electronic experience to give back confidence to battered cultures.

Create competitions and award web cams to those who come up with the best use of them to communicate with others and customers.

Put up discussion boards and let people chat about what matters to them.

Encourage and promote a fun culture at work. Coming to work should be fun!

Customer experience thinkers

It's not good enough just to be different. You've got to be different in ways that involve trade-offs with other ways of being different. In other words, if you want to serve a particular definition of value, this must be inconsistent with delivering other types of value to other customers. If not, the position is easy to imitate or replicate.

MICHAEL PORTER, EDITOR OF *CAPITAL CHOICES: CHANGING THE WAY AMERICA INVESTS IN INDUSTRY* (MCGRAW-HILL, 1994)

... you must learn how to reinvent the existing competitive space you are in, and there are a variety of ways in which you can do that. Essentially it is by changing in some fundamental way the rules of engagement and the basis for competitive advantage within an existing industry – as Wal-Mart did in retailing in the US, or as Ikea did in furniture retailing in Europe.

… a company must learn to create fundamentally new space, so that you can satisfy a need that individuals or companies didn't even realize they have.

GARY HAMEL, CO-AUTHOR WITH C.K. PRAHALAD OF *COMPETING FOR THE FUTURE*
(HARVARD BUSINESS SCHOOL PRESS, 1994)

We showed that meaningful growth – which Wall Street demands and everybody else is pretty fond of, too – can be stimulated at the store level without having to expand the empire, an expensive strategy that always runs out of gas sooner or later.

PACO UNDERHILL, AUTHOR OF *WHY WE BUY: THE SCIENCE OF SHOPPING*
(SIMON & SCHUSTER AND ORION, 1999)

" A new age is taking form throughout the entire civilized world; civilization is taking on new aspects. We are only now starting to realize, perhaps, that this modern, mechanistic civilization in which we live is now in the process of perfecting itself. **"**

JOHN MOODY, 1928

Do it, do it now, and do it again – next steps

You know so much and have such great hopes so it's time to figure out how to share your vision and get a team of believers ready to deliver the ultimate experience

YOU NOW KNOW ALL ABOUT THE WONDERFUL WORLD of the e-customer experience. We have discussed the reasons for this experience being the key difference between a customer using your electronic services and either staying in the real world or spending time elsewhere online. We have examined the mind and needs of the customer and how the experience can be adapted to fit the characteristics and aspirations he has. If you were convinced that it works, it would be a waste to just let your convictions grow old, tired, out of date, and go untested. Do something about it, and do it now.

Where to start? Only you know where your business is, how it's doing, and how far you will have to travel to reach the idealized experience your customer wishes to buy. You know (or need to find out) how your colleagues and your organization think and act. You are aware (or need to become aware) of the resources, characteristics, and attitudes toward change. Do not convince yourself that creating the ultimate experience will be easy, or natural, or anything less than radical. You can start with small steps and quick wins but, however you divide it up, it is still a goal that will demand a great deal of the business that chooses to implement it.

I recommended that you start with the following, two-part approach as a basis for action. First, you need to prepare yourself and your business for the demands of the changes inherent in creating an effective online customer experience. Second, you will get on with the continuous, valuable, and prioritized improvements that will deliver a complete experience that your online customer considers worthy of his investment.

PART 1: prepare, prepare, prepare

1: describe your vision and identify opposing and supporting forces

You have read the book and so should now be able to describe your vision for the experience that your business can provide to the e-customer. Write it down and sketch it out so that you have taken a few steps more than your colleagues. In this way, you will be able to lead them with confidence.

Once you have described your vision, you need to identify all the reasons that your business and colleagues would give or accept to both support and oppose such a vision. It is only natural that there will be opposition – it happens in all things, so expect and plan for it.

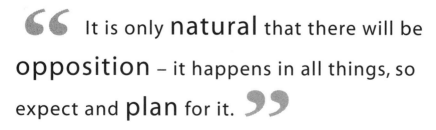

" It is only natural that there will be opposition – it happens in all things, so expect and plan for it. "

As you follow the next steps outlined in this chapter, keep referring back to the vision. Use it to communicate with all those people you need to ensure that the vision stays consistent throughout. As you gain insights from discussions and debate, go back and modify it. When the project becomes formally recognized, you can publish the vision and invite comments from the wider community. Of course, there will be critics, but get them out in the open by encouraging public, electronic debate of all the ideas. Criticism can be a great spur to the improvement of ideas, and using it constructively is just as important as framing the idea constructively in the first place.

Pay particular attention to the forces of light and dark that you have identified. It should not become simply desk or hard drive clutter. It should be a constant reference point that is altered as your knowledge of the situation grows and as you find ways to turn opposing forces into supporting forces.

Beware – do not make this list personal. It should not, must not, include names of individuals, even if you thought of individuals when you compiled the list. Why not? First, one or more of those named will always find out, and this can be fatal to the project and hurtful to the person involved. Second, naming will make you think of good guys and bad guys – it will get you in a fighting mode – and this is against the culture of cooperation that will be necessary to the success of the experience.

2: Create a network of believers

You cannot act alone, so you need to share your vision and grow a team of believers with whom you can work to communicate the principles and practical aspects of this book. This includes colleagues – those in your own team and representatives from other disciplines who can provide greater perspective on and scrutinize your vision from a different angle, be aware of factors you might not have thought of. It also includes customers, who can see the benefits of what you are proposing and can add strength to your vision, either directly or via a survey, suggestion, or user group results.

Cast around, gently at first, for those who are willing to understand the importance of the "experience"-focused business. Finding those who are active users of electronic channels is a good place to start, and the best way of doing that is electronically! It provides a useful filter for "resumé fillers" – those who want to include a new project on their resumé, but do not use the channels themselves. You might want to post a web address on the business drinks machines and noticeboards, then ask people from the site that you have created to send an e-mail if they are willing to share their knowledge of the web.

You also need to identify influencers in the business whose opinions are followed by others. There is always a "top dog" in every group, profession, and department, and they are not necessarily the manager or executive. These people matter because they are the real experts who understand how the business works and the part that their skills play in keeping it going. Identify as many of them as you can, then establish where to start creating a vision with them that is not only accepted by them but a product of their work.

Don't think that this is just a ruse to create "ownership" (although that helps!) – it is a serious way of improving the quality and effectiveness of the experience. Creating the ultimate experience is beyond the expertise or capability of any one person. The organization has to learn to share information, cooperatively build knowledge, and work across traditional boundaries for the good of the online customer. This step, if successfully worked through, will provide the basis for the kind of business culture that you will need in order to attract, bond, and build those relationships with the customer.

> ❝ The **organization** has to learn to share information, **cooperatively** build **knowledge**, and work across traditional boundaries for the good of the **online** customer. This will **provide** the basis for the kind of business culture that you **will need** in order to **attract**, bond, and build those **relationships** with the customer. ❞

3: get top-level support – form your network of angels

With your vision sketched out, the opposition identified, and the benefits of reviews from your network of believers, you are ready to lobby and obtain top-level support. Success in this step will bring not only a budget and the authority to proceed, but also a "network of angels" that can step down from above to clear obstacles, share wisdom, and protect you from attack.

Holistic improvement of the end-to-end experience will naturally cut across boundaries and responsibilities. Although you can start with quick wins, as discussed in Chapter 2, eventually the implementation of the vision will demand decisions that only the most senior executives in your business can provide. Even if you are the chairman or CEO, the blessing of investors and as many of the executive team as possible will be essential.

Right from the start, consider how to communicate the essence of your vision to people who may not have very much (if any) first-hand knowledge of using electronic channels of any kind. Our research shows that usually only 1 in 20 could be considered to be an experienced internet user. This is an alien world to many of them and you will have to find a way of explaining what it means, why this is not just another dot com investment, and how they can help all along the way. Expect to find high levels of skepticism, a strange relief among some that many initiatives have failed, and a great desire to finally make some money from all this investment.

4: organize an "experience" action team

With the support of your angels, organize an experience action team that will provide the nucleus of the project over at least its first year. Some of its members will be part of your original network of believers, but it is wise to also include new recruits who can join the movement while being supported from outside.

It is worth stating the obvious here, because picking the right combination of team members is vital. It needs to include the full range of interests and skills. It needs to be representative of the overall business. Ideally, team members need to have hybrid characteristics at the onset of the project and, if they do not, then training, reading around their blind spot subjects and studying this book will help. Select for *attitude* ahead of skills, rather than the other way around – you can add skills and include specialists in the design, build, and delivery teams later.

> " Picking the right **combination** of team **members** is vital. It needs to include the full range of **interests** and skills. Select for *attitude* ahead of skills, rather than the other way **around.** "

Try to gather a team that is as reflective of the diversity in the online customer population as possible – your team will be attempting to think on behalf of the customer, so the more diversity it has, the more effective it will be at achieving this objective. You need old and young, fat and thin, male and female, able and disabled, experienced and inexperienced. It is very difficult to create something of interest for someone whose interests are beyond our personal experience. It is much smarter to just get team members who are closer to the target than you are! Even if your target group has narrowly defined characteristics, remember that they still reside, eat, sleep, and drink in a family and friends network you desperately need insights into.

5: complete a gap analysis between the existing situation and the vision

With a team around you, it is time to look again at what you want to achieve and the gap between that and what you have today. How will the success of your project be determined?

First, by the accuracy with which your vision matches the needs of your customers while differentiating you from your competition and delivering it at just the right time to exploit that difference. Don't deliver too much, too soon that the customer will not pay for.

Second, the accuracy and effectiveness of the route map that your team draws between the existing experience and that vision. It needs to consider far more than technology, far more than new products, far more than advertising, and far more than customer service. It's the whole deal.

6: Understand possible cross-project friction or overlap

The project to implement part or all of your vision for an improved experience will not take place in a vacuum, but, instead, in the context of competition for limited resources and of established loyalties and political rivalry. With your network of angels, believers, and action team, it is essential that you identify and assess as many as possible of these sources of friction, competition, and overlap.

Pay attention to this advice! Too often, we have seen the poor results that come when projects established to improve the experience chose to ignore anything outside of their immediate control and somehow hoped that anything that was ignored would have no damaging impact. Poor deluded fools.

> 66 Poor **results** come when projects established to improve the **experience** chose to **ignore** anything outside of their immediate control and **somehow** hoped that anything that was **ignored** would have no damaging impact. Poor **deluded** fools. 99

PART 2: go, go, go

If you have followed Part 1 of the plan, you are now all prepared, with your network of angels, a network of believers, and a team of experience creators. You know where you are now, where you want to go, and when you need to arrive there.

The preparation is not simply an excuse for inaction, but a set of activities that, if put in place, give your project the best chance for success. It provides a foundation that the vast majority of projects appear to completely lack so that when they get to implementation, the project is on shaky ground already. Internal and external project teams sit on their hands until the kick-off date and then work like crazy, almost as if they liked late nights and failure.

> 66 The **preparation** provides a **foundation** that the vast majority of projects appear to **completely** lack. Internal and **external** project teams sit on their hands until the **kick-off** date and then work like crazy, almost as if they liked **late nights** and **failure**. 99

1: plan the plan and give that vision some direction

Da plan (don't worry that *was* slang) is often hidden in that place we like to call "the project planning software" and there it lurks, periodically being allowed back into polite society in the form of summary charts or even the mother of all detailed flowcharts that covers walls of dedicated players of project planning tools. The task of producing these mammoth and futile efforts is delegated to a "project coordinator" who tries to make sure that every individual part and subproject reports back on what has been achieved so that overall "progress" can be reported to the project progress meetings and endless steering groups and committees. It is usually out of date, often confused, usually based on layers of guesswork, and, every now and then, if it is used to track expenditure on consultants, causes arguments about payment.

This is not what I mean by planning. These may be useful tools for individual projects to use (let them make that decision), but such a process is not a great way to create adaptive experiences or have any fun or reach consensus or change the way that you build relationships or see clearly how best to pull the vision into a timeline. The true – the only – plan is the way of giving the vision the direction it needs.

With everyone in the room and a skilled facilitator at work, there is no reason for the planning process to be incomplete in its breadth. Just agree, approximately, the characteristics of the existing experience, agree what the future looks like, and post the two descriptions at opposite sides of the room. Next, determine a checkpoint in the future that will allow you to know whether or not you are making stunning progress toward the vision. Get someone (other than you) to write up the list of changes you want to make to the experience (any component of it) by the date of the checkpoint. Then the fun really begins as each member of the action team contributes to the planning by listing tasks that he feels are necessary to achieving the checkpoint objectives.

2: prioritize the plan (now, soon, later)

The next step is to look at the list of tasks to be completed and start prioritizing them into three groups. This has to happen rapidly, with members of the team "authorized" to make real decisions. If the time gap between discussion, decision, and action is anything other than fast, then it will be difficult to ever know if the original improvement would have been successful if it had not been delayed.

Priorities should be based on a number of criteria and these work best when the group has the key facts. First, what can be achieved with the elapsed time, people, skills, and budget available to the business and the experience project? Second, what will bring the greatest benefits? Third, which tasks are prerequisites for other tasks and must be done?

By asking these questions, the team can start to put the priorities in order, out in the open, subject to scrutiny and debate rather than behind the scenes. It can also determine criteria by which success should be judged for each of the initiatives, tasks, and improvements.

3: organize "customer experience" councils as widely as possible

Who owns the customer? The customer owns himself. Who delivers the customer experience? Everyone.

Each person involved in every project and every activity that is associated with the business delivers some part of that experience. His involvement can help or hinder its effectiveness and your project can turn an attitude from one that is too often neutrally lukewarm into one that is excited to be involved. I know that this may run contrary to what your experience (and that of your cynical peers) has taught you, but have the faith to put this into practice.

> **❝** Your **project** can turn an attitude from one that is too often **neutrally** lukewarm into one that is **excited** to be involved. **❞**

Establish what we call "customer experience" councils, but you can call them anything you like. The end goal is to ensure that every person working for the whole business participates every two weeks in a 45-minute council to share customer wisdom and figure out how the experience should, could, is, and has been improved. The nominated leader of the group (on a rota basis) spends five minutes preparing and ten minutes writing up the results of the meeting before sending them to the experience action team.

Think it's too much work? Do you think that there are people in your business just not capable of understanding what your customers need? Do you think that there are people who are just too busy or too important or too specialized to spend time figuring out solutions to problems that real customers want? I hope not, for the sake of your business.

4: improve the experience – understand, figure, council, deliver, stay fresh

Go back to Chapters 3, 4, 5, 6 and 7, repeatedly, as you implement the five-step approach that surrounds the e-customer experience framework. This is an iterative process if you can just get through it once!

Consider strongly the kind of quick wins that are described in Chapter 2 so that you get the team working together, build belief, and get some real benefits flowing through to improve the experience for the customer and the business.

5: measure success and gather feedback

To measure success, you need to have determined your form of measurement, and that is why it is mentioned in Step 3 above. Don't forget to build into everything that is done some simple metrics that can be easily understood and used to adjust and adapt the organization's experience interface with the customer. Suggested metrics include:

- satisfaction levels, measured by surveys online and off-line;
- numbers of new customers recommended by existing customers;
- lengths of time taken to complete a simple and a complex order;
- number of complaints from online and off-line customers;
- comparative satisfaction levels between users of your electronic channels and those of key competitors.

Equally important is direct feedback from those impacted by the improvements, overall experience, and business' performance. You need criticism, compliments, complaints, suggestions, and observations from customers and the experience councils. You need to know how your experience compares with that of your competition.

All this feedback will educate the team, business, and its councils so that you can all work smarter toward intelligent, valuable objectives, rather than work longer hours to some ill-defined, unappreciated, end.

> ❝ You need **criticism**, compliments, complaints, suggestions, and **observations** from **customers** and the experience councils so that you can all work **smarter** rather than work longer hours to some **ill-defined, unexpected**, end. ❞

6: back to the beginning – never be mediocre again

Plan for the long term if you want to create the ultimate effective online customer experience. This means completing all the steps that are set out above. It also means having fun, relaxing, learning, and avoiding prolonged periods without sleep, family, and friends. The path to excellence (I still believe in it) in customer experiences requires you to be fresh, energetic, and optimistic, and this will not come if you view everything as your personal burden. Smile and the customer will smile with you!

> ❝ The path to **excellence** (I still believe in it) in **customer** experiences requires you to be fresh, energetic, and **optimistic** ❞

Fortunately, you will start to enjoy the benefits of working for the good of other people. It will do your soul good to do your part in helping the business to build healthy, profitable, two-way relationships that endure. You never have to be mediocre again. Your business can compete with the very best if it can learn the infinitely valuable qualities of listening and changing.

You've come a long way baby

That was the easy bit. You are a true believer (if not, read it again!) That's why I included the theory, examples, real customer comments, insights, and analysis.

The tough part is putting such an all-encompassing vision of the way business should be in the internet era into practice. That's why we included the experience model, systematic plans, checklists, and activities. There is more than enough to move your electronic experience far beyond that of any other business that exists today – if you get your head around how radically different your business would look if it was adapted to fit the priorities and focus of the e-customer.

The next part is tougher (it's also fulfilling), but if you have read this far (or are you just sneaking a peek at the ending?), you can do what it takes. You can work past the setbacks and grow stronger as a result. I hope that you are going to buckle your seatbelt for the adventure of a corporate lifetime. Become a lover of people, connect to the minds and cultures of all those people you do business with, and then make every possible effort to put the humanity and skills of your colleagues into the direct service of your online customers. That can be fun. It's also far more likely to let you survive the downturns and surf the upswings of our global market because, when you get it right, you will always be adapted to create profitably what the customer still wants to buy!

> **❝** Make every **possible** effort to put the **humanity** and skills of your colleagues into direct service of your online **customers.** That can be **fun. ❞**

What you will achieve will be historic. It will create a new breed of hybrid businesses that use technology without nervousness and without geekishness to create adaptive, cyborg interfaces that reshape themselves around the characteristics of real (people) customers. This way leads to less waste, more enjoyment, greater respect, and more control. It's a winner, and you can be part of it, so write it down, keep the history, record the performance of your team, channel, department, or business, before and after. It will make you smile when you read it in a year's time, ten years' time. It is the start of great things.

So, that's it. My best shot, our best shot, at providing you with a route guide for creating the ultimate online customer experience. It's got everything that we could possibly include for this edition, but the next edition will include even more. How do I know that? Well, first of all, I am one of the world's only prescient consultants – I can actually see the future – and, second, because we have already started the research projects that will help the fledgling science of online sales and service to give you, the experience creator, even more help toward your goals.

Help the research along by spreading the word among your friends, family, and colleagues. They are all either e-customers, potential e-customers, or involved in the creation of e-customer experiences. You can share your thoughts, insights, first-hand knowledge, successes and (relative) failures via e-mail, and we will share them with the world.

Let me say it one more time:

be different, inspire the e-customer.

Experience study

Spiegel.com – "shopping at the speed of life"

"Shopping at the speed of life" is quite some promise, even for a 135-year-old company that has been doing business direct via catalogs for 105 years and via the internet since 1995. It has been successful – into e-commerce early, with three different online retailers (Eddie Bauer, Newport News, and Spiegel), each focusing on a different lifestyle by offering, in its own words:

> A shopping experience that delivers total customer satisfaction.

How well does the shopping experience do?

Its visual design follows the standard of e-commerce in the late 1990s. It has the usual categories at the top of the screen and opts for a neutral only tone with little, or no, variation in tone. Clicking on "Kids," as an example, reveals that the section is aimed at parents of kids, not children themselves. This is a shame (the wish list is similarly restricted) as the kid does the recommending – it could easily become a shared experience, with children suggesting and shopping with their parents at hand with credit cards.

FIGURE 9.1 Spiegal in pictures.

Despite this, many customers will find Spiegel's site easy to navigate and the choices wideranging, although not as comprehensive as the catalog (does that make sense?) It makes good use of product pictures to illustrate the categories to appeal to the visual senses of its customers. Text categories tend to allow customers to find what they already wanted, while pictures are more likely to be browsed and to attract attention to impulse buys.

The customer is left to make all the approaches with the free phone numbers, e-mail addresses, and a question feedback form with a set of preset question topics. There is no live help or community. There are no discussion boards, additional information, and stuff to do, news, or chat rooms.

Spiegel offers a good example of a wish list that customers can use to:

> File away those little somethings that you need to think about for a while. Come back and purchase them when you're ready. Or send your Wishlist to family and friends.

This is potentially a good way of pulling the customer into the center of the experience and pulling in his network of family and friends with him. Warning! This will not automatically work and is not top of the customer's priorities. If you want him to use the service, then you will have to sell it to him rather than expect him to look for it.

First, add other services that make the wish list more likely to be used. Spiegel has provided a personal address book and a gift reminder service to increase the attraction of the service to customers. These are all services that are combined into "My Spiegel," where customer's details, billing and shipping information are stored so that they can be automatically used to simplify new purchases.

FIGURE 9.2 Spiegel's well-organized services.

To help encourage natural buying, Spiegel includes its charge card and corporate incentives on the same list of services. The customer is helped to feel like this company is on his side, working for him. The issue of paying for such assistance is not an issue when the help is so timely and well-organized.

Spiegel backs these services up with a guarantee that is such a good example of clarity that it is worth reproducing here. Is your own guarantee so clear-cut?

> We want you to be totally happy with every Spiegel.com purchase. 24 hours a day, 7 days a week, we're dedicated to making online shopping fast, convenient and worry-free. If you're not completely satisfied with your order, return it for a full refund. If there's a problem or complaint, please call our Customer Satisfaction Helpline at [XXXXXX] or fill out the form below and we'll make things right.

Equally clear is the online help offered in the attractive "Ask Spiegel" feature. It provides a choice between intelligently organized answers to frequently answered questions and the facility for the customer to ask his own questions in his own natural language. The result is a comforting feeling that Spiegel is a smart shop assistant who is knowledgeable, approachable, and happy to help.

Spiegel states that it was built on the concept that shopping at home is a great idea. It also claims that shopping at home is, "better than ever with Spiegel.com." The experience is uninspiring but simple, pleasant, and convenient to use. Spiegel did well.

FIGURE 9.3

Spiegel's
online help is
actually helpful.

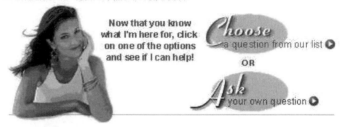

The online
resource to get answers
quick and easy!

How can we help?

"Ask Spiegel" is a customer service feature providing you with instant answers about all things Spiegel. Select a question from our list or ask your own. We'll search our database to find the answer. If we can't find it, please send us an e-mail, and we'll get back to you promptly.

Now that you know what I'm here for, click on one of the options and see if I can help!

Choose a question from our list ○

OR

Ask your own question ○

Stuff to think about

books, articles, TV shows, and websites

Webpartner.com

Founded in 1998, Web Partner is a privately held, venture-backed company that offers support to customer experience optimization, including the assistance of customer experience analysts and web-monitoring tools to aid you in customer experience management.

Ecompany.com

With one of the best set of electronic columns in the industry, you just have to sign up. Trouble is, you won't have time to read them all. Try "Future Boy," "The Conference Spy," and the "Talent Monger" to start with.

Fastcompany.com

Currently being blamed for a lot of the hype surrounding the new economy, its catchphrase is "Ideas that matter. Tools that work. Everything fast." It's still fun and cool. Just make sure you check the same ideas out from other less enthusiastic sources – ft.com for example – to be sure that the gushing has some substance.

Activity 9.1

Next steps: project plan checklist

Here is the project plan checklist for our proposed two-part approach as the basis for your action. Make sure that each deadline is met and that responsibilities concerning each task are assigned. Enjoy the ride!

Completion date: _____

75% done ☐	100% done ☐	Tasks	Who will do it? (initials)	By when? (date)
		Part 1		
		Write down and sketch out the vision.		
		List vision's supporting arguments.		
		List vision's opposing arguments.		
		Keep referring back to the vision.		
		Publish the formal recognized vision.		
		Invite feedback from wider community.		
		List ways of turning opposing forces into supporting ones.		
		Find those who are active users of electronic channels.		
		Post a web address on the drinks machine and noticeboards.		
		Invite people to share their knowledge of the web on the website.		
		Identify the opinion influencers in the business.		
		List skills and specialities required in the team.		
		Put the team together.		
		Sketch out the gap between existing experience and vision.		
		List steps to go from existing experience to vision.		
		Identify sources of friction, competition, and overlap capable of affecting project.		

Part 2

Determine what's the checkpoint in the vision.

List the tasks necessary to achieve
checkpoint objectives.

Prioritize tasks.

Establish "customer experience" councils.

Use metrics to adjust and adapt the
organization interface with the customer.

Invite feedback on experience
improvements from customers.

Invite feedback on competition's experience
from customers.

Activity 9.2

Next steps: people, teams, and networks

1 Write down the name of the primary believer, the person responsible for
overseeing the completion of tasks by each group member, and keeping the
whole team on track.

Name and title: _____

2 Where are the resources for this project coming from?

_____

_____

3 List all the believers who will be responsible for accomplishing the tasks
listed throughout this book. Your team of believers is built around the
following groups: experience visioneers, experience designers, experience
component makers, and experience deliverers.

Groups	Name	Initials	Department	E-mail *
Experience visioneers				
Experience designers				

Experience component makers		
Experience deliverers		

*If you don't have these addresses you're in serious trouble!

Customer experience thinkers

We have to make our own sense, our own future. And organizations have to make their own futures. The world is up for grabs. That's both frightening and yet very exciting. To make the future happen we need to be self-confident and to believe in our own worth. That's what schools should teach us.

CHARLES HANDY, AUTHOR OF *GODS OF MANAGEMENT: THE CHANGING WORK OF ORGANIZATIONS* (SOUVENIR, 1986)

Another belief I have is that, if a company is interested in finding the future, most of what it needs to learn it must learn outside its own industry. That's a very radical thing to say when most managers view strategy as taking place within well-defined industry boundaries.

GARY HAMEL, CO-AUTHOR WITH C. K. PRAHALAD OF *COMPETING FOR THE FUTURE* (HARVARD BUSINESS SCHOOL PRESS, 1994)

I have a very simple observation which is based on something I have seen in many companies: if you think you're good, you're dead.

The essence of successfully going forward is humility – a recognition that the world has changed so much that the formulas for yesterday's success are almost guaranteed to be formulas for failure tomorrow.

I think it will be an open-minded humility, and a recognition that we have to reinvent ourselves for the customer, that will be the difference between those who survive and thrive in the twenty-first century and those who become footnotes in the history books.

MICHAEL HAMMER, AUTHOR OF *BEYOND REENGINEERING: HOW THE PROCESS-CENTERED ORGANIZATION IS CHANGING OUR WORK AND OUR LIVES* (HARPERCOLLINSBUSINESS, 1996)

Complete checklist for all activities: get them checked off!

Chapter 1	The e-customer experience – what's it all about?		
Activity 1.1	Starting to think about the e-customer advantage	☐ Yes	☐ No
Activity 1.2	E-customer vision: stuff to get the team arguing, thinking, and agreeing	☐ Yes	☐ No
Chapter 2	Get this thing on the road		
Activity 2.1	Get thinking (quickly)	☐ Yes	☐ No
Activity 2.2	Something for everyone: a taster	☐ Yes	☐ No
Activity 2.3	Thought shocking: what changes do we want to make?	☐ Yes	☐ No
Activity 2.3	*(a)* Prioritizing the improvements to the online experience	☐ Yes	☐ No
Activity 2.3	*(b)* The transition plan: vision meets reality	☐ Yes	☐ No
Activity 2.4	Would you buy from you?	☐ Yes	☐ No
Chapter 3	Understanding *your* e-customer		
Activity 3.1	E-customers: listening, watching, and glad-handing	☐ Yes	☐ No
Activity 3.2	E-customers: a letter from a stranger	☐ Yes	☐ No
Activity 3.3	E-customers: home front	☐ Yes	☐ No
Activity 3.4	Team stuff: talking, arguing, fighting, agreeing	☐ Yes	☐ No
Chapter 4	Creating the e-customer offer		
Activity 4.1	Back to the primitive: the e-customer proposition statement	☐ Yes	☐ No
Activity 4.2	Thought shocker: something less boring instead?	☐ Yes	☐ No

Activity 4.3	E-customer proposition value: feed me!	☐ Yes	☐ No
Activity 4.4	The lost art of keeping a secret	☐ Yes	☐ No
Activity 4.5	Putting the online customer in rich context	☐ Yes	☐ No
Chapter 5	Creating the ultimate e-customer experience		
Activity 5.1	Your very own experience curve	☐ Yes	☐ No
Activity 5.2	The nuts and bolts of bricks and clicks	☐ Yes	☐ No
Activity 5.3	Right to reply	☐ Yes	☐ No
Chapter 6	Experience creation teams – the individuals, culture, skills, and the stress		
Activity 6.1	Taking the temperature	☐ Yes	☐ No
Activity 6.2	Would this happen in your business?	☐ Yes	☐ No
Activity 6.3	Teams checklist	☐ Yes	☐ No
Activity 6.4	Killer skills checklist	☐ Yes	☐ No
Chapter 7	Trends and technologies for creating experiences		
Activity 7.1	Experience technology rapid check	☐ Yes	☐ No
Chapter 8	Keeping it fresh, staying in business		
Activity 8.1	Keeping it fresh checklist	☐ Yes	☐ No
Chapter 9	Do it, do it now, and do it again – next steps		
Activity 9.1	Next steps: project plan checklist	☐ Yes	☐ No
Activity 9.2	Next steps: people, teams, and networks	☐ Yes	☐ No

The e-customer manifesto:
an open letter

WARNING! There are hundreds of millions not like me. Who don't dress like, talk like, act like me, but, in the end, they want just like me. Figure that out and make your fortune..

Dear strangers,

You don't know me. I'm the e-customer. You talk like you know me, invested as though you understood what I really want. The government paid for the first 20 years of the internet, investors paid for the next 10 years. Who is left? I am the only one who will pick up the tab for your future e-commerce plans.

So, open up your heart and hear this. There is no joy to be found in doing half a job for me and there's very little money either. You need to get into my mind, and I'm legion, multiple, distinctive, and ever-changing.

You can't force me to feed. I'm hungry, but not for tasteless slop. Electronic channels need to open up each of my six senses to a better world. They exist because of the relentless need of the inventive to build a better way, but if they do not improve my world then shut them down, turn them off.

Just stop
I am telling you to stop throwing away the legacy of the e-generations. Believe what you are offering is worth more than it costs to provide. Make your profits the honest way. Create stuff that I really appreciate and value more than any alternative use of my money.

Adopt the hacker's perspective. Build things that matter. Give back to me. View waste as evil. Expand your mind. Let in my dangerous thoughts. You can do anything for me in this post-DNA world. Everything is possible so I want you to think of everything for me.

I will never stop wanting it all. So make the desirable feasible. Turn the impossible into the profitable and be sought-after. I will come to you if you have what I want before everybody else. If you always have it first, then the trust between us can start to deliver supernormal profits (and that's what you want, right?)

Be the friend I can't live without. Present loving arms that hide the technology. Be my robo-nanny, my techno-host. Welcome me in. Serve me and turn my demands into revenue. Match my whingeing with your wisdom. Align yourself to my desire to be smarter with less effort and you will experience infinite growth.

See and serve me multidimensionally. Link the real world and the virtual world with bridges that offer handrails and an easy gradient. Let my diversity and that of my fellow online customers flood into your organization. Respond with a team that can, through expertise and experience, represent me. Designing for my priorities, my eyes, my ears, and my world. Use my tone. Speak my language.

Free agency. Choice. Accountability. Life-affirming values and the most effective way of coping with the legion of personalities that arrive at your electronic door. Don't depend on convergence to allow you to limit the play list. You will never guess what we all want, so let us make our own world. Guide us to it. Play the part of mentor.

Don't call me baby!
Don't rush me on the first date. There is time to pop, sparkle, and slide messages past my eyes and into my brain. First, I have to be open to the new ideas and most online customers ain't ready when we are acclimatizing ourselves to your little place. It's a new world for some of us, so take it easy.

If it isn't usable, then it isn't useful to me. If it isn't useful, you won't be able to give it away. Oops! Did you try to give it away? I bet that hurt! Get to the point. Make it clear how you can help to solve my problems. Say it in less than 20 words, then keep on saying it through the design of every picture, paragraph, and pointer.

Don't spread yourself too thin or lay it on too thick – you really cannot be the best at everything that I want – but it may be easier to get it from you than click my way to the competition if you tidy up your offer and unclutter your rhetoric. It is better to be known for a little of something than a lot of nothing.

Make sure that your team understands all dialects of e-customer gibberish. The stuff you don't understand about me can still kill you. Keeping the blindfold on won't stop the bullets. Learn a smattering yourself so that you can at least follow my conversations. Having smart interpreters in alien worlds is good, but relying on them for the basics makes you look foolish. The faster I change, the more you will need to know. Keep the learning habit and get past the addiction to the way it was.

Being afraid of what is to come or greedily trying to get your piece of net pie is insufficient – it will not sustain you in the hard times to come. When the flurry of easy money has evaporated, when the world starts to see things as they really are, ignorance, fear, and covetousness will be unmasked.

I am returning to my profoundest desires and my most outlandish wishes. I want the real thing. And, more than the real thing, I want experiences. To find a life. I no longer believe that life can be bought or that the purpose of life is in celebrating its pointlessness. I am moving beyond modernism and postmodernism to a post-ironic peak. I aim to get a life by living. If you can help me to get connected to the world, you are in a business worth being in.

When I get mad, simply channel my passion into a relationship with your service. My anger is not something I want. It is frustration caused by not getting what I want. I raise my voice or move to capital letters when I feel that I am not being heard. Give me alternatives and bond.

Rise above the lists and above the possible providers. I belong to me and I will choose my friends. Be my best friend. Really! Work for me and I will pay you for the effort. Don't take me, or be taken, for granted. You earn your right to be considered worthwhile, just as I pay for the right to have your help. If the exchange is good for both of us, then we have a chance of staying together.

Like the Fogdog promise to get whatever I want, whether or not they stock it, at no extra cost or the sweatshirt jam-packed with intelligence, reflecting light, transferring sweat, and reducing my drag coefficient. Like my e-kids being able to choose from 76,000 Barbie doll combinations. Like cybiko, koszmo, customerstore, Napster, paypal or amihotornot, interactive news from Sky or 192. They all get some of it right, but I am far from fulfilled. Give me more time, give me more friends, give me more wisdom.

No more flukes

Don't build your future plans on the successful flukes of the past. If you can't remember why your business is successful then I will eventually forget you. It's going to be tough to avoid becoming irrelevant or upgradeable. Keep the focus on the simple benefits that you bring into my life and you'll have a chance. Change the style and substance of the stuff that you do for me as my lifestyle and expectations change.

Keep it real. Get in among the crowds. Hang out where I hang. Experience my life. Talk to me in text, voice, and 3-D chat rooms. Glad-hand and listen. The bigger my hang-up, the bigger the payoff to you for solving it. Change yourself, your team, your systems, and your business. It's a relationship thing. I want real trust, real relationships, and real integrity. Anything less than transparency of intent and implementation will create suspicion. In my open world, there are no walls, and there are no secrets.

Unshrink the people who work with you. Let their personalities out to fill up the place with humanity. It's the most valuable, priceless, attractive part. The network gives the world back its interaction. What else is being multimedia, two-way, and real time about? People: hundreds of millions, then billions, until the air is used to connect every last one of us. Be part of making that work better and enjoy the ride.

So that's it. My impassioned plea to do more for me. To think further. To believe that what you can offer is more than exists. That your life's work can make more money by making the world a better place. Build your kingdom where the e-customer has his heart.

Be different. Inspire me.

Faithfully,
but not yours, yet,
E-customer

Music that produced this book

Gorillaz **by Gorillaz** Debut album from the virtual band represented by its cartoon characters when it was unknown and by its real-life members now that it has been successful. Featuring Brit Pop's Damon from Blur and some very nifty, creative hybrid tracks. The CD also features an interactive multimedia portion that takes us into the world of "Murdoc's Winnebago" and a link to a pretty cool website – gorillaz.com

Corrosion **by various artists** Compilation album featuring Pitch Shifter, The Suicide Machines, Creed, and a bunch more hard, emotion-filled tracks. You have to love music that includes lyrics like these, that fill your head so full that you can ease any worry in the world. Not, you understand, that I ever worry. Not with this available, anyway. A stomping adrenaline rush.

Parachutes **by Coldplay** Put it on and lose yourself while working for hours, and hours, and hours. I can barely tell sometimes if I like it or not but it is enchantingly positioned between being clever enough to keep those brainwaves changing but simple enough to let concentration stay with the task at hand.

The Optimist LP **by Turin Brakes** The cover is full of suitable praise with which I am forced, from the strength of the musical experience itself, to agree. The group focuses on its song-writing strength that is described by *Mojo* magazine as "an undoubted gift for crafting goose-pimply melodies" to inhabit what *NME* called "a space that is entirely their own, full formed and brutally emotive." Listen to anytime, but especially when you want to get back to loving life.

La vita è **by Nek** An Italian's album about life. Why? Because, like Charles Handy, the English business philosopher, said, "the process of living is actually quite a full-time occupation. In Italy, just living – the talking, the shopping, the cooking, the eating, the family and all that goes with it – actually consumes a whole day. It's a miracle that Italians ever get any work done. But it makes life rich; there's a texture to it, and more of a point." The album brings to my mind "la dolce vita."

Supernatural by Santana The album is a cool mix of different beats, cultural influences, and languages. It's quite useful to get me through a rainy day in England, where sunshine is a very rare commodity. Long live Carlos Santana!

Silence Becomes It by Silence 4 The album's title is a very good description of any creation process. It is by the Portuguese band Silence 4 who sing most of their songs in English. Their lyrics are pretty amazing and profound. They make us ponder what is really important in life and the effect we have on other people's lives. Definitely something to listen to when working on a book about creating amazing experiences for customers.

Notes

Here is a chapter-by-chapter breakdown of the notes that give you background details and references linked to quotes, case studies, statistics, and anecdotes used throughout the text. I am a self-confessed enthusiast of such notes. First, they keep the flow of the narrative going. Second, because they provide somewhere for me to put some of the valuable material I couldn't fit elsewhere in the book. Third, because I always find so many insights in the notes in other books that most readers just do not see. What the majority miss, you can enjoy.

Preface

1 Although online shopping more than doubled in size to an estimated £1.4 billion, this still represents less than 1 percent of all retail sales, according to Verdict Research (2001).
2 Quoted in *The Economist*, October 14, 2000.

Chapter 1 The e-customer experience – what's it all about?

1 KANA, 2001.
2 *New York Times*, September 20, 2000.
3 "The Myers Programming Report," April 20, 2000.
4 *USA Today*, April 25, 2000.

Chapter 2 Get this thing on the road

1 John Dawson, journalist, *Retail Systems*, **5**, 2, February/March 2001, commentating on what he felt were the all too obvious contents of Ernst & Young's report on global online retailing
2 "Portrait of the artist as a brand," *The Economist*, February 10, 2001.

Chapter 3 Understanding *your* e-customer

1 Ernst & Young's "Survey of Global On-line Retailing," 2001, found that 64 percent of customers want good merchandise selection, 65 percent want competitive prices, 42 percent want ease of use, and 34 percent want high product availability.
2 *Computing*, February 15, 2001.
3 "We have lift-off," *The Economist*, February 3, 2001.
4 "The Defogger," *Analyzing Chat*, Dylan Tweny
5 *Wired*, March, 2001.
6 Shopping flopping, *The Economist*, January 13, 2001.

7 "In Helsinki's Virtual Village," *Wired*, March, 2001.
8 "Counter-culture," *The Economist*, January 6, 2001.

Chapter 4 Creating the e-customer offer

1 "We have lift-off," *The Economist*, February 3, 2001.
2 Warren Berger, "The cool thing about aggregation," *Wired,* October, 2000.
3 "The big telecoms bust," *The Economist*, December 16, 2000.
4 "We have lift-off," *The Economist*, February 3, 2001.
5 "Another kind of net work," *The Economist,* March 3, 2000. Because prices fluctuate during the day and vary according to the 17 landing spots, deciding about a price offer was just guessing before. Now they call to find out. In the fish markets, agents, handlers, and traders are also equipped with mobile phones. Technology does provide the means to more efficiency, for example, now the carrier boats are only summoned when there is something to deliver, saving expensive fuel. Does this all seem too good to be true? The reality is that all of the big boats carry mobiles, but few of the smaller ones do it.
6 Nielsen Ratings, April, 2001.
7 Over 1.4 billion unique pages are available via the search engine Google alone, and that's before we consider all the real-world locations and pastimes.

Chapter 5 Creating the ultimate e-customer experience

1 *Wired*, December, 2000.
2 "New formula Coke," *The Economist*, February 3, 2001.
3 "Corporate Finance," *The Economist*, January 27, 2001.
4 According to a Greenfield Online survey of 1000 internet users in 2001, reported on cyberatlas.com.
5 *Wired*, March, 2001.
6 This is supported by a survey of 2000 people carried out by the UK-based Consumers Association. It revealed that 42 percent didn't think complaining would change anything, 14 percent were too busy, 12 percent didn't think it was important enough, 9 percent were planning to make a complaint soon, but 6 percent didn't even know who to complain to.
7 "A picture of health," *Internet Works*, February, 2001. Auravita.com is a successful business-to-consumer site, launched in October 1999. The company's philosophy is customer service and personalization:

> If you let clients down they don't come back, so we will go to the ends of the earth to make sure that anybody who uses the site is not only given the best information possible, but is given the best service and best aftercare service. It is absolutely imperative.

As for personalization, customers can build up a "favorites" section as they browse, making it easier to select products at a later date.

8 "Finding a real person," *Sales Director*, January, 2001.

9 Andersen Consulting looked at 445 orders made with 162 dot com companies across Europe in early 2001. It monitored each company's ability to capture and fulfil orders, process payments and refunds, and handle returns. Good points? The websites successfully helped shoppers to complete online purchases, two-thirds of the sites surveyed provided order confirmations, and a third told customers when their goods had been shipped. The bottom line? They are failing to tell customers if products are in stock, delivering late, and are not catering for returned goods. Of the total orders made for the study, 39 percent were incomplete transactions, with a third of them not fulfilled due to technical or procedural problems. The remaining two-thirds were due to purchased goods not even being delivered.

10 "Noise 'R' Us," *Wired,* August, 2000.

11 Dave Barry, *Miami Herald*, April 8, 2001.

12 In a survey carried out by Which.net, 48 percent either thought that prices were the same in the real world as the internet or did not know the difference. Meanwhile, 67 percent disagreed that they received better customer service electronically than in the real world, while only 11 percent thought it was the other way around.

13 "Shopping flopping," *The Economist*, January 13, 2001. The era of big margins is over, according to Richard Hyman, chairman of Verdict Research, because customers are used to ever-falling prices as a result of low inflation and the internet. At the same time, the growth in general consumer spending is slowing down and customer demand is shifting from goods to services.

14 "Kid gloves," *The Economist*, January, 2001.

15 "It's a funny old game," *The Economist*, February 10, 2001.

16 Manutd.com lists as its partners Sun, UUNET, Coral Eurobet, Informix, Lotus, and Sports.com, but the experience is lacking in any kind of character – a perfect match, some have said, for the team itself.

17 Women say twice as many words as men in a given day, but the average telephone call between two women takes 24 times as long as a call between men (KPN Telecom, 2001).

18 From a survey by Worldlingo, the free translation service, 2001.

19 Percentage of content in each language: English 76.59 percent, Japanese 2.77 percent, German 2.28 percent, Chinese 1.69 percent, French 1.09 percent, Spanish 0.81 percent, Korean 0.65 percent, Italian 0.62 percent, Dutch 0.36 percent, Portuguese 0.35 percent, Swedish 0.32 percent, Finnish 0.17 percent, Danish 0.14 percent, Norwegian 0.14 percent, Hebrew 0.02 percent, Icelandic 0.02 percent, Other/unknown 11.98 percent.

20 The question is asked in advertising from Accenture, stating that, *"Now it gets interesting,"* but it still doesn't explain why the name is so unclear.

21 "New formula Coke," *The Economist*, February 3, 2001.

22 *The Wall Street Journal*, May 3, 2001.

23 The California-based Lunar Design has developed Blu, a concept jacket made of digital fabric, according to Tad Toulis: "Information is like any material – wood, paper, plastic." Riffing on work done with fashion houses such as DKNY and tech giants Motorola and Hewlett-Packard, Lunar ended up with a flexible and tailored screen with a high-speed processor and a 24/7 wireless connection. Applications: clothing-as-advertisement, clothing-as-navigation device (bike messengers' jackets display a street map and track their wearers' progress via GPS (*Wired*, January, 2001).

24 Once a product has been bought in the virtual world, it has to be physically transported from the warehouse to the recipient in the real world. Developments such as DespatchLink from Neopost can allow your business to centralize the courier service management in your despatch center or mailroom. Your team can then liase with individual courier companies via the internet and use a single computer (instead of one for each different courier) to run rate comparisons and select the best-value courier (*Manufacturing and Logistics IT*, winter 2000/2001).

25 Kevin Maney, "Net is getting weirder," *USA Today*, January 17, 2000, and a whole bunch of other reports, including those on DigiScents' own site, if it's still open.

26 "Sweet, Scents and Nonsense: Does Aromatherapy Stink?," *American Council on Science and Health*, 9, 4, 1997.

27 Ernest Lilley, "Innovations 2001," Byte.com, January 15, 2001.

28 "The sky's the limit," *The Economist*, March 10, 2001.

29 Like the "trusted shop" seal, and many others like it, developed by consumer protection agencies in Europe by government organizations and backed up by Gerling Insurance Group. The scheme is EU-endorsed, offers 24-hour online customer support, and money-back guarantees on purchases in the event of non-delivery or failure to refund returned goods (reported by *Internet Works*, February, 2001).

30 CNET User Opinions said 96 percent love it compared to only 4 percent who didn't, based on 141 votes.

31 All the worlds we looked at allowed free access, but some charged for additional services – typically the ability to change avatars or store changes made to the world.

32 Khanh T.L. Tram and Antonio Regalado, "Websites bet on attracting viewers with humanlike presences of avatars," *The Wall Street Journal*, 2001.

33 According to worlds.com chairman, the company has been increasing revenues but also increasing its losses. This is apparently a result of one of its customers defaulting on its contractual obligations. Even if worlds.com goes out of business one day, as with any other example, it is still a valuable study into the possible directions of electronic experiences ("Worlds.com Reports Record Revenues for Fourth Quarter," *Fiscal*, 2000).

34 *Net*, March, 2001.

35 Deborah Michel, "Customer service on the web: good, bad and ugly," msn.com

Chapter 6 Experience creation teams – the individuals, culture, skills, and the stress

1 "IT creates distinctive customer experiences," *Computerworld*, April 30, 2001 – the CEO is Jim Champy, chairman of consulting at Perot Systems Corporation in Cambridge, Massachusetts.

2 *Wired*, March, 2001.

3 "Delhi calling," *The Guardian*, March, 9, 2001.

4 "Crunch times for General Motors," *The Economist*, December 16, 2000. The world's biggest car company is facing serious problems. England's Luton car assembly is closing and losing 2000 jobs, Opel's Russelsheim factory, near Frankfurt, is reducing its production capacity in Europe by 400,000 units by 2004. GM is directing production to lower-cost regions, such as Poland. Oldsmobil, the oldest of GM's brands, failed to capture younger-generation customers. GM does not face horror alone, however. Ford is struggling in Europe, too. That is why Ford Europe is spending heavily on the company's global research and development budget.

5 "The penguin gets serious" and "Authentic hero," *The Economist*, January 27, 2001. Linux is a free computer operating system choreographed by Finnish student Linus Torvalds and developed by thousands of volunteers/hackers collaborating over the internet. That is the amazing thing about it, and about the internet itself. The internet's nature is propitious to communities and development. Linux and other open-source products are as disruptive to the traditional software business as the internet. The internet and open sources reinforce each other as the internet makes possible new models of collaborative working and the open sources support the internet's preference for open, non-proprietary standards. Linux software is becoming more solid and more suitable for corporate use.

   The Open Source Laboratory, an independent, non-profit research center financed by IBM, Intel, and Dell, intends to accelerate the adoption of Linux in business computing and allow developers to test their software on the largest systems. Linux's presence in the market for operating systems that run the millions of small- to medium-sized server computers that offer web pages handle e-mail and do countless other routine administrative tasks is already very strong and more ubiquitous than equivalent versions of Windows.

6 Ricardo Semler, "How we went digital without a strategy," *Harvard Business Review*, September–October, 2000.

7 Emile Henry Gauvreay, journalist and military historian (1891-1956).

8 The site whywork.org is full of arguments against working at all – worth a read to challenge conventional thinking.

9 This excerpt is from BOFH, "Who Put the Mug in Smug?" by Simon Travaglia, posted December 3, 2000, at 14.51. Don't worry Simon, we didn't mess with your copyright!

10 The *New York Times* on the web, Wednesday, May 9, 2001.

11 John Wanamaker was born in 1838 and is most famous for the quote, "I

know half the money I spend on advertising is wasted, but I can never find out which half." He introduced innovative marketing (advertising, money-back guarantees) and was recognized as a religious pillar of the community. He was a customer experience pioneer.

12 International Data Corporation (IDC), October, 2000.

13 *Computing*, February 15, 2001.

Chapter 7 Trends and technologies for creating experiences

1 In 2000, CSC interviewed 1000 UK consumers and 100 marketing professionals within bricks-and-mortar UK corporations in the financial services and retail sectors. Of the marketing professionals 24 percent of them felt that a lack of integration was the chief barrier to more effective customer management, 8 percent felt that the scale of tasks stopped the business from making a start on improving, and 9 percent concluded that a lack of investment made the task impossible. That's a grand total of 42 percent who feel that technology is the problem. Over on the people side, 11 percent thought culture was the problem, 5 percent felt that there were not enough good people, 3 percent said that poor training stopped those people becoming good enough, and 18 percent felt that the market was changing too fast for the people to cope. In other words, *everything* is a barrier to customer management. Your job? To get everything working together.

2 *Retail Systems*, 5, 2, February/March, 2001.

3 "In Helsinki's Virtual Village," *Wired*, March, 2001.

4 "A LAN line," *The Economist*, January 13, 2001.

5 "Whole world in the palm of your hand," *The Times*, January 29, 2001.

6 Everybody thinks so, including the writer of "Banner-ad blues," *The Economist*, February 24, 2001.

7 There are many such surveys, but this one was reported in *Retail Systems*, 5, 2, February/March, 2001.

8 Erich Luening, "Microsoft tool 'Clippy' gets pink slip," news.cnet.com, April 11, 2001. The article describes how, "The long-despised feature of Microsoft's popular Office suite of business software, is the star of a new web marketing campaign. The campaign and a companion website trumpet Microsoft's forthcoming Office XP software as so easy to use that Clippy is out of a job. The website, designed and hosted by Microsoft, serves as a mock layoff notice and resumé for Clippy. 'I've taken over this space to share my pathetic story and show off my skills as a web designer. Not bad, huh? Know anyone who's hiring? Office XP works so easily that it's made Office Assistants like me useless. Obsolete. And, I'm told, hideously unattractive,' Microsoft has Clippy saying on the website." What's the bet that Clippy becomes an anti-hero?

9 From an interview with Alan Meckler by Karen Lake, *Strategy Week*, April 5, 2001.

10 *Wired*, April, 2001.

11 "Information furnace" was a term used in the article "The PC is dead – long live the PC," *The Economist*, December 16, 2000.

12 *Wired*, March, 2001.

13 Rage *v* Maniax, *The Economist*, February 3, 2001.

14 The feedback was sent at 1.50 pm, April 25, 2001.

15 The Future Foundation, 2000.

Chapter 8 Keeping it fresh, staying in business

1 Christopher Mines, senior manager with Forrester Research, outlining what he felt was the key to success for telecommunications companies in the article "When big is no longer beautiful," *The Economist*, December 16, 2000.

2 Moving into data-based services for corporate customers, broadband internet access for consumers, and into mobile and voice data has cost a lot and hasn't generated returns at the expected pace.

3 Cisco is laying off up to 8000 workers, Intel is cutting 5000 jobs and announced a decrease by 25 percent in its revenues for the present quarter. Motorola is cutting 7000 jobs and Ericsson announced a pre-tax loss of $513 million in the quarter "The falling feeling," *The Economist*, March 17, 2001.

4 "Productivity, profits and promises," *The Economist*, February 10, 2001.

5 *Wired*, March, 2001.

6 "Online education," *The Economist*, February 17, 2001.

7 *The Economist* defined "post-crash realism" as "The bracing sobriety that has swept the dot com world, leading many to be more cautious about their choice of projects and their techno-utopian prognostications." Of course, it really misses the point.

8 Liz Bailey, "Cyber Bitch," *T3*, May, 2001.

9 Stan Gibson and Michael R. Zimmerman, "Cisco: bad luck or bad attitude?," eWEEK, May 11, 2.48PM ET, 2001.

10 Dr Adam Johnson from the Open University – the world's leading virtual university – believes that e-mail communication can actually help rather than hinder the creative process because it enables people to put forward ideas without fear of being judged. According to him, brainstorming via e-mail results in more ideas being produced than when sitting face-to-face because people are not so self-conscious.

11 On the other hand, look at the struggling M&S – there is a lack of confidence and confusion about what M&S stands for (*Telegraph Magazine*, November, 2000).

12 "Bridging Europe's skills gap," *The Economist*, March 31, 2001.

13 Katrina Brooker, "I built this company, I can save it," *Fortune*, Monday, April 30, 2001.

14 *Wall Street Journal*, May 8, 2001. Cisco Systems posted a deep fiscal third-quarter loss, largely due to a restructuring charge to cover layoffs and excess inventory as sales dropped from a year earlier.

Index

3-D experience 176–180
3-D Worlds.com 176
Abbey National 133
Activeworlds.com 177
Adaptive experience membranes
      123–125
Adverts, power of 92
Airline tickets, buying 131
Amazon 90
Ananova.com 268–270
Art meets the net 26–29
Assessing a site 193–194

Back to basics 162
Banner adds 92
Boo.com 176
Buying experience, your 36–37

CD-Rom,
   sample, experience of 10
Channels layer 125–126
Characteristics layer 159–180
Chat rooms 46–47
Checklist, complete 318–319
Choice and direction 93
Consensus building 16–17
Content versus connectivity 91
Control and freedom 45–46
Country of origin and residence
      164–165
Cross-project friction 304
Customer alchemists 89
Customer experience thinkers
      18–19, 37, 80–81, 107,
      195, 230–231, 276–277,
      296–297, 317

Customer service 226
Customers,
   delivering the online experience
      4–5
   expectations of 2
   finding your 46
   five steps 6, 7
   loyalty 5–6
   meeting the needs of 6
   online initiative 2
   reliance on 1–2
   support lines for 145–148
   understanding your 3

Design considerations 126–127
Digimon.com 94–95
Digital generation,
   behaviour of 44–45

ebates.com 139–143
e-customer,
   advantage 16–17
   behaviour of 54–55 61–62
   collecting details on 42–43
   defining your 53–54
   experience framework 110–114
   imagining your 76–77
   location of 43–53
   manifesto 320–323
   model, creating a 18
   needs of 56–57
   questionnaire 30–31
   recognition of 55–56
   understanding your 31, 39–42
      78–79
   universe 114–116

vision 17
e-customer team,
    creativity 210
    customer service, obsessed with
        218–219
    emotionally connected 209–210
    empowering your 227–229
    experience builders 221
    experience component makers
        204
    experience culture 207–209
    experience deliverers 205–207
    experience designers 204
    experience visioneers 199–203
    killer skills checklist 229
    listening and learning 219–220
    measuring your 224–226
    minimal rules and trust 213
    positive and highly-principled
        214–215
    putting together your 8, 31, 198
        et seq.
    relationship-driven and people-
        focused 212
    valuing people 220
    visionary 218
    working conditions for 216
e-family, at home with 64–66
e-generations, meet the 62–64
Ego layer 158–159
Enhanced TV 11–13, 127–128
Experience action team 303
Experience curve 137–138, 191, 193
Experience interface 120–123
Experiences,
    comparing the 103
    creating the ultimate 109 et seq.
Eyestorm.com 26–29

Feedback, assessing your 104
Financial websites 51
Firstdirect.com 270–273
First-hand experience, gaining
        75–76

Flash cartoon 48
FoxKids.com 94–96

Gambling 49–50
Gaming 47
Gap analysis 304
Gateway.com 291–292
Gen Y 50
Gender and sex 162–163
Google.com 222–224

Habbohotel.com 179
Human intelligence, applying 69
Hunger layer 154–157
Inside track, working your way to
        the 66
Interactivity 128
Interests and hobbies 161–162

JCPenney.com 185–188

Keeping it fresh 279
    affiliate scheme 282
    change and grow 285
    checklist 294–296
    pooling of effort 281
    relax and grow 288–290
    sell and grow 287
Loyalty 5–6, 58–60

Mobile electronic experience
        129–130
MOPy fish 56
Music swaporiums 48
Network of believers 301–302

Offer,
    appreciated value analysis 85
    content of 84
    creating the 83–94
        steps to 87–88
    marketing 85
    product and service design 85
    types of 148–151

Online experience,
   improving the 34
   transition plan 35
Organizational layer 133

Palm.com 70–72
Politics and philosophy 165
Portals 49
Postmodernist society, impact of
      67
Preparation importance of 300–301
Procedures and rituals 60–61
Product to fun 67–69
Putting it all into practice 305
   improve the experience 308
   measure success 308
   organise the customer
      experience 307
   people teams and networks 316
   plan the plan 306
   prioritise 306
   project plan checklist 315
Quick starts 21–22

Race, language and heritage 164
Research and play 43
right to reply 194–195
Role and profession 163

Secrets, discovering 105
Senses and sensibilities layer
      167–173
   fair play 174
   hearing 169
   sight 167
   smell 172
   taste 173
   touch 169
Shopping 50–51
Spiegel.com 311–314

Starting small 25
Stealth approach 23–25
Structure and flow 134–137
      143–145
Survival layer 153–154

Taster 31–32
Team building 79–80
Technical aptitude and attitude
      165–167
Technology,
   accessibility of 265–266
   bandwidth 251–253
   boundaries, blurring of 257–259
   buying 245
   checklist for 275–276
   e-mail management 242–243
   games get serious 259–260
   humanization 253–256
   interaction 238–242
   interactivity 264–265
   mix 152
   selling 243–244
   tracking 246
   transparency 247–248
   trends and 234–237, 246
   virtual grid 260–262
   wireless age 248–251
   WYDIWYG 262–264
Thought shocking 32–33

Usability 160–161
Video streaming 48
Vizualisation 116–119
Voyeurism 51–52

Web rings 48–49
Worlds.com 181–185
Xmenthemobilegame.com 97–99
Yahoo! 90

The customer experience framework

See page 111

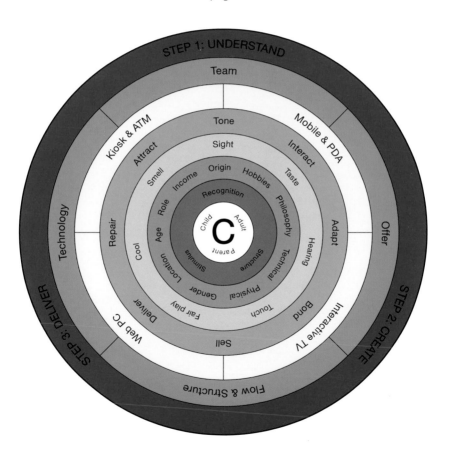